THE UPPER ROOM

Disciplines

2010

D1540258

UPPER
ROOM BOOKS®
NASHVILLE

AN OUTLINE FOR SMALL-GROUP USE OF DISCIPLINES

Here is a simple plan for a one-hour, weekly group meeting based on reading Disciplines. One person may act as convener every week, or the role can rotate among group members. You may want to light a white Christ candle each week to signal the beginning of your time together.

OPENING

Convener: Let us come into the presence of God.
Others: Lord Jesus Christ, thank you for being with us. Let us hear your word to us as we speak to one another.

SCRIPTURE

Convener reads the scripture suggested for that day in Disciplines. After a one- or two-minute silence, convener asks: What did you hear God saying to you in this passage? What response does this call for? (Group members respond in turn or as led.)

REFLECTION

• What scripture passage(s) and meditation(s) from this week was (were) particularly meaningful for you? Why? (Group members respond in turn or as led.)
• What actions were you nudged to take in response to the week's meditations? (Group members respond in turn or as led.)
• Where were you challenged in your discipleship this week? How did you respond to the challenge? (Group members respond in turn or as led.)

PRAYING TOGETHER

Convener says: Based on today's discussion, what people and situations do you want us to pray for now and in the coming week? Convener or other volunteer then prays about the concerns named.

DEPARTING

Convener says: Let us go in peace to serve God and our neighbors in all that we do.

Adapted from *The Upper Room* daily devotional guide, January–February 2001. © 2000 The Upper Room. Used by permission.

THE UPPER ROOM DISCIPLINES 2010
© 2010 by Upper Room Books®. All rights reserved.

UPPER ROOM®, UPPER ROOM BOOKS® and design logos are trademarks owned by THE UPPER ROOM®, a ministry of GBOD® Nashville, Tennessee. All rights reserved.

The Upper Room Web site: http://www.upperroom.org

Cover design: Left Coast Design, Portland, Oregon
Cover photo: Joe Allen
First printing: 2009

Revised Common Lectionary copyright © 1992 Consultation on Common Texts. Used by permission.

Scripture quotations not otherwise identified are from the New Revised Standard Version Bible © 1989, Division of Christian Education of the National Council of the Churches of Christ in the United States of America. Used by permission. All rights reserved.

Scripture quotations designated RSV are from the Revised Standard Version Bible, copyright 1952 (2nd edition, 1971) by the Division of Christian Education of the National Council of the Churches of Christ in the United States of America. Used by permission. All rights reserved.

Scripture quotations designated NIV are from the HOLY BIBLE, NEW INTERNATIONAL VERSION. NIV®. Copyright © 1973, 1978, 1984 by International Bible Society. Used by permission of Zondervan. All rights reserved.

Scripture quotations designated as THE MESSAGE are from *The Message* by Eugene H. Peterson, copyright © 1993, 1994, 1995, 1996. 2000, 2001, 2002. Used by permission of NavPress Publishing Group. All rights reserved.

Scripture quotations designated NCV are from the New Century Version, copyright © 1987, 1988, 1991 by Thomas Nelson, Inc. All rights reserved.

The week of March 22–28 was published in *Disciplines* 2007.

The week of October 18–24 was published in *Disciplines* 1998.

ISBN: 978-0-8358-9977-2
Printed in the United States of America

CONTENTS

FOREWORD

CARPE MAÑANA—THAT'S THE TITLE OF A BOOK I FOUND ON A friend's bookshelf. It's a play on words, of course. The Latin phrase *Carpe diem* urges us to seize the day. *Carpe Mañana*— the title of the book if not its subject—calls for something else altogether. It could well sum up for many of us the challenge we face in our quest for spiritual nurture and discipline.

We know we should read scripture and pray daily. We know this because we've been taught that spiritual disciplines are an important part of a Christian's life. We know this because it keeps us centered and whole. Most of all, we know that prayer is important because *we hunger for God's company*.

In spite of our hunger, we sometimes put off until tomorrow— or the day after—to begin daily prayer and study. It's not quite intentional. We *do* desire to grow closer to God. But we procrastinate all the same. We want to seize (and be seized by) our relationship with God—but sometimes those intentions end up on our "tomorrow" list.

Disciplines offers you a way to make time and space for God: to still yourself, to meditate on scripture, to pray, and to listen.

Each week, *Disciplines* features scriptures from the Revised Common Lectionary, a guide or table of readings used weekly in public worship. Each week a spiritual leader or writer reflects on a different set of scriptures, explores its meaning, and suggests a way to meditate and pray. This daily practice of scripture reading, reflection, and prayer is a powerful means of grace and spiritual growth.

There are countless ways to approach a daily discipline of scripture reading and prayer. Quiet time in the morning can be calming and centering for you; this may be the best time for study and prayer. Or, you may need time in the evening to pause, reflect, and pray. You may decide to read *Disciplines* just before you exercise; prayer and meditation are sometimes deepest when people swim, walk, or run. No matter what form your spiritual discipline takes, scripture is clear that God begins with you wherever and however you begin.

Begin—or begin again—today. Seize this time, now, to be with God. As you read scriptures, reflect on your faith, and pray throughout the year ahead, remember that you are in good company. Thousands of believers all over the world have read these same scriptures, reflected on the mysteries of this same faith, and prayed to this same God, the God who hungers for your company and who waits for you today.

— Helen R. Neinast
Author and Consultant • Upper Room Books

Essentials for a New Year

JANUARY 1–3, 2010 • REBECCA DUKE-BARTON

FRIDAY, JANUARY 1 ⁓ *Read Psalm 8*

When my son Daniel was two, my husband and I left him in a hotel with my parents while we stayed in another room. His granddaddy was trying to settle him in the bed, and Daniel kept saying, "Mama, Daddy . . . " My father assumed he was asking for his parents, and he reassured Daniel that we were not far away and he could see us in the morning. Daniel, restless, kept insisting.

Finally Daniel sighed and began saying, "Mommy loves, Daddy loves . . ." Every night we list the people who love him before he goes to sleep. Suddenly understanding, his grandfather joined him, "Mommy loves you; Daddy loves you; Granddaddy loves you; Grandmother loves you; Aunt Margie loves you . . . " and on through our final words, "And most of all, God and Jesus love you, so you can go to sleep knowing you are surrounded by love." With that assurance, Daniel rolled over and went right to sleep.

Daniel, even at two, understood the need for assurance that God still cares about him in the midst of a strange situation. He could only find rest knowing he was surrounded by love.

As we look forward into the new year, we may have moments when we feel small and alone. Yet the psalmist sees the work of God's hand as a reminder that God *does* care for humans. We can rest in the assurance that, whatever the new year may bring, the Lord of creation cares for us. We are surrounded by love.

God, thank you for the way that you surround me with love.
Let me rest in that assurance throughout this year. Amen.

Adjunct professor of religion at Andrew College, ordained elder in the South Georgia Conference of the United Methodist Church, and mother of three children under age six

I spent the past month engaged in Christmas celebrations: shopping, wrapping presents, attending parties, traveling to see family, baking, extra choir practices, and special services. There is never enough time, yet somehow I managed to fit all of these extra activities into my life.

What will I do with all of my free time now? Of course, when I look at my brand new calendar, it doesn't feel that I have any free time. I have three children under the age of six, I teach two college courses, I am married to a minister, and I myself am a minister on family leave. The calendar is already full of doctors' appointments, church meetings, and birthday parties.

Even normal days are hectic. The simple task of preparing a meal becomes a carnival as I try to cook with twins climbing in the refrigerator. At the end of the day, when the children are finally in bed, I look around the house and know there are dishes to do, toys to pick up, and always laundry. Any other projects that I want to accomplish, such as writing or Bible study, also have to fit into this window of opportunity. And sometimes I'm too tired even to think about those things.

The passage in Ecclesiastes, however, indicates that in God's plan for our time, it is God's gift that we would "take pleasure in all [our] toil." With this, I am given a sense of purpose, of calling, because I know that in the mundane activities of my life, I am building a future for my three children.

As you fill in the blanks on your calendar, how will you choose to use your time? What is your sense of the business that God has for you right now? In order to find pleasure in our toil, we need to keep our calling from God in focus.

O God, in all of the pressures on my time, help me remember the call and passion your Spirit puts in my heart. Amen.

SUNDAY, JANUARY 3 ~ *Read Matthew 2:1-12*

In one of my first lectures in my introduction to the New Testament class each semester, I bring in a Nativity scene, complete with Mary, Joseph, Jesus, shepherds, angels, wise men, and lots of animals, all gathered together in a stable. I then have the students compare that traditional picture to the Christmas stories in the Bible. My students are generally surprised to discover that Luke's shepherds and Matthew's wise men did not all arrive together. In fact, the wise men visit Jesus in a house, up to two years later. The celebration of Epiphany twelve days after Christmas recognizes the time gap in the scriptural witness. The problem for most of us is that we try to compress the whole story into one day.

It always strikes me that we do ourselves a disservice by ignoring the later arrival of the wise men. Reading about their arrival today invites us to take another look at the story: the celebration of the coming of Christ doesn't end when the Christmas decorations come down; the celebration is really only just beginning.

The wise men had a star to lead them to Jesus. I've wished at times in my life for a star to guide me, or a burning bush, or a dream to instruct me in what to do. I have never gotten any of these signs, but I have found guidance in the discipline of reading the Bible. Though the wise men had a star to lead them to the Christ, I have the Bible. I want to read the scriptures anew this year, paying attention to what the Bible says and not simply what I have always heard about it. In the reading I hope to find the star that can guide me to a genuine encounter with God as revealed through Jesus Christ.

As I begin this new year, God, I pray for your guidance. As I search the scriptures, let me encounter you in a new way. Amen.

Walking with *el Pueblo**

JANUARY 4–10, 2010 • CRISTIAN DE LA ROSA

MONDAY, JANUARY 4 ~ *Read Psalm 29:4-9*

An elder in the United Methodist Church, I have been in transition for the last two years from pastoral ministry in local settings to teaching in the Hispanic institutes of local congregations and in mainline seminaries. From these vantage points, I've had interesting and contrasting experiences related to listening for the voice of God.

Young Hispanic people are eager to learn and go out into the mission field full of the knowledge that God is calling them to serve *el Pueblo*. I am amazed at the powerful voice of God in the testimony of older persons—without recognized degrees or institutional ordination—who seek knowledge to continue in their ministries. I have been most surprised by those who leave well-established careers and comfortable homes to answer the powerful voice of God.

In mainline seminaries, my experience has been very different. Many students there are either second career individuals preparing for ordination with a mainline denomination, or they are young people searching for meaning that transcends institutional churches. I hear the powerful voice of God in the students' passionate opinions, comments, and questions in class. The lively intergenerational discussions help me understand that God's majestic voice reaches across cultures, time, and space. God's voice comes to each of us in powerful ways if we only make the time and space to listen.

God, help me hear you, so that I may be ready to walk with your people in ways that I might not expect. Amen.

* Spanish for "town" or "the people"

Director of the Hispanic Youth Leadership Academy at Perkins School of Theology in Dallas, Texas;

"Where was God when children were being massacred?" This question started a powerful and poignant discussion in a class I was teaching in a seminary last year. We were considering a reading that tells of a massacre of Jewish children in Germany during the Holocaust. Most of the class members who lived during that time were surprised that they did not know hear about it in this country. Those who came from other countries or were born after the event were also surprised that with all the information available about the Holocaust, this was new information.

I come from an immigrant family. We are very familiar with the struggles of families from other countries and the experience of Hispanic ministries within the context of new immigrant communities in this country. Firsthand stories of massacres in Central America, especially Guatemala and El Salvador, have been part of my formative ministerial practice (and the reformulation of my theology). The massacre of Jewish children was familiar and in line with the processes of war that destroy life in Latin America.

It was the question of "Where was God?" that surprised me. In the context of ministry with immigrant communities, it has been clear to me that God is present. God's voice is heard so clearly and in so many ways as the community survives, finds hope, and affirms life. God is there in the surviving witnesses and in the telling and writing of the story. God's voice echoes across the oceans as a song of hope and victory over death as we read and tell the stories and especially as we dialogue and claim a God of life who nurtures and protects *el Pueblo*.

We thank you, God, for this earth and its peoples, **sus pueblos.** *We remember the words of the psalmist and proclaim that the Lord gives strength to the peoples of this earth and blesses them with peace. Amen.*

WEDNESDAY, JANUARY 6 ~ *Read Isaiah 43:1-7*

EPIPHANY

The struggle and the suffering of immigrant families, especially those from Latin America, have been evident in the ministry of Hispanic congregations for the last five years. Immigration reform, raids, and constant profiling of those who appear to be the "other" dramatically increased the suffering and fear within new immigrant communities. The themes of strength and survival against fear and death fill our sanctuaries and are dominant topics for Bible studies and ecumenical dialogue.

It is so easy, even among us Christians, to ignore the suffering of the "other" in the context of this economic crisis and a predominantly anti-immigrant atmosphere. I find it impossible to believe that the Creator of a diverse humanity, the God of all life, would discriminate among human beings, agree to a dividing wall between nations, or support immigration laws that separate children from their parents.

The image of the prophet Isaiah passing through fire remind me of the Central American *pueblos*, the wars in the last ten years in that region, and the sanctuary movement organized by people of faith in the 1980s to rescue and protect life. I consider the scriptures for today and remember that the promise of God is to protect *el Pueblo*. Isaiah writes "I have redeemed you; I have called you by name, you are mine." As I consider today's scripture, I know that in the "other" we find the face of God.

Thank you, God, for my life.

O God, give me today the courage to search for your face in the face of the "other." Help me understand that in my relationship with the other, I am loved and honored by you. Amen.

The readings for today bring to mind images of the people of African descent in this country. Memory and suffering in *el Pueblo* know neither time nor space. I am reminded that my own struggle and memory of suffering as part of a Latin American *pueblo* resonates with the struggles and memory of suffering of African-American brothers and sisters.

Isaiah's image of passing through deep waters reminds me of the suffering of African people crossing the ocean as part of the slave trade: people of God treated as a commodity by other people of God. It is difficult to imagine. We cannot think of it taking place today in the same manner. However, the dynamics of power that made this possible continue to survive within our global economic systems. We talk about surplus people who must accommodate our systemic needs. We take undocumented immigrants for granted and fail to provide decent housing and working conditions.

It is very difficult to discern the voice of God in our own time. It seems impossible to know what a meaningful and relevant ministry is today, since technology and globalization make everything much more complex. However, the memory of suffering is there in *los pueblos* (in the peoples of every corner of this earth that suffer), and it interrupts history. These interruptions can help us claim our humanity as people of God—again listening to the voice of God and recognizing the accompaniment of God as we walk with those who suffer—in our own suffering or our memory of suffering.

Creator God, help me reflect upon my own reality and the suffering around me. Empower me to walk in your reality as I remember the suffering of others. Amen.

In my twenty-plus years of ministry I have always been intrigued by the power of *acompañamiento el Pueblo* (the accompaniment of the people). There have been many times that I had no answer, resources, or appropriate ritual for critical circumstances. However, as awkward as it felt, simply being there with the people facilitated transformation not only for them but for me and my ministry as well.

In today's reading Peter and John are emissaries from Jerusalem. Their encounter with the people of Samaria will be one of great consequence. The community had received the word of God and were baptized in the name of Jesus but "the Spirit had not come upon any of them." Somehow the Holy Spirit required a face-to-face encounter and the accompaniment of those who facilitated the word of God.

I like to imagine that the apostles in Jerusalem sent Peter and John with the necessary resources—spiritual as well as material—to encourage and support the new community of Samaria. As a Hispanic pastor in the context of a predominantly Anglo denomination, I want to think that this is a good model for the support of new ministry, especially in diverse settings. The elements of recognition (the apostles recognized that the people of Samaria had received the word of God within their own context), accompaniment (the apostles sent two of their own to accompany this new community; the presence of Peter and John facilitated an encounter), and prayer (it was in the prayer and the laying of hands that the new community received the Holy Spirit) are the highlights and marks of God's process of *acompañamiento el Pueblo.*

Our Creator and Redeemer, help me today to feel you walking with me. Help me to discern the accompaniment I need to provide as I walk with others. Amen.

In my pastoral ministry I try to strengthen the hopes of people, especially those who suffer at the margins of society. However, it is always difficult to minister with marginalized communities where there seems to be so much need and concern for everyday survival. I hope to at least nurture the hopes of people so they themselves, in community, can bring about new life. As a preacher I try to imitate the preaching of John the Baptist and suggest new images for our discipleship.

The main images in this reading are baptismal water and fire. Having seen immigrants walk across the Arizona desert, I visualize Christ turning the heat of the desert into a warning for those of us who refuse to be hospitable and who do not offer water to the suffering. I am reminded of my responsibility to care for life as part of a faith community that claims to serve the God of life. And yet, ironically, by offering water to a thirsty immigrant, I am seen by some as helping a criminal.

New questions come to me as I consider a relevant and meaningful ministry in the tradition of the Hebrew prophets, John the Baptist, and Jesus the Christ—one that can raise the hopes of *el Pueblo*. At what level am I implicated in the suffering of others? Does the legal rationale for not providing help and hospitality for immigrants become a legal mechanism allowing others to die? Can we, as Christian leaders today, facilitate hope for *el Pueblo* while we encounter the realities of new immigrant communities?

God of life, help me remember my baptism. Help me welcome and claim the power of the Holy Spirit to be transformed and to be part of life-giving processes that bring about new realities for others. Amen.

SUNDAY, JANUARY 10 ~ *Read Luke 3:21-22*

BAPTISM OF THE LORD

Luke makes an interesting point about Jesus' baptism in relationship to the baptism of the other people. Luke notes that Jesus was baptized *after* all the others. This differs from the other Gospel stories. And that leads me to ask why Jesus waited until last and why John did not decide to begin the baptizing that day with Jesus as an example for the people.

Out of my own Hispanic tradition it is almost as if Jesus is the *padrino for el pueblo* (the godparent for the people). I imagine him there, accompanying the new followers who accepted the invitation to participate in the building of a new reality and were open to hear the message and the voice of God. In the context of Latin American theology one can also say that this confirms the option (the preferential care for the poor) for *el Pueblo* .

The primary image of this passage is the care Jesus takes with the people as if one by one their baptisms affirm the practical aspects of his ministry and strengthen his commitment to facilitate the redemption and salvation of this creation. His commitment is soon blessed by the voice of God stating, "With you I am well pleased." This passage reminds me that Jesus now takes on the suffering of the people as a way of preparing for the cross. Somehow I think that as he accompanied *el Pueblo* that day he restored hope by receiving—at the end, in his own baptism—the suffering and pain of the people. The voice of God also offers the approval of this practice by Jesus anticipating his important encounter with humanity—on the cross.

In this new day, O God, as I remember the baptism of Jesus, I ask for the clarification and affirmation of my own call to sacrifice in the processes of facilitating new life. Amen.

Be More Beautiful

MONDAY, JANUARY 11 ～ *Read Isaiah 62:1-3*

Think of a time when something or somebody made you happy—really happy. Perhaps it was when your child rushed home from school with a drawing she'd made just for you. Maybe a great performance or speech moved you to a very deep place. It might be the kindness of a stranger that turned your day around and made you smile. Perhaps, in a moment of quiet prayer, God came to you with new power and strength.

These kinds of moments, this depth of feeling—Isaiah's exuberant praise can never come close to capturing the glory of what God has done and what God will do. Yet he is compelled to try. At this point in Israel's history, the people have likely returned from exile and are about the work of rebuilding. Given their past hardships and their present hard work, this kind of joy is astonishing. The contrast between their terrible troubles of the past and their bright hope for the future makes their joy in the present even more striking.

But the joy is not ours alone. God too is jubilant and joyous.

Joy, then, is part of the covenant God has established with us. In our daily walk with God, we embrace it all with joy. And in the joy God has bestowed on us, in the joy that God shares with us, there is something holy.

God, grant me the grace to celebrate the joy of your relationship with me. Permit me to dwell in your delight today. Amen.

Director of Hispanic/Latino Ministries of the North Carolina Conference of the United Methodist Church; wife and mother of four children

If we think of our life on earth as a journey, we might imagine the turning points and stopping places as parks or museums, dusty back roads or crowded interstates. Some of the stops on our journey might represent our good deeds or accomplishments. Other times, the stops on our journey evoke pain and betrayal, disappointment or failure.

During our journey, no matter how long or short it's been, no matter how plain or elaborate, no matter how tranquil or troubled, we have acquired a history with God and a history with others. That history tells our story as clearly as if it were written in big letters up in the sky. That history—our history—is under God's care, whether we have known it or not. Isaiah knows it. He knows God's joy is powerful and irrepressible.

And his words tell us that our journeys can be transformed by the God-given joy that accompanies us every day. Prayer, worship, scripture, celebration of the Last Supper all nourish our relationship with this joyful God. In that relationship we discover fresh portions of love, love that should be celebrated. God has claimed Israel—and us—as a groom claims a bride. With joy. With exuberance. And with much rejoicing.

God, help me uncover the joy and exuberance that is part of who I am. Thank you for making me capable of so much happiness. Amen.

I couldn't resist asking, "How much do you love me?" "As big as this whole house!" my children would answer. Sometimes my son Diego would add, "No wait! As big as the whole universe!" Isn't it amazing how children define love in such grandiose measurements? Yet, when we look at the scriptures, we find that same grandiose affirmation of God's firm and far-reaching love.

God's love, the psalm says, extends even to heaven. It's that big, that wide, that high. The immensity of God's love is staggering. God's love reaches from earth to heaven. And it is a steadfast love.

When my son was preparing to go to be with Jesus after a long battle with cancer, we were deeply grieved because we knew his death was only a few days away. We tried to look strong and be discreet about our grief, but we had our tears; and Diego noticed. He was young—just two days shy of his sixth birthday. But we soon discovered he was old enough to tell us, clearly and emphatically, in his most firm voice that he wanted us to stop crying.

"I just want to go to heaven so that I can run and jump and play with Nemo!" As far as Diego was concerned, his four-legged playmate that had been hit and killed by a car and died was waiting for him, probably somewhere near the feet of Jesus. Diego had not been able to walk or run for a long time because of his illness. He was ready to take on the streets of heaven with his puppy at his side. For him heaven is a place of healing and wholeness. It had been for Nemo, and it would be for Diego. A boy, a puppy, and heaven. What could be more divine than that?

God, you are my Lord, the Lord of heaven and earth and all created things. Remind me, O God, that your love is steadfast and never ending. Amen.

It is good to read scripture slowly and thoughtfully. In this case, the words "steadfast love" merit a close look. To be steadfast means to be firmly fixed in place, unchanging, determined. Most of us, if we reflect on our lives, can identify times and places where God has been faithful and steadfast, unchanging, determined to stick with us. Are we steadfast or "firm in belief" that God is faithful, even when we can't fully understand why difficult things happen to God's children?

When the sun is shining, our car is running well, and our home is not in need of any emergency repairs it is easy to take God's steadfast love for granted. It is when we are suddenly confronted with a tough change in life or a great loss that we question God's love and just how steadfast it is.

Knowing God well, finding the strength to affirm God's steadfast love for us in *all* circumstances, remembering that God is with us even when we don't feel it—all these things don't just happen by themselves. They happen when we live in community with other Christians and when we practice the spiritual disciplines faithfully and consistently.

God promises us refuge, no matter what. The "shadow of your wings" is that place of refuge. This is where God nourishes us with food and drink for our soul, so that we might continue in our steadfast relationship with God.

These are gifts for us to help us on our journey. The road is sometimes more difficult than at others. But, no matter what comes our way, God is indeed steadfast.

God of my salvation, thank you for your generous love. Walk with me this day. If difficult times come for me, let your Holy Spirit remind me that your love for me is steadfast. Amen.

You may have heard it said you should "keep your friends close, and keep your enemies closer." In an odd way, this could apply to this passage from Paul. But the friend/enemy dichotomy may not be an outside one, but one within each one of us.

Paul begins with the contrast between the previous lives his converts lived and their lives now as Christians. He reminds his readers that the idols they worshiped before their conversion were mute. Not all spirits are of God. People pretended these idols could speak, but they couldn't. By contrast, in their new lives as converts, the Holy Spirit bestowed upon believers the power of speech to confess the lordship of Jesus. This was true speech.

This is why Paul reminds the Corinthians of their past history as pagans. He wants to make sure the Corinthians understand that the confession of Jesus as Lord is the only cornerstone of the community. This confession is the one that binds the believers together and gives them the power to discern between that which is spiritual and what only pretends to be.

It is through the gift of Jesus Christ that God restores us to relationship with God. In today's passage, Paul is concerned about the gifts and spiritual manifestations that were being witnessed and experienced in Corinth. Paul did not want his new believers to be taken in by false idols.

So he tells them they must carefully measure and discern the difference. And, he says, the measure of whether or not a person or practice is truly spiritual is this confession: Jesus is Lord.

God, we thank you for the gift of your Holy Spirit to guide us and help us find our way in this world. We pray for discernment and strength to follow your Spirit and to stay close to you. Amen.

This passage, with its image of interconnectedness and whole-ness, calls to mind the picture of a body with many parts, all of them healthy and functioning properly. This satisfies our images of a good and healthy body. It also goes along with Paul's teaching here that the Spirit manifests itself in the life of each believer by imparting some different but complementary gift. It was when some in the early Christian community started to believe their gift was superior to someone else's that the trouble began. That's why Paul used the analogy of the body as the faith community and individuals its parts. It was a striking reminder that all are honored equally.

But let us consider this passage through a different lens. Let's think about a body whose parts may not meet our tradi-tional definition of a whole and functioning. I am a part of the military community, so I am sensitive to the increasing number of individuals with artificial limbs or wheelchairs or other devices to assist persons in their daily tasks. Amazing inven-tions enable people to do many of the things that I take for granted. Would we say that these persons are not a functioning body because of their dependence upon alternate body parts?

Technology is starting to restore to wounded veterans func-tions that, in an earlier decade, would not be possible. We see and read amazing stories of many documentaries and read many stories of brave young men and women who are adapting to a new life with arms, legs, or hands with moving fingers.

In an odd way, these veterans' "different" bodies lend a new and poignant way of looking at Paul's assertion that all are honored and all are needed. God gives us grace and gifts simply because God loves us so much.

God, for the gifts of grace, community and an ever-widening community, we give you thanks. Amen.

Be More Beautiful

I love the story of the mother of Jesus going to a wedding in Cana. How did she feel that morning when she woke up and knew she had a good reason to make her hair pretty and wear her nicer clothing? Her beloved son, Jesus, now a grown man, was also in town. He would be attending the same wedding with his friends!

As you get into it, the story gets better. The wine runs out, and Mary discreetly whispered into the ear of her son, "They have no wine, Jesus." Why did she do that? Of course, Mary knew Jesus well because he was her son. But what does she mean by this? It's a question that has many answers—and no answer at all.

Jesus was very specific in his performance of this first official miracle. When Jesus asked the servants for jars, he asked for some very particular jars. He wanted the stone water jars used for purification. Jesus had the servants add more water so that each was filled to the very top. The servants were then told to take some out and bring it to the chief steward.

Those who drank did not know where it came from but they knew it was very good wine. Why was it saved for last? Why had it not be served at the beginning of the wedding when flavor would be most noticed? Why would Jesus perform his first miracle at a wedding? His miracle didn't heal a child or bring sight back to an old man. It just gave partygoers more wine to drink. Why is that? What's going on here?

Many people have tried to answer these questions, and it is interesting to try. But most of the answers to these questions remain a mystery. What's not so mysterious is this: Jesus' generosity is abundant. The gifts he brings to us are beyond our imagination.

Jesus, thank you for your generosity. Help me this day to recognize the kindness of your gifts to me. Amen.

Joy and Strength in the Word

JANUARY 18–24, 2010 • KAY NESMITH

MONDAY, JANUARY 18 ～ *Read Nehemiah 8:5-6*

As a teacher's assistant in a kindergarten class in my small town, I am thrilled to witness my students learning something new every day. The room fills with squeals of delight when a puzzle is completed or when that stubborn shoe is finally tied!

Jack is the one who showed me true joy in learning. He had a tough home life with many challenges for a child so young. I often wondered how he even managed to get to school.

All year long, the class had been working on reading—learning the sounds letters make in preparation for reading. Jack lagged behind most of his classmates, but he kept at it. By March, he was reading simple words. I will never forget the day he came barreling over to the teacher and me with a crumpled paper book held high above his head. From the look on his precious face, we knew he was finally reading! Yes, the words were short and the story simple, but Jack had a blinding smile on his face as he shouted, "I can read this, I can read this!"

As joyous as we were at Jack's discovering he could read, so too were the people gathered who heard Ezra read the words in Nehemiah: their souls were renewed, they were blessed with understanding of the law.

As it was for Jack and as it was for those present for Ezra's reading, so may it be for us. May we be joyous in reading and understanding God's word. May we come to know God's word as our source of strength.

God, help me to find joy and strength as I read your word. Show me truth and wisdom. Enlighten me and give me joy. Amen.

Educator, wife, and mother of two daughters, living in the northeast Georgia mountains

When I was a new bride, my husband and I attended a small but growing church in the northern part of our state. It was full of young families, many of which were tied to the patriarchs and matriarchs of the church. There was a strong feeling of love and connection in that church that I have not felt since.

Miss Marion was a long-time member of the church. She always worked behind the scenes, especially when a meal was served. She was a true southern lady with the gift of hospitality, revealed most tangibly in what we called simply "Marion's covered dish." Her fried chicken or coconut cake often almost caused a scuffle as people rushed forward to grab a piece before it was all gone.

Miss Marion didn't teach Sunday school or keep the nursery. She wasn't the organist or the church secretary. She just did what she did best: cook delicious food to share with the community of Christ. God truly blessed that congregation with Miss Marion and her ability to cook and lovingly share with others.

In the body of Christ today, the call goes out for those who will share with others in the ways God has blessed them. The soloist with the amazing voice, the loving grandparent who keeps the nursery, the gifted teacher who opens the word of God Sunday after Sunday—all are needed to lift up the body of Christ.

It is the word of God that gives life to the community, and the gifts of the community that bring the word to life. We are blessed—no matter who we are or what our gifts—to be part of one body.

God, show us how to use our gifts as tools of service. Allow us to surrender ourselves to the movement of the Holy Spirit within us. Make us humble servants both in our churches and in the wider world beyond. Amen.

WEDNESDAY, JANUARY 20 ~ *Read Luke 4:14-21*

We've often heard the phrase, "You can't go home again." I remember the first time I returned to the university from which I graduated. I eagerly anticipated walking around campus, visiting some of the old classrooms and labs and even peeking in my old room at the sorority house. But so much had changed in the years I'd been away. Streets were now blocked off so I was unable to drive a familiar route; the classroom building where I'd spent countless hours had been torn down and replaced with a sleek new structure, and I was met with odd stares from very young women at the sorority house. I felt like a stranger in my old hometown. Stepping back in time is highly overrated! Driving home, I was more determined to look ahead and embrace my current life with new resolve.

Jesus began his public ministry by returning to a synagogue in Nazareth where he had been brought up. His teaching met with a mixture of wonder and rejection. Similar reactions to these same teachings continue today in our world. Jesus was appointed by God and anointed with the Holy Spirit to minister and to preach. His ministry was a prophetic ministry. And this news is nothing short of revolutionary: captives will be released, the blind will receive sight, those who have possessions and money will share with those who do not.

Following in Jesus' steps and proclaiming his message, we too are called to bring good news to the poor. And, no matter how we are received, we know that Jesus has walked this road before us. We know that Jesus sustains and strengthens us for our witness in the world.

God, keep me in your ways as I witness to the power of your words. Favor my lips with the good news Jesus preached and lived. Amen.

I've passed many dark nights sitting quietly on the deck of my house with my eyes on the heavens. A variety of feelings drive me to this tranquil place: worry, restlessness, desire for peace. From that comfortable and familiar vantage point, up through the prickly Georgia pines, God's creation slowly becomes visible. As I sit in anticipation, looking at the inky black, a true spectacle reveals itself, moment by moment. The stars appear to brighten, and before long I can trace my favorite constellation. This once-darkened sky fills to overflowing with sparkling light!

And so it is when I try to live my life fully dependent upon God. I may feel as though I am stumbling along in the dark—the job isn't fulfilling anymore, the kids act as though they are from another planet, someone I love just got a troubling report from the doctor, daily pressures squeeze the joy from life. The next step seems shrouded by fear, uncertainty, doubt or disobedience. Yet, if I remain still, God sheds the light I need to take the next step. The light may appear dim, but if I am faithful in my waiting, God too is faithful to reveal grace and mercy to brighten the way.

Without speaking a word, creation declares God's glory and presence. Without speaking a word, the heavens and the firmament interrupt our anxiety and worry with a powerful witness to God's power. Nothing, not even our daily cares and concerns, is hidden from God.

The psalmist says it clearly: God's law is perfect. It revives our soul. God's commandments enlighten our eyes and bring us vision.

It is these words that visit me as I sit on my deck at night. It is these words that challenge me, give me comfort and show me righteousness.

Thank you, God, for creating the heavens, for creating me! Shine the light of your word and the light of all creation on me so that I may know peace and joy. Amen.

I grew up with an older brother. I wanted to be everywhere my older brother was, all the time—much to his dismay. Whenever my brother played army in the backyard with his best friend, I would trail along with my dolls and a tiny American flag, ready to set up the nursing tent should anyone be wounded. He was so embarrassed by my presence that once, when I stuck my head into the tent where my brother and his friend were, he hit me in the nose with his metal toy pistol. He broke my nose, and I got two black eyes. As punishment, my brother not only had to play with me every day for the rest of that long hot summer—he also had to set up my nursing tent in the backyard and "tend" me until I got better. It was an *awful* summer, as he recalls.

In our world, as it was, no doubt, in Jesus' world, brothers and sisters sometimes act in holy ways—and sometimes they do not. In any gathering of Christians, there are some whose behavior is not exactly Christlike. When we face crises at work or challenges with our children, do we react in ways that look just like the world's reactions, or can people see there is something different about the ways we respond? Do we leave hard feelings and anger in our wake, or do we offer the peace and joy we say we seek as Christians?

For too long, the "body of Christ" has been seen as exclusionary—the very opposite of what Christ intended. Each of us is called to represent Christ, to reach out warmly to those around us. Christ has blessed us with forgiveness and peace. We can do no less for others.

God, you have so richly blessed my life. Show me today ways I can bless others with a kind word or deed. Make me a true member of the body of Christ. Amen.

My husband and I vacationed in southern Germany with his parents. We planned to take a bus tour through Italy down to Venice. Keith and his dad purchased the tickets in town. We rose early, eagerly anticipating the trip. We boarded the bus for the daylong journey and took our seats just as the tour guide began speaking . . . in German! We waited for the English translation, but more German followed. Slowly we realized we were on a tour to Venice, but one with a small glitch—this was a German language-only tour, and we didn't speak German!

Just as we would have benefited from a translator on our tour, so also the people in Nehemiah 8 needed Ezra to help them understand the Torah. When Ezra helped them understand what the scriptures meant, the truth became clear: the word of God must not only be read, it must also be interpreted. It was only by understanding the meaning of what Ezra read that the people could rejoice in the actual *rediscovery* of God's word.

God gives us the Bible for meditation and study, for instruction and practice. However, we, like the community in Nehemiah, need help understanding the Bible. We may be unfamiliar with how to study the Bible, or we may lack the discipline to spend enough time in meditation and study. We may have heard some passages so often we don't listen to them anymore; we may not have read unfamiliar passages because they seemed too difficult.

We need to read the scriptures within our faith community. We need leaders who can interpret God's word and make it real in our lives. The word read, studied, and interpreted gives meaning to our lives, gives us reason to rejoice.

God, thank you for loving us so much by giving us your word. May we honor you by spending time with your word each day. Amen.

Every time I look at the big blue plate on the bookcase I think of my grandmother, long since gone to be with the Lord. She and my grandfather had been married over sixty years when he died. They lived a simple and happy life—he in sales and she as a homemaker in the best sense.

My grandmother baked for ladies' luncheons in the small kitchen where the plate originally hung over the window. I spent many mornings "helping" and soaked up her answers to my numerous questions. Only now do I realize how much she was teaching me about love, life, and the Lord during those baking sessions.

The unusual plate had been a wedding gift and until it was passed along to me, I didn't realize that it had been dropped, cracked, and repaired many times.

When I questioned her about the plate, she told me of the couple who had given it to her and my pappy. The couple was childless and saddened by that fact, but they blessed others by their gentle and kind spirits. Out of their broken dreams, they gave so much to so many. They gave my grandparents their love and care.

We are not unlike the big blue plate. We have been broken by disappointment, unrealized dreams. And, like that big blue plate, God has repaired us in our broken places, brought our dreams back to life and given us into one another's keeping.

And so it was in Ezra's time. The broken community was put back together by the reading of God's word. Instead of weeping over their broken lives, the Israelites heard the word of God and knew the "joy of the Lord."

Sometimes redemption comes in the form of a blue plate. Sometimes it comes in the form of God's word, interpreted and made plain. But healing does come.

Loving God, healer of my brokenness, show me today someone who needs your healing love. Amen.

A Standing Invitation

JANUARY 25–31, 2010 • RAY WADDLE

MONDAY, JANUARY 25 ~ *Read Jeremiah 1:4-10*

Jeremiah opens with one of the great mysteries of the life of faith: the sense of calling, mission, vocation. Jeremiah's just a young man when God calls him to the task and ordeal of a prophet. Bamboozled by the idea, he insists on his unworthiness, but God knows better. God knows Jeremiah's potential.

The scarcely conceivable notion that the Maker of the Universe is tapping you for an amazing journey, a new identity or public witness, a revolutionary course inducing joy and sacrifice—well, it happens. As a journalist, I encounter people every day who've heard such a call for themselves, a divine beckoning. How did it come? Every sort of way: the bolt-of-lightning experience that makes page-one news or a sudden whisper or a persistent dream or, as often as not, a long, slow turning in personal perspective, years in the making.

Some people say they literally hear a voice. Was it God? Or conscience? Or the soul's own cry? Perhaps the divine calling breaks in on a person's life when the literal and the metaphorical become one and the same, a vision of justice and kindness; the effect is life-changing.

Then there are the believers who aren't called in a dramatic flourish, who see the mission before their eyes and go about it without fanfare. Jeremiah discovered his way, one of the most famous reckonings in human history. Everybody faces the prospect of a calling, whether it makes front-page news or not.

Eternal Spirit, keep me alert to the signs and wonders of your will, and lead me where you will. Amen.

Columnist, author, and editor writing about faith and culture; former religion editor for the *Tennessean* in Nashville; now living in Connecticut

We baby boomers are getting on up there, getting older, just plain old getting old. This psalm, the plea of a person crying out in old age, might one day be the baby boomers' unofficial theme song, the psalm to cherish in the twilight.

A boomer theme song? The vast boomer demographic—78 million Americans, the first wave now closing in on their 60s—always had a complicated relation to faith. About a third of the boomers left church and never came back. Another third wandered away but eventually returned. The other third never really left in the first place. Boomers grew up riding a golden age of pop songs and prosperity. Nostalgia, the sweet memory of the way things were, could be the tempting religion of old age.

The writer of Psalm 71, while reflecting on past deliverance and refuge, lays down a challenge to proclaim the living God in the present. The psalmist has not had an easy time of it. He cries out from feeble health and vulnerability, offering poignant details. The psalmist has been faithful to God during a long lifetime, but now enemies mock. He was once perhaps a teacher in the faith, but his strength is spent. Yet now, reaching deep inside once more and fighting back doubt and fear, he finds a reserve of trust in the divine, a vision of joy. A few verses later, the psalmist asks God for strength enough to proclaim God's might to all the generations to come. It's a big-hearted request, a generous way to spend the remaining fragments of one's old age, taking harp and lyre in hand to proclaim God's wondrous deeds.

We boomers have had a good run. We should remember our privileges with gratitude, search our hearts, and muster the courage to proclaim the faith again—"for you are my rock and my fortress"—for all to hear.

Holy Lord, you are the rock of refuge no matter how uncertain the times we live in. I pray your name with gladness, thankful for the gift of life. Amen.

The psalmist testifies that it was God who took him from his mother's womb, a declaration of great intimacy and faith. It has echoes in Jeremiah's cry that God knew him in the womb.

What a breathtaking image: God was there when our tiny hearts and minds were yet unformed and now waits patiently for us to come around. Some of us get the message early on, seeing our parents praising God and reading scripture, and we follow suit. Others of us arrive at the party way later, after decades of spiritual sleepwalking or confusion or anger or plain bad luck. God's governance isn't altered by our false turns or inertia. The divine patience arcs across the span of one's whole life. A standing invitation beckons us to step into the drama of redemption.

In Psalm 71, the psalmist declares a lifelong trust in the Lord. But now in old age that lifelong relationship feels tested as never before. Poor health, cruel enemies, and corrosive doubts torment him. There's a momentary slip of resolve: Do not cast me off in the time of old age.

But the logic of divine presence is clear enough—the God who was there in the womb, when we're helpless and silent and unaware, is there at the other end of life too. The psalmist summons determination, puts aside fear, gathers a lifetime's verbal tools of faith, and goes out with a bold witness of praise to God. An entire life is traced here, from womb nearly to tomb, from the prenatal heartbeat to the music of a last leave-taking. When the final credits roll on his life, the psalmist makes sure Who gets top billing.

Dear God, you've been constant from the beginning, a presence our whole lives, even in the shadows of old age. Grant me the voice to praise you with ever-renewing force to the last. Amen.

This is one of the great passages of all scripture. Every time I read it, something fresh leaps out at me, usually: "Love is patient; love is kind." My wife and I read this passage at our wedding. It remains a foundation document for matrimony.

Some days other passages clear their throat and take center stage: "If I have all faith, so as to remove mountains, but do not have love, I am nothing." This is startling to hear in a nation of so much official religion and doctrinal competition to see who can market the strongest faith.

At the moment, though, yet another passage chimes forth with alarming authority: "For we know only in part, and we prophesy only in part." Our knowledge is imperfect. In the world of religion, many of us are reluctant or afraid to admit we don't know the mind of God after all. We're afraid such an admission would look like weakness or spiritual laziness or look bad on the annual evaluation.

But there it is in the Holy Bible, permission to state the obvious: We don't know the whole picture, not yet. We peer, all of us, into the mirror dimly, the glass darkly. Our doctrinal knowledge cannot be perfect. To insist that it is perfect opens the door for arrogance, vanity, and violence. Better to trust actions over words, the actions urged by Paul in First Corinthians: Love is the ultimate action, the needed thing, the grown-up thing in a grieving world.

Dear God, you give us love, and you give us each day to fill with love. May I be a worthy instrument of your love. In Jesus' name. Amen.

Do you take the Bible literally? Many people declare the whole Bible is literally true, and they mean it. For others, *literally* is one of those litmus test words—a gotcha term in religious debate when one side tries to outdo the other for first place and top ranking in the Bible-believer playoffs.

Usually literalism focuses on the six-day creation story in Genesis or on Jonah in the belly of the fish or on the miracles of Jesus. Such debates never get around to this famous passage on love written by Paul in his first letter to the Corinthians. But what if everyone indeed took this passage literally; that is, took it to heart, as if the words had the unflinching, nonnegotiable, divine quality of authority, which they do?

What would the world look like then? What would Christianity be like? Imagine: Ideological tensions would cease. Energy would shift from doctrinal haggling and committee work to incessant acts of random kindness. The culture wars would be mothballed. Religious and ethnic bitterness would lose relevance. Each faith would feel safe enough to trust its own best insights and gifts to the world—the triumph of love, right action over righteous talk, results and not speculation. Divine love would be a verb again and not a pious abstraction. Literally.

Heavenly God, I thank you for your word, laid down in the pages of scripture across the many centuries, speaking to us plainly. Help me read it with courage, that it will enter my heart and move me forward to action. Amen.

From the start, Jesus was acquainted with rejection, even at his birth in Bethlehem where there was no room in the inn. And now, near the beginning of his public ministry, rejection stands ready to isolate him. Speaking to the home-turf congregation in Nazareth, he has just announced a world-shattering manifesto, the old words from Isaiah made new: release to the captives, sight for the blind, freedom for the oppressed. But it doesn't take. People are alarmed and getting mad. The acceptable year of the Lord is anything but acceptable. By any earthly measure, his is a disastrous hometown debut.

Jesus' words always had a way of rubbing people the wrong way. Only committed followers got the picture, and even they misunderstood much of what he was saying. So Jesus never stayed anywhere for long. After preaching, he slipped through the clutches of doctrinal hostility, finding daylight, moving on. Divinity on earth is no easy fit. Anything Jesus said was likely to be met with befuddlement or irritation except to a disciple's heart.

Nothing much has changed. It's no easy thing for a preacher to stand in the pulpit and read these subversive words from the old Holy Bible and declare the acceptable year of the Lord, even in the year 2010. Release to the captives. Freedom for the oppressed. Hard sayings indeed. They imply rearranging personal values and questioning public priorities. More than two thousand years after Jesus' ministry, divine messages and earthly life mingle uneasily still. Somehow, though, the good news keeps arriving. It's being fulfilled in our hearing today, every day.

What will I do today to help make this the acceptable year of the Lord?

One brief scene in a Nazareth synagogue changed the world. Jesus stood and read from the prophet Isaiah, then sat down and declared that God's time had come to be fulfilled. When Jesus spoke, a vision of compassion, healing, action, and redemption was released into the world. It's been circling the globe ever since, looking for a place of welcome.

It must have been an astonishing moment to hear these words from Jesus, this compelling new testimony to life's possibilities. Afterward, a silence surely filled the room, a long moment of silence, as the words sank in. But it only lasted a moment. The protest from his audience was almost immediate.

They knew this man, his family, his ordinary daily circumstances. He was local, surely too local and familiar to be an honorable prophet.

After Jesus escaped Nazareth, he went to Capernaum and preached out of the synagogue there. It became a base of operations where he performed mighty acts of healing, though even there he was eventually rejected. Years ago I visited the ruins of the Capernaum synagogue near the banks of the Galilee, the likely spot where Jesus himself preached. It was a disorienting experience—such a small place, crowded, tourist-centered. My tour group was tired and on a tight schedule. Bus fumes were everywhere. How could such a headachy scene be ground zero for history-altering news of spiritual import?

The joke was on me, of course. I was letting everyday irritations get in the way of a biblical truth. From this humble place, Jesus' message of kindness and decision was released all those years ago like the dove freed from the ark after the great flood, a vision of compassion still looking for a place to light its feet.

Dear God, it's my privilege to share this earth and walk this world for a time. I rejoice in the power of your Son, his words, witness, and resurrection. Amen.

Epiphanies

FEBRUARY 1–7, 2010 • V. H. "SONNYE" DIXON JR.

MONDAY, FEBRUARY 1 ～ *Read Isaiah 6:1-13*

In the year that King Uzziah died, I saw the LORD sitting on a throne.

The prophet Isaiah recalls the timing of pivotal moments in his life journey according to how they fall, date-wise, to a significant death in his community. I do that too. For example, whenever I recount the events around my high school graduation, the first thing I recall is that year was the same one my father died.

This week marks the forty-six year anniversary of a culture-altering event for people of my generation. On February 7, 1964, the Beatles arrived in the United States. I was one of the estimated seventy-three million people who tuned in to *The Ed Sullivan Show* that Sunday night to see John, Paul, George, and Ringo.

I have two memories from that night. First, when the Beatles were singing, I turned to my African-American mother and said, "I want to wear my hair like that." A loving, indulgent parent, she took me to a department store and bought me a Beatles wig.

The second memory was more bittersweet. Three months before, US president John F. Kennedy had been assassinated in Dallas. It was the end of an era for my nation—and the world. Like many, I had wondered that November day if I would ever smile or celebrate again. But the world continued to spin, and the nation began to recover. A few months later the Beatles landed and that night in front of the television, I cheered and danced.

I have looked back on that night many times to remind myself that God does bring about new mercies.

O God, as we near the end of this Epiphany season, we give you thanks that you still reveal yourself to us. Amen.

Lead pastor of Hobson United Methodist Church, an intentionally diverse, inclusive, and reconciling congregation, in Nashville, TN

With the exception of Holy Week and Easter, the season of Epiphany is my favorite time of the liturgical year. Even though I am not fond of the bitter cold that comes with January and February, my spirit is filled with the promise of this Christian season. At my best, I spend the whole year seeking Epiphany, seeking the living God to reveal God's self to me.

It would be great if God would appear as this scripture imagines: as "the Master sitting on a throne—high, exalted!—and the train of his robes filled the Temple. Angel-seraphs hovered above him" (THE MESSAGE). While I'm looking for pomp and glory, though, I suspect that I have missed some important moments of revelation because God has instead, come to us as God appeared to the Magi—in the form of a child.

Even as I seek God in the faces of children, I could miss the revelation of God's incarnation if I look only in a well-funded private school; God might also be in an inner city public school that has failed "No Child Left Behind" standards.

According to the Gospel of Matthew, Joseph and Mary took the child Jesus to Africa to escape persecution. So, maybe the One I'm seeking is the child of Somalian refugees living in exile in a homeless shelter. Or a child whose parents are undocumented residents trying to escape economic or political collapse in Latin America.

We are reminded at Epiphany of the divine. The Divine One calls us to take divine love and divine justice into the streets, back alleys, and fields—or wherever children of God suffer because others of God's children have failed to live out their faith. Epiphany calls us to seek and find God in unlikely places, for that is when God's light shines more fully in our lives.

Lord God, reveal your light to me. Give me the boldness and courage to travel to those places where I can see it best. Amen.

I love to drive through the countryside, looking for small, rural church buildings that dot the landscape. I remember one church I discovered on a drive through Appalachia in Kentucky.

The church was surrounded by a beautiful garden of flowers, and the cemetery was as well manicured as any I have ever seen. I stopped in front of the church to take pictures, and a man in his seventies came out of the church. At first I was a little afraid. After all, I was a black man riding around in the foothills of Appalachia. He didn't seem friendly—probably, like me, his fears and stereotypes colored his perceptions. So I blurted out, "I'm just admiring your lovely church. Are you the pastor? I'm a pastor."

"No, son. I'm not the preacher. You need, 'im?" he asked

"No. I was just looking," I replied

"You said you are a preacher?" he asked, a little more relaxed.

"Yes, sir." By that time we were close enough to shake hands, so we did; and we both began to let down our barriers. He told me the small church was one of five on a single circuit, and they met only monthly for worship. I wondered aloud how they could afford to maintain the church and grounds.

My new acquaintance explained that when he was a teenager he felt a call to ministry. His pastor, who was trying to discourage him, said he must first learn to serve. So the pastor gave him the job of mowing the church lawn and cemetery and promised one day to talk to him about becoming a minister.

That was sixty years ago, and he's still mowing. Caring for the church building and grounds became the man's ministry. That day I *saw* one of the best sermons ever, and I recalled the text for this day, "The LORD will fulfill his purpose for me; your steadfast love, O LORD, endures forever."

O Lord, I know you will fulfill your purpose for me. I give thanks for the ministry to which you have called me. Amen.

During a recent session of vacation Bible school, I revealed to a group of children that my favorite movie of all time has always been *The Wizard of Oz*, starring Judy Garland.

I recounted for them my favorite scene, when Dorothy and friends discovered that the wizard was not really a wizard. "Pay no attention to that man behind the curtain!" I repeated, using my best imitation of the booming voice of the magic man's voice. "Go! The Great and Powerful Oz has spoken!"

One boy interrupted me, "What's a wizard?" I explained that a wizard was like a magician. That week we had discussed the miracles of Jesus. The lesson for that day was Jesus feeding of the multitude. So I was not shocked when the boy blurted out, "Jesus was a magician! He fed all those people!" Before I could correct him, a girl next to him sharply said, "No, he wasn't! If Jesus had been a magician he would have made all the people disappear when he found out they didn't have any food!"

Too often, we find ourselves stymied when we teach the miracles of Jesus. We look for safe, scientifically sound explanations. But that's not relevant. Jesus was not a humbug or fake wizard but the Messiah promised and sent by God. Yes, the stories of his mighty acts are incredible. His very manifestation, which we celebrate at Epiphany, defies easy explanation. Its truth has sustained us for more than two thousand years. It was not magic but the power of the living God that fueled Jesus' works on earth.

Paul encouraged the early church to "hold firmly to the message . . . unless you have come to believe in vain." Our faith is grounded, not in fairy tales, but in the matchless power of the God of the ages. That power may defy human understanding, but it is real.

God, I am sure of one thing: you are real, for I can feel you in my soul. Amen.

Usually controversy accompanies any reported estimated numbers of people in a crowd, particularly at a public demonstration or political event. I first noticed this in reports about the August 1963 Poor People's March on Washington. United States government officials recorded the crowd at just over 200,000, while organizers of the march boasted over 300,000 people attendance. Media reports hovered in between. The official government estimate of the crowd at the inauguration of US president Lyndon Johnson in 1965 was 1.2 million; Republicans said less than a million people attended. Attendance at the Million Man March in 1995 was estimated by organizers at over 1.5 million. Mall police reported 655,000.

I'm a stickler for accurate reporting, so these variations in the numbers annoy me. It's the same when I read the Gospel accounts. So, Jesus reportedly fed 5,000 men, not counting women and children? Some scholars estimate the total number of people fed was around 20,000. This is hard for me to accept considering the total population of Jerusalem at that time was about 80,000. Could Jesus have fed one-fourth of the community at one sitting?

Another number story that bugs me is found in 1 Corinthians 15:6. That passage says that Jesus appeared to more than five hundred at one time. Really, *five hundred at one time?* That would have been a lot of people. What troubles me is that neither Luke nor Matthew includes this claim, so there seems to be no corroboration.

I can almost hear the apostle Paul yelling, "Stop! What difference does it make if Jesus appeared to a few dozen or if the number exceeded five hundred? What matters for your faith is not numbers, but this: "that Christ died for our sins . . . and that he was buried, and that he was raised on the third day in accordance with the scriptures."

Sweet Jesus, forgive me when I focus on the numbers and not on you. Thank you for dying and rising. Amen.

O ne summer while attending a meeting in Atlanta, I was eating dinner when a woman came in and sat next to me. She ordered a glass of wine. She sat there for about fifteen minutes just holding the glass. Her silence and motionlessness made me so uncomfortable that I asked her if something was wrong. She didn't answer, just continued to stare at the glass.

When I got ready to leave, I asked the waiter for my check. I told him to place her wine on my ticket because she it seemed she didn't want it. Only then did she turn toward me. I could see the tears brimming in her eyes. Sensing her pain, I said, "I hope things get better for you." Then this fragile soul replied, "This is my two-year anniversary of sobriety; I don't think I can make it."

I resisted the temptation to ask why or what was wrong. Instead I simply said, "You will make it." Then I did something uncharacteristic for me, particularly in a strange city away from my congregation. I asked her if we could pray together, which we did. Afterward, she walked away, leaving the glass.

The next summer when I was back in Atlanta for that same meeting. I saw her again, but I didn't recognize her until she spoke. She introduced herself and said, "I am the woman you prayed with last summer." She told me that had been a difficult time for her. In the new place she had felt invisible, and the temptation to drink was great. She had even questioned whether or not God knew she existed. She said that during our prayer she felt God watching her.

After reading today's passage, people have asked, "Why did Simon, James, and John immediately leave everything and follow Jesus?" I believe they did it because he offered them a word of hope. We, like Jesus, must have the courage to bring hope to others. The potential impact is incalculable.

O Lord, help me to be aware of those around me today. Give me the courage to offer words of hope to those who need it. Amen.

I preached a baccalaureate service using this text. The sermon title was "Plans Do Change." I wanted the young men and women in audience to know that even though they had their lives all planned, sometimes plans change.

I am convinced when Simon, James, and John "finished school," they expected to spend the rest of their lives on the Gennesaret Lake fishing. But those plans changed the day they encountered Jesus on the shore.

These fishermen were coming in after a long night of unproductive fishing when Jesus got into their boat to escape the crowd that had begun to press upon him. Exhausted from the night, Simon was probably too tired to deny Jesus' request to push out from the shore so he could address the crowd.

Luke doesn't tell us the content of Jesus' teaching, but I imagine Simon was amazed as he sat next to Jesus listening to every word. But Luke does tell us about what happened when Jesus finished his teaching. Jesus said to Simon, "Let's go fish in the deep."

Simon, an experienced fisherman, probably knew that they weren't going to have any luck fishing in deep waters in the late morning. But Simon replied, "Yet if you say so, I will let down the nets." Simon's plan—to get back to shore or to talk more in-depth with Jesus—changed because his catch was so great that it nearly broke his nets. Instead of talking to Jesus, Simon had to call his friends to assist him in getting the catch to the shore.

Luke tells us that Simon sensed his plans were about to be changed because he said to Jesus, "Go away from me, Lord." We know change is scary. It was to Simon. He probably said to Jesus, "I know you probably are going to ask me to go with you, but I'm trained to fish." Sensing Simon's apprehension Jesus spoke to him, "Do not be afraid; from now on you will be catching people."

Plans do change.

O Lord, when you call, help me answer and follow. Amen.

Inspiration and the Glimmer of Glory

FEBRUARY 8–14, 2010 • SALLY DYCK

MONDAY, FEBRUARY 8 ~ *Read Exodus 34:29-35*

The transfiguration of Moses is a mysterious story. It's been debated throughout history. What does it mean? Why did his face shine so brightly when he came down off the mountain with the law? John Wesley believed Moses' face shone because Moses "carried his credentials in his very countenance."

When something significant happens to us, we too "carry it in our countenance." Our whole bodies reveal whether we're sad or happy. Likewise when we claim to believe in the transforming power of Christ, shouldn't our faces as well as our very beings come alive with the palpable presence of God?

Cornelia (Connie) Wieck is a United Methodist missionary with the denomination's General Board of Global Ministries. She teaches college-aged students who will become teachers in the rural countryside. She never said anything about her Christian faith to her students. She simply sought to inspire in them a sense of service in teaching.

One day the mother of one of Connie's students came to her to tell her that her daughter wondered why Connie cared so much about people. The mother told her daughter that Connie was a Christian. The daughter exclaimed, "If Connie is a Christian, I want to be one too."

Without words, Connie's faith shines through her smile, her actions, and her love of people and the world. It's contagious!

O God, shine through me this day so that others may be compelled to know you and follow your son, Jesus Christ. Amen.

Resident bishop of the United Methodist Church's Minnesota area

I've always wondered if Jesus got up one morning and said to his followers, "I think I'm going to climb that mountain over there. Would anyone like to join me?" All eyes around the campfire looked toward what scholars think might have been Mount Hermon. The disciples would do anything for him but climbing a 9,300-foot mountain seemed a bit extreme.

Yet Peter, James, and John went on an extreme adventure with Jesus. It was a rough trip for these disciples, and the physical aspect was the least of it. Yet even as they bumbled through, they grew in their discipleship. They encountered Jesus in a way that they had not experienced before. He was transfigured, changed, transformed, and metamorphosed right before their eyes. They were awed and silenced before this new experience of Jesus. Climbing the mountain with Jesus was extreme discipleship; seeing his transfiguration had an extreme impact on their lives.

Like the disciples, we are called to extreme discipleship too. It's so much more comfortable down at base camp with the others, but then we find ourselves wondering why we don't glow with the palpable presence of God, why our faith doesn't grow as it's stretched to new heights, and why our lives don't go in new and life-changing ways.

Jesus calls us to grow in our willingness and also in our skills to follow him wherever he will lead us. Physically, mentally, emotionally, and spiritually our Christian faith challenges us—or it should—every day to stretch ourselves to new limits of compassion, service, justice, and love.

O God who reveals yourself to us: help us to follow Jesus that we might grow in our faith, discipleship, and joy. Amen.

Peter just didn't know what to do. Peter knew that what was happening on the mountain was important, significant, and even profound. Jesus was changing right before his eyes, and he was being joined by Moses and Elijah. Light was flashing everywhere. Was it lightning, and what was this cloud enveloping them? Peter didn't exactly stop and think about it. He reacted.

Peter wanted to concretize the moment and make it last. I've always imagined that if Peter were in this situation today, he would take out his digital camera and try to line up Moses, Elijah, and Jesus for a shot. He'd take the picture home and show his family and friends. He'd look at it from time to time. Put it in a book. Keep it as a memento.

In essence, that's what Peter suggested to Jesus that he do. He wanted to make the moment last forever by building a monument to commemorate it. By so doing he was distancing himself from this profound moment instead of letting the power of God's glory in Jesus fill his life.

At significant times in life—weddings, baptisms, family gatherings of joy or sorrow and even at spiritual moments— we can distance ourselves from them by taking a picture, trying to hang on to them, clinging to the moment. We like our monuments and booths, our photos to tell the story, instead of entering into the profound experience with God and others and letting it wash over us and change us forever.

O great and glorious God, who comes to us in all the experiences of our lives; help us to embrace your presence, fixing it in our hearts and minds so that we may grow closer to you and others. Amen.

A braham Joshua Heschel, the twentieth-century Jewish mystic, philosopher, and reformer of Judaism, repeatedly wrote that awe precedes faith. This simple phrase reminds me why we in our modern, technological, automated lives struggle so with faith. What takes our breath away at its beauty and wonder?

Every morning I like to go for a run in my neighborhood or wherever I am. Even though I have lived and run in the north central states, including Minnesota, with cold, wind, and snow, I don't like to run indoors. I run partly to be outside each day. Otherwise I could go days without going outside except for a few paces from my car to the office or to the grocery store.

When I run through the tall trees and the changing seasons, see owls and critters, and hear the rushing creek or feel the falling snow on my face, I am reminded of a transcendent God who brought mountains as well as people into existence. I experience the transcendent God each morning as I run.

The transcendent God revealed in Psalm 99 calls us to extol the name of God because it is God who has made the heavens and earth as well as the people who inhabit the earth. It is the transcendent God who can "execute justice and righteousness."

It's both humbling and a huge comfort to be reminded that I am not God every day as I run through nature. As I look up— if not to the mountains, at least to the tops of the trees to see the brightness of a new sunrise—I give thanks to God. I may not worship God at God's "holy mountain," but I worship God in the great cathedral of nature each day.

O transcendent God: lift our faces to see your glory in creation around us, lift our minds to recognize how great you are, and lift our hearts to bless your holy name. Amen.

Mother Teresa received what she called her Inspiration. It was a "calling within a call" to serve the most destitute and poor of Calcutta. It gave her strength and determination as she moved through the many levels of bureaucracy, resistance and uncertainty in making her Inspiration a reality.

As she was persisting in bringing her Inspiration to reality, she felt the presence of God intensely within her. It lifted her spirits and made her face shine. Her Inspiration helped her to give her whole life to the poor for Jesus' sake, and she did not "lose heart" as she served others.

When the Inspiration became a reality and the mission was begun in Calcutta and across the world, the glow within her seemed to die away. People were shocked after her death to discover that she had felt darkness of spirit for years as she worked tirelessly to care for the poor and to carry out her mission.

While she felt she had lost the inner glow of Christ, she came to see it in others. In every person she met—no matter how poor, sick, alone and offensive to all sensibilities—she saw the glow of Christ reflected. And the poor saw Christ reflected on her face whether she felt the glow within or not.

Moses' face glowed when he received his Inspiration of God's word. While the glow remained with him, he also experienced the tedium, disappointment, and struggle with God as he led people through the wilderness. Like Moses and Mother Teresa, we may not always feel the glow of God's presence within us. But it can be seen on the faces of others, and they may see it on ours when we follow Christ in our love and service.

O Great Inspiration to us all, unveil from our lives whatever keeps us from revealing your face to others so that through us others may see you. Amen.

E ven Jesus needed to know that he was God's own beloved son so that he could face the cross of suffering and death.

But it's not just Jesus who needed to know who he was and whose he was. We all need to know our identity as the children of God and be assured of God's love for us. There's no more poignant example of the need for this assurance in our lives than that of Sister Helen Prejean's experiences with several men that she visited over the years on Louisiana's death row.

One of her inmates, Robert Willie, was about to go to his death. She was his spiritual counselor, and as she was sitting with him in his last hours, she was at a loss for words. All she could think to say at one point was, "You are a child of God."

This hardened, heinous criminal looked up at her with surprise in his eyes. He said, "Ain't nobody ever called me no son of God before." He smiled and sadly said that he'd been called a lot of things before, "but never no son of God." No, not every one of us is the son of God as Jesus was, but we're all children of God—the sons and daughters of God.

Imagine if we treated every child as a child of God. Could it make the difference in the way in which a child views himself? Could it remind each child of the best within herself rather than the worst?

O Parent of all your sons and daughters, thank you for your beloved son, Jesus, whose life, death, and resurrection make it possible for us to be your children. When I meet a child today, help me to speak and act as your child toward one of your children. Amen.

SUNDAY, FEBRUARY 14 ~ *Read Luke 9:28-36*

TRANSFIGURATION

I'm reminded of another man who climbed a mountain to glory and then used that glory to love and serve humanity. Sir Edmund Hillary was the first to scale Mount Everest, the world's tallest mountain peak, in 1953. His glory was won with his Sherpa guide, Tenzing Norgay. They climbed the mountain without all of today's special fabrics and equipment to protect against wind and cold. It was truly their courage and skill that put them at the top. The world often asked which one of them got to the top first, but Hillary refused to say; they shared the glory.

Imagine the glory of the sun shining upon the snow-covered mountains and the glory of decades of fame. But imagine also that Hillary spent the rest of his life using his fame and glory to raise money and provide schools, hospitals, and other infrastructure for the people of the Himalayas. He established twenty-seven schools, two dozen hospitals, a dozen medical clinics, numerous bridges over wild mountain rivers, and freshwater pipelines through villages.

Until his death in 2008 at the age of eighty-eight, Hillary poured his life, passion, and fame into the lives and livelihoods of people the world will never know and who could never repay what he did for them.

Once God's glory touches us, it is in many ways beyond our control. God's glory will lead us where God desires; we simply respond to God's glory with discipleship and service.

If our lives have any glimmer of glory in them, let us use them to enlighten minds through education, lighten hearts that are suffering with joy, and illuminate the world with the witness of Christ.

O God of glory, help us to use opportunities, gifts, and graces, that come our way in order to serve others. Amen.

Lent's Stark Realities

FEBRUARY 15–21, 2010 • BEVERLY J. JONES

MONDAY, FEBRUARY 15 ~ *Read Joel 2:1-2, 12-17*

The storm clouds were brewing, low and dark across the horizon. Churning slowly they moved closer and closer. Their churning was silent from the place I was standing; the air around me was quiet and still. I knew what was moving toward me was nature's hydroelectric power, ready to unleash a dangerous mix of wind, water, lightning, and hail.

Judah faced the mass of migrating locusts once again. The slow undulating waves approaching had power to destroy crops ready for harvest and, with them, all security and hope. Mincing no words, the prophet Joel declares, "Wake up you drunkard and weep . . . Mourn like a young woman in sackcloth . . . Despair you farmers . . . the harvest of the field is destroyed." There are circumstances that cut to the quick human plans, desires, and hopes.

Ash Wednesday invites us to a bright awareness of the stark reality of our situation: the deep knowledge that all is not well in the world and we are not as secure as we thought. I am not as blameless and innocent as I pretend to be. To us Joel shouts, "Blow the trumpet! Sound the alarm! The day of the Lord is coming!" It will be a day of clouds and thick darkness, unleashing the truth about us, about faith and faithlessness. A shadow is cast toward Black Friday. Experience alone teaches us that this week's harsh truths will turn out to be good.

God of life and death, in the Lenten days ahead, cast your loving judgment toward my life, that I may turn my face to yours and be saved. Amen.

United Methodist minister and member of the New Mexico Conference; serving as a district superintendent

I watched as snow covered the landscape, blanketing the rough ground beneath it: rocks and stones, brittle sage in the sandy soil . . . and trash. The trash of this landfill is the place people seeking a better life had purchased "property" to build the simplest of homes along the Mexico-U.S. border. No matter how much trash is removed, there is another layer beneath it. The shifting winds blow away the sand and dirt to reveal a new layer of discarded trash. Bits and pieces of trash poke through the sand to the layer where life is lived.

Some of the items uncovered had been of great use in their time: a toy for a child, plates and cups for family meals, shoes to protect tender feet. Other items were trash from the beginning: plastic bottles, cellophane bags, disposable diapers. Day in and day out, families diligently work to keep their yards free of trash. They are determined to have a home and a better life for their children.

Our work and God's in the Lenten season is to allow the signs of brokenness to come to the surface of our lives. It is not easy work. It may be difficult to distinguish that in our lives which from the beginning was trash, from those things which were once useful but have long since not done us or anyone else any good.

Clearing one layer of sin from the surface may serve only to reveal another that will take time and energy to clear away. No blanket of snow can remove our troubles, no magic wand—or prayer—will clean up our sins, no sacrificial ritual will give us wisdom. Only God's steadfast love and abundant mercy can do that. It is not easy work. Not for God. Not for us.

God of love and mercy, give me patience this day to sustain a willing spirit and to join in the witness of others who never give up on your love and your hope for their lives. Amen.

ASH WEDNESDAY

The lights were low and the candles bright on the altar as we filed one by one to receive the burnt ash of last year's palms; a mark that let us know that repentance is a sober thing. I felt humbled and dependent upon God. My life was in need of some turning around, and I was getting my courage up to make those turns. I knew it would take an extra push, and I hoped for a "holy moment."

As much as I was seeking a holy moment, a feeling that would confirm my need and commitment, I soon realized that the power of Ash Wednesday is not to be found in that feeling of religiousness and security we get from participating in its ritual. Oh, do not be mistaken. There is a great feeling of power to be found in well-done ritual. Through ritual we have the opportunity to bring our whole selves into the present moment. This is the power of singing the school fight song as the team takes the court or the procession of the turkey to the Thanksgiving dinner table. Ritual offers us the invitation to embody the focus of our attention.

Jesus no doubt understood and affirmed the power of ritual to strengthen our relationship with God. But he also understood the power of ritual to manipulate people into a self-centered religion designed to gain the security of social status. He easily spotted such "spirituality." And, he offered a counter measure to those who would follow God. He is simple and direct. Give in secret. Pray in secret. Fast in secret. We find our treasure and our holy moments there in the quiet and deliberate disciplines that need no outward show.

Jesus, be with us as we seek the holy moments that come when we are alone, in secret, with you. Amen.

A Levite mother fearful of the death threats of Pharaoh placed her infant son into a small basket sealed with tar and pitch and placed it among the reeds of the River Nile. Did she know that she put the saving grace of God into that basket that day? Certainly her hopes for the child welled up as Pharaoh's daughter took him in. Could she see the possibilities and the risks of letting him go?

The book of Deuteronomy is written in the form of a sermon from Moses to the people of Israel as they prepare for their entrance into the promised land. Their journey has been long and arduous. Freed from the pharaoh's yoke of slavery, they realized they were free to wander in the wilderness that held at once hope, fear, temptation, and deliverance.

Now, perched near their God-given goal, Moses tells them about something they are to do down the road when he is long gone. He offers them a litany to be enacted by the people and the priest once their feet are planted on solid ground and the crops they have planted are fully grown. The litany retells their past and confirms their present. Moses knew how prone his people were to forget, to get distracted, and to fall into ruts they had cut in the wilderness. He could see the possibilities and risks of letting Israel go into the future without him.

Jesus pointed his face and feet toward Jerusalem. He knew what he was doing. Each step for him was the incarnation of the possibility and risk inherent in a life worth leading. Each day of Lent invites us to that same possibility and risk.

What risks and possibilities would you include in a life worth leading? What risks have you already encountered in your faith life? What possibilities?

The moment of decision. While it is an act of the will, it is often experienced as the free gift of grace. Something wings its way into our spirit, and we act. I watched in awe as the 2008 Olympic divers took their place on the platform in the aqua cube to make their dives as the world watched. Taking the platform from the ladder with a slight jerk of the arms, shaking out the nerves and awaking the muscles, then finally stepping forward.

The spirit quiets. The mind at first works to focus its attention. There is an ingathering of the moment, every muscle tuning itself to an inner beat that comes from a finely honed impulse. This is the moment. The core of the self knows. The decision is made "corporately." Body, mind, and spirit fuse into unity, diving with a rhythmic harmony that expresses itself in pure grace. The moment of decision overrides the value of any score that the outside judges can make. To let the power of their judgment take hold is to flinch into the abyss of chaos.

"Jesus, full of the Holy Spirit, returned from the Jordan and was led by the Spirit in the wilderness, where for forty days he was tempted by the devil." Seeking to take full advantage of Jesus' diminished physical state, the devil attempts to confront and attack Jesus from the inside; quoting beloved scripture to distract Jesus from his relationship with God; attempting to goad Jesus into using his power as a defensive option; inviting Jesus to step into an awesome display of his power, now.

Jesus knew better. The core of the self knows. Decision is an intentional act of the will. Its most powerful moment is the freeing gift of grace.

O God, as I seek to follow in the steps of Jesus in this season of Lent, help me to do your will in my body, in my mind, and in my spirit. Amen.

Ifound myself frustrated that some parents had decided that Sunday morning worship was the right place and time for their children to eat their fast-food breakfast. It was an unholy distraction. I, as a child, had been taught to enter the sanctuary in the silence of holiness and with a reverence for ritual that made the elements of Holy Communion and an occasional cherry-flavored cough drop the only food to be consumed in the sanctuary. I was getting used to the benefits of informal worship, but a sausage biscuit was to me, in a word, ridiculous.

Any number of things can stir up in us our self-righteousness based on our experiences. Some may be well founded, others simply shortsighted. Either way, they can become the real stumbling block to worship. Distractions creep in. We take our eyes off Jesus. We fumble the ball, losing it for ourselves and for others.

We are not saved by our own righteousness, the apostle Paul proclaimed. We are saved by grace, all the way. At first, this idea of grace offends our sensibilities. "I know what proper behavior is in the sanctuary. I know how the Lord should be treated here."

To "be reconciled to God" is to relinquish our claim to righteousness, taking into full account the power of sin and the power of God to overcome it. This is not the same as ignoring real problems or insights. Paul sought to help the church to discern the real issues in what it meant to be the body of Christ. Sorting out the power of God's grace, especially in church, will involve some sleepless nights, sorrow, and defensiveness. Truthful speech, patience, and kindness do not come easy. Did Jesus ever say that they would?

What behaviors at church irritate you? How can the temptation to self-righteousness be tempered by the gospel of grace for you? for others?

SUNDAY, FEBRUARY 21 ~ *Read Psalm 91:1-2, 9-16*

First Sunday in Lent

Trust. Sometimes fragile, sometimes the strength of a fortress, we venture into each day with trust; trust in people, trust in life, trust in God. In Psalm 91 the psalmist professes that the Lord is "my refuge and my fortress; my God in whom I trust." The psalmist gives personal testimony to the claim that God is trustworthy—able to deliver, protect, and satisfy.

The Gospel writer of Matthew drew upon Psalm 91 as he undertook to relay the story of the devil's attempts to tempt Jesus in the wilderness. Into the devil's mouth are put the psalmist's words: "On their [angels'] hands they will bear you up, so that you will not dash your foot against a stone" (Matt. 4:6; Ps. 91:12). Matthew hopes to show how Jesus proves the devil's use of scripture is wrong and that Jesus' trust is in God alone. The writer of Matthew is also planting literary seeds that lift up Jesus as the fulfillment of Israel's hopes for a messiah. In this way the reader is at once invited to join Jesus in dwelling fully within the profession of trust found in Psalm 91. We are also invited to see Jesus speaking to us through the psalm.

As we read the Gospel narratives through the season of Lent, we know the end of the story from the beginning. Whether we are fragile in our faith or strong as a fortress, we walk with the one who loves, delivers, protects, satisfies, and saves to the very end. To the very end, which is our beginning.

O God, our refuge and our strength, lead us into the truth of Christ, that whatever befalls us this day will be a reminder of him in whom you dwell and through whom you dwell in us. Amen.

Be Careful What You Hope For

FEBRUARY 22–28, 2010 • BRENT WATERS

MONDAY, FEBRUARY 22 ～ *Read Genesis 15:1-6*

Abram, that great pillar of faith, is anxious. He is worried about what will become of him and his family. What is most remarkable is that his anxiety is prompted by a vision in which the Lord tells Abram not to be afraid for the Lord will protect and reward him.

Specifically, Abram is worried about the future. He is afraid that all his efforts and hard work will come to nothing, for he has no children to inherit his estate. His legacy will not live on among his descendants.

The Lord tells Abram that he will not remain childless. An heir will be born to him. Moreover, the Lord promises Abram that his descendants will be as numerous as the stars in the sky. Abram is assured that his legacy will live on.

Note, however, that Abram is given a promise that he will never see fulfilled. He will not live to see these accomplishments. All he is given is a promise. All Abram can do in response to what the Lord has promised him is to reply, "I believe you."

Like Abram, we too may be anxious about the future. We may not worry about a lineage, but we nonetheless fret if our lives will come to nothing. Will our work make a contribution to future generations or prove futile?

Despite our best efforts the future always remains out of our control. Like Abram, we too must place our hope in a future that we will never live to see fulfilled. We too have only God's words of promise to assure us.

Lord, we are anxious about the future. Help us to trust you. Amen.

Stead professor of Christian Social Ethics and Director, Stead Center for Ethics and Values at Garrett-Evangelical Theological Seminary, Evanston, IL

The Lord has promised Abram that he will be blessed by innumerable descendants, so presumably his anxiety about the future has been alleviated. Not quite. Abram learns also that his descendants will possess a land and establish a new nation. The Lord has raised the ante.

Abram is rightfully troubled. If he is to be the founder of a new nation he wants to know exactly where this land is and whether his descendants will be up to the task of possessing it. He needs a sign, and the Lord gives him one. Through a ritual that to us may seem bizarre, Abram learns the exact boundaries of the promised land. And, more importantly, the Lord establishes with Abram a covenant to seal the promise. So long as his descendants are faithful to the covenant, they cannot fail. Abram now has a tangible sign, for he can travel about and see the land that will be inhabited by the nation he has established in covenant with the Lord.

Like Abram, we too want some visible signs of the covenant. We want to see some evidence that God is keeping God's part of the agreement, be it property, fame, fortune, upstanding reputation, good health, and the like. We need some solid reassurance.

But as the subsequent history of Abram's descendants demonstrates, the signs of the covenant can become distorted into idolatry. The signs of promise become idols to be served and worshiped. We too face the temptation of idolatry. We may come to serve and worship our material blessings rather than receiving them as gifts entrusted to our care. Signs are meant to be reassuring . . . but the temptation to shape these into something other than God intended can be dangerous.

Lord, we need signs of your covenant. Help us to see and interpret them correctly. Amen.

Abram's descendants possess the land that the Lord has given them. They dwell in peace and security, for since the Lord is their light and salvation they have nothing to fear. They cannot, however, do with the land whatever they will, for it is the sign of the covenant—ultimately it is the Lord's land and not theirs. They are tenants and not landlords. Consequently, the land is to be regarded as a tabernacle: a place where songs are to be sung to the glory of the Lord.

Like Abram's descendants, we too need a place to dwell. We need a place to find food, shelter, and rest. It is in such places that we see the signs of God's covenant and care. God has provided us with the material necessities to sustain our lives. They are good gifts of God's love and grace. And like Abram's descendants, we too should regard our dwellings as tabernacles in which we sing praises to God who sustains our lives.

To be good and faithful dwellers, we must resist the temptation of seeing these signs of God's care as entitlements we deserve rather than as gifts to be gratefully received. Again, this idea of promised land may be expanded to include material possessions, wealth, fame, good health, and the like.

When we come to believe that we are owed these things, we become unduly anxious because we must protect what is rightfully ours. But in doing so, we also become unfaithful dwellers. For these things are not ours but God's, and we must use them to fashion our lives as tabernacles in which God is honored and praised. It is in such tabernacles that we are called to dwell because it is here that we are freed from fear. God is the stronghold of our lives, our light and our salvation.

Lord, we need a place to know and praise you. Help us to be faithful dwellers. Amen.

Abram's descendants dwell in the promised land. Yesterday's reading exudes confidence. The land is *the* sign of the Lord's favor and clear indication of the Lord's protection. There is no reason to fear any enemy, because the Lord will protect the people. The land itself has become not only a sign but also *the* object of hope.

Today's reading, however, reflects a subtle, yet significant, change in tone. The confidence is more muted and less exuberant. The Lord is not always immediately present. The psalmist uses such metaphors as the Lord's face being hidden and the Lord forsaking and turning away from the people. The psalmist appears to be entertaining the unthinkable possibility that the Lord might abandon the land and the people dwelling in it.

Yet underlying this dreadful prospect is a remarkable spiritual insight. When the Lord is absent rather than present, the people can and must wait. And waiting does not require a particular sign or place; they can and must wait wherever they may be. The Lord's presence is not confined to any material sign, such as land and the nation dwelling in it. It is the Lord alone and not signs that is the proper object of hope.

We may no longer see the land in which we dwell as a sign of God's favor, but we nevertheless have other signs, such as our work or possessions, in which we have placed our hope. Upon close inspection we too may find that God is not present in these signs. What, then, should we do? As the psalmist reminds us, we must wait wherever we may happen to be. To paraphrase Simone Weil, when we encounter God's absence, our task is not to set out to find and replace what is missing but to wait and allow God to find us and enfold us in God's mercy and grace.

Lord, we invite your presence. Help us to wait. Amen.

Jesus is on his way to Jerusalem. He has gained a reputation of being a troublemaker. King Herod would prefer that he stay out of his city, so he sends a messenger to deliver a threat. Perhaps he can frighten Jesus away. But Jesus cannot be put off so easily. He tells "that fox" that there is nothing he can do to prevent him from fulfilling his mission. Like the prophets before him, he too will die in Jerusalem.

There is also great pathos in Jesus' words. He longs to care for the residents of this city as a hen cares for her chicks. Jerusalem is the royal city, the crowning glory of the land promised to Abram's descendants. If any place should be receptive to God's presence, it should be Jerusalem. Sadly, this is not the case. Jerusalem has had a long history of killing prophets who proclaim the word of the Lord. A city which should be a sign of God's abiding presence has instead been deformed into a symbol of earthly power that cannot tolerate prophetic words of judgment and calls to repentance.

Jesus, however, is not just any prophet who proclaims God's word. He is the incarnate Word of God. He comes not just to proclaim judgment and repentance but to become a permanent resident that embodies a divine presence. God now dwells among the people.

As Christians, we know how this story ends: Jesus will die in Jerusalem and then be raised from the dead. God, not Herod, will have the final word. We should not be smug, however, just because we know the story. Even as Christians, in this Lenten season we, as dwellers in our modern Jerusalems, are again confronted with this troublemaker. We too will need to decide once again whether we will welcome Jesus gladly, or join those who slay another troublesome prophet.

Lord Jesus Christ, we welcome you as the Word made flesh that dwells among us. Help us to be hospitable. Amen.

Paul, never one to be accused of false modesty, urges the church at Philippi to join with their fellow sisters and brothers in Christ in following his example. He has set the pattern for how the life of the Christian should be lived—a life which embodies the virtues of faith, hope, and love. These virtues are the signs of the new life in Christ. Since God in Christ through the Holy Spirit now dwells among the people there is no longer any need for signs such as land, cities, or possessions to disclose God's presence. Indeed, such objects may prove to be distractions. Wherever two or three are gathered in Christ's name, God is present. And God is encountered in people whose lives are shaped by faith, hope, and love.

Paul, never one to miss an opportunity to admonish, also offers a dire warning. Those failing to follow this pattern are living lives that are heading toward a destiny of destruction. Effectively, they have become enemies of Christ. The problem is not that they are inherently wicked people, but their minds are set on worldly things. They live lives that are oriented toward themselves rather than toward God and neighbor. In short, they have fallen into the trap of idolatry by placing their hope in the false gods of materialism and sensuality. Consequently, their faith is banal, and their love is small and shallow.

Lent is a time of introspection to reassess and realign our priorities. As Christians, are we living lives oriented toward ourselves, or toward God and neighbor? Are we living lives of faith, hope and love, or lives of self-indulgence and excessive consumption? These are some of the questions we must ask ourselves as we prepare once again to encounter Christ crucified and Christ risen.

Lord Jesus Christ, we want to live as your faithful disciples. Help us to conform ourselves to the right pattern. Amen.

SECOND SUNDAY IN LENT

We are citizens of heaven. The church of Jesus Christ is unlike any nation or earthly association of people. It is not bound together by bonds of political affiliation or biological kinship. Rather, the church is a gathering of people called out from every nation and family across the globe, bound together by their faith and allegiance to Jesus Christ. As Christians, we are citizens of a realm that has no land or capital city to call its own. The church's physical place and space is wherever Christians gather in their Lord's name.

Consequently, Christians are always an unsettled people. Following Augustine, we are sojourners or pilgrims, for our destination, our destiny, is eternal fellowship with the triune God. Christians know they are not entirely at home in the world and are therefore always a bit restless.

Being sojourners, however, is not synonymous with being nomads. Christians do not simply wander about aimlessly. We are instead pilgrims on a journey heading somewhere. Along that journey we are not oblivious to our surroundings; we often pause for extended periods along the way. Practically, this does not mean that the bonds of nation, family, friends, and colleagues are dismissed as insignificant concerns or annoying encumbrances. Rather, we acknowledge that these are important, but nonetheless lesser loyalties in comparison with our greatest or highest loyalty to God.

Lent is a season when Christians reaffirm our heavenly citizenship. Or in other words, Lent is a time when we check to see if our pilgrimage is heading in the right direction and take care to avoid dead ends and routes heading in the wrong way. Lent is a time when we reassess and realign our lesser loyalties and allegiances in line with our greatest or highest loyalty to God.

Lord Jesus Christ, we have placed our hope in you. Help us to order our lives accordingly. Amen.

Invitations, Decisions, Repentance

MARCH 1–7, 2010 • MARIELLEN SAWADA YOSHINO

MONDAY, MARCH 1 ~ *Read Isaiah 55:1-9*

During a worship service, when the worship leader calls out: "The Lord be with you!" the congregation responds, "And also with you." Or "*Gloria a Dios!*" In some churches the response is dry and rote. In others, it is full and heartfelt.

A call requires a response. An invitation begs an answer. An offering of affirmation or assurance deserves acknowledgment. Whatever reply the faithful make to a call, invitation, affirmation, or assurance, the response is always predicated on a decision. Is my decision wholehearted, or do I hold something back?

This week's Lenten scriptures focus on such decisions. The prophet Isaiah issues an invitation to the fullness of life. The Psalm offers an affirmation of faith. Paul's writing affirms assurance of God's faithfulness. And Jesus' words sound a call to repentance.

Each is a call to decision. Now, this third Sunday in Lent, we are called to make faithful responses to the scriptures before us. We must get serious, fortify our faith, and listen to God's call and claim on our lives.

The question is not insignificant: Will we use this week to grow closer to Jesus on his way to the cross? Can we prepare ourselves to respond to Jesus' gift of himself to us this Lent?

Holy God, in this holy season, take us deeper into our faith. Help us hear your call and invitation to follow more closely and to give our hearts more fully. Amen.

Ordained elder and district superintendent in the California-Nevada Conference of the United Methodist Church

A couple of years ago, I got sick, really sick. In the end, I had to learn to sit, stand, and walk again. I had to relearn to feed myself. I even had to teach myself again how to "text."

In the midst of the treatment and rehabilitation, a friend gently asked me, "So, are you mad at God for this?"

"Why?" I asked. "Should I be?"

Perhaps if I were to think that God caused my illness, then, yes, I could be mad at God. If people believe that God is the instigator of harm, then anger would make sense. If they see God as one who metes out divine suffering in the form of illness or pain, then, yes, I could get mad right along with them.

I almost feel bad for God, receiving such blame from us, the very ones whom God has created. How must God, the one who adores us and loves us so much, feel about the recriminations and complaints we sometimes heap on God?

The people with Jesus must have been wondering about God too. Should they be mad at God for the suffering of the victims at Pilate's hand? Should they blame God for the toppling of the Tower of Siloam? It is easy for us, as it must have been for the people with Jesus, to get caught up in fear and blame. To do that, however, crowds out what is most important in this Lenten season.

So Jesus redirects his companions and us. "What is important," says Jesus, "is that you choose repentance for your life. There is no life without it. You have a choice beyond the madness, beyond the blame."

Choose repentance. Or not.

Dearest Lord God, you know us so well. Forgive us when we seek blame instead of understanding. Help us to realize our need to repent and, through your grace, to receive new life through your son, Jesus Christ. Amen.

In today's scripture lesson, Jesus tells a story about a fig tree. Some believe this scripture is about a person's soul. Others say it refers to Israel. But most certainly, this story refers to the harsh judgment of God, the landowner in the story. Or so I thought.

But then I moved to California's lush and fertile Central Valley. It was there, in the town of Hanford, that I met Jim, a man who tends his orchard of walnut trees. "We growers," Jim says, "are eternal optimists. We do the best we can as the stewards of our land. We have to take care of our trees. We have to be diligent in pruning out the old growth, diligent in the watering of our trees, and diligent in knowing the yield of our trees. When we're not farming our trees right, they don't produce and we have to take them out."

In Jesus' story, the landowner tells the gardener to take out a tree that had not produced any figs for three years. It's not an unusual order, as my friend Jim taught me. However, the gardener asks for a reprieve for the tree—one year, one more chance for the tree to produce and live. Another year could be all the tree needs. So the landowner softens his judgment, for one year. After that, the tree will be judged.

It's hard to know exactly what to make of this story. Is God the landowner? Are we the gardener? Or the fig tree? There are many different interpretations. But the message has a clear focus: we must repent. We must show the fruits of our faith. And we must be ready at any time to receive God's judgment.

For it will come.

Dearest God, who has called us to faithful, may we be diligent and ready today. Help us cultivate our faith, that we may be an encouragement to others. Amen.

The scripture in Isaiah 55 is given to the children of Israel while they are still exiles in Babylon. Through the prophet Isaiah, God urges the exiled people to make the decision to leave the lifestyle to which they have grown accustomed and to begin instead to live in the way God has planned. If Isaiah's words are heard as an invitation, they seem grand and generous. But if they are heard as a command, Isaiah's message seems more daunting and doubtful.

Miyo has been a Bible study teacher in her small town's congregation for at least fifty years. She tells me that the new pastor of her church is preaching about new things. She says that the pastor is preaching about her congregation's need to "get out of the box" and be the body of Christ in new ways.

"Getting out of the box," Miyo reflects, "must be like the disciple Peter getting out of the boat to walk on water." She recalls that when Jesus said to Peter, "Come," Peter made a decision. He got out of the boat and went to Jesus. Whether by invitation or command, Peter made a decision. He responded to his teacher, friend, and Savior. He did what Jesus said to do.

Miyo showed me her congregation's new mission statement. Her congregation has heard the invitation. The members have heard the command. And they have decided and are responding.

Through the prophet Isaiah, whether a call, invitation, or command, we hear God's words to "Come . . . drink . . . eat . . . live." We realize God's desire for our lives. How shall we respond—with action or inaction, with faithfulness or fear, with passion or apathy?

Will we live out the plan of God? Or not?

Great and amazing God, you have spoken words we need to hear. You have issued an invitation and given us a command. May we act with passion and courage. Amen.

Paul writes to the Christians of Corinth, "So if you think you are standing, watch out that you do not fall." Perhaps Paul is saying to the people of New Testament times, "Watch out. Be alert. You never know when you might slip up, make a wrong decision, or be deceived by a falsehood."

A magnificent tree grows in the Sequoia National Park, known as the "General Sherman" tree. Approximately 274 feet tall, this particular giant is said to be the largest tree in the world. Its circumference is over 102 feet.

No one knows the true age of this tree. Most estimates range between 2000 and 2700 years. The tree, for all human purposes, has always been here, and will continue always to be. No one could imagine that this healthy, magnificent tree would ever be damaged or threatened.

But in January 2006, a limb of the tree broke off. The limb itself was bigger than many trees. The break was unexpected and unexplained. It was a major blow to those who know and cherish the sequoias.

None of us stands nearly so tall as a giant sequoia; yet, we often believe ourselves to be "high enough" to be above falling to idolatry, breaking apart from God's will, or losing ourselves to temptation. It's as though we think that we will stand tall forever.

Such thinking may be our undoing. It is not we, Paul reminds us, but God who is unswervingly sharp, strong, and sound. It is God who stands amidst any trial.

We have a choice. We can rely on the God who "provides the way." Or we can rely on ourselves.

And so we must choose to rely on our faithful God. Or not.

Dearest Lord of us all, we stand in awe of your divine stature. Let us rely on you and your strength rather than that of our own. Amen.

Each church congregation has a unique potluck. At the various churches I visit, I am treated to everything from chicken and long rice to barbecue beef, pot stickers to kimchi, lasagna to sushi. I enjoy Jell-O of every color and cookies in every shape. I eat enchiladas and three-bean salads, prize-winning chili and green bean casseroles. And of course, there is my potluck favorite, deviled eggs.

Congregations take pride in their gathering of food. At church, the potluck table is a metaphor and reality of blessing and fellowship. When gathered, prayed over, and shared, the food is certainly a blessing from God.

This food might be described by the Greek adjective *pneumatikos*. *Pneumatikos* is the Greek word that means "of the Spirit." Paul uses this word to describe the food and drink given to the Israelites while they were in the wilderness. Paul reminds the early Christians in Corinth that the children of Israel "all ate the same spiritual food and all drank the same spiritual drink."

Paul continues the story. Even though the Israelites ate this great food and drank this grand drink, still, they became idolaters. Even though the Israelites were greatly gifted with *pneumatikos*, gifts, they chose to do what was displeasing to God.

They took in *pneumatikos* sustenance but did not follow with *pneumatikos* living. Don't follow suit, Paul tells the Corinthians, Don't take advantage of the blessings. Don't just eat, and then abandon the generous Host.

Paul's message is still appropriate today. The *pneumatikos* blessings are all around us. Just as Paul challenged the people of the New Testament, he challenges us on our Lenten walk.

We may decide to take advantage of our blessings or to be faithful with our blessings. That decision will be described as *pneumatikos*—or not.

We praise you, God, and thank you for your gifts to us. May we show our gratitude by living lives of faith. Amen.

SUNDAY, MARCH 7 ~ *Read Psalm 63:1-8*

THIRD SUNDAY IN LENT

What inspiring words for this Sunday morning! The composer of this psalm surely has his life in order. Obviously he lives amidst good will and abundance. If only each of us could be in such a place of perfection and peace.

And yet, this psalm's intent is at odds with our initial reading. The title gives it away: "A Psalm of David, when he was in the Wilderness of Judah." The wilderness of Judah was no lap of luxury. It was a place without ready food or drink. It was a place of the fearful unknown. It held the dark nights and harsh natural elements.

This was hardly the place of perfection or peace.

"There was hardly peace in our community during this last freeze when most of the oranges in the orchards were destroyed," laments a pastor from Lindsay, California. "There was great concern and worry about this emergency."

"While most of the fruit was lost, people kept working long hours out in the fields," explains the pastor. "The days and nights were long for everyone in our community."

"And yet," she related, "that was when our community came together. That was when the churches worked to provide help with food and basic needs. And of course, we came together in prayer. That was when we felt the power of God in our midst. That was when we praised God mightily."

Even—or especially—in the times of life's troubles, we are offered the peace that passes all human understanding. We, like the psalmist, must choose to sing praises and seek God, "who is our help." We, like the people of Lindsay, must choose to cling to God, "whose steadfast love is better than life."

Sustainer of all life, help us claim the peace you offer. Let us live each hour giving thanks for your saving love. Amen.

Your History: A Valuable Past

MARCH 8–14, 2010 • STEVE BARSE

MONDAY, MARCH 8 ~ *Read Joshua 5:9-12*

Members of the Kiowa tribe of Oklahoma have much in common with the people of Israel. We can be an obstinate and contentious people. We are a tribal people, driven by tradition. We have pulled from the edge of extinction many of our dance societies and warrior organizations. We value family bloodlines.

The first chapter of Joshua makes reference to being courageous. A Kiowa word for courage is *tain-ah-day* or "strong heart." The Hebrews would well have understood that word.

Also, like the Israelites, the Kiowa are firm believers in the importance of ceremony, whether within the dance arena or in the tepee of the Native American church. A segment of the Kiowa tribe still makes an annual pilgrimage to the ten Holy Icons of the Kiowa people, the sacred Ten Grandmothers.

The Kiowa waited to receive allotted lands—as did Joshua's people. The promised land would require great courage of its new inhabitants. They would have to acknowledge their covenant with God and adhere to certain ceremonial rites.

For us as believers, what does this snapshot of history mean? The book of Joshua calls for courage, or as the Kiowa say, to have a strong heart. But, I don't always heed the promises of God. I can falter and lose sight of the promised land. Then I am called to return to the ceremony of prayer, to seek out other courageous believers who can provide encouragement, support, or simply inspiration.

Examine your own history and the strengths it might bring to your everyday walk.

Community liaison for the Oklahoma City Indian Clinics, active in Norman First American United Methodist Church, member of the Kiowa Tribe

The Kiowa ethos is captured in the mythic character of Saynday. Saynday was sent to earth by the Great Mystery, and according to *Kiowa Voices: Myths, Legends and Folktales* "his survival and that of the tribe often depended on cunning, cleverness, prowess, and a shrewd ability to do the right thing at the right time." These traits became the shared values of the tribe and brought meaning to everyday life. But, sadly, Saynday developed a dual personality. He brought the Kiowa people from underneath the earth and into a world of light. He brought them through many difficult and troubling times. Yet, he developed a trickster side that brought him—and the tribe—agony and embarrassment. This Saynday mirrored the disintegration of the world the Kiowa people once knew.

The writer of Psalm 32 makes clear that the blessings of God come to those "in whose spirit there is no deceit" (v. 2). Cleverness and cunning may get us out of a sticky situation or get us something we want now and then, but in the long run, such character traits will leave us empty.

I had the great fortune of being able to spend a good deal of time around my father in his later years. He was a member of the Sisseton-Wahpeton Sioux Tribe. Through his long years of life, he developed such great strength of character that his tribe bestowed on him shortly before his death the rare honor of the "making-of-chiefs" ceremony or *we-cha-sh'tah-yah-don-pe*. My father was too ill to attend so my older brother stood in for him. In the ceremony, three objects were given to him to symbolize the importance of character: an eagle star quilt, an eagle headdress, and a ceremonial staff. I have the staff; it is a constant reminder to me of the importance of fostering a spirit of good character where "there is no deceit."

Where do you sense guile in your life? How do you attempt to purge it?

It occurred to me a number of years ago that guilt, in a way, is God's gift to us. Those of us fortunate enough to be raised in homes that taught moral and ethical guidelines carry an imprint within our conscience that distinguishes the right and wrong of things. Scripture too is invaluable in helping us make those distinctions between right and wrong. Careful reading of both our conscience and our Bibles can alert us to sin in our lives by a healthy sense of guilt.

Having said that, though, I am aware of the dangers of inappropriate guilt. Certainly there are people racked by guilt to the point of being dysfunctional. The problem though, according to Psalm 32, is keeping silent about the guilt: "While I kept silence, my body wasted away" (v 3). Unconfessed sin is a heavy burden to bear.

I think God has a purpose for all of us. That purpose is not unlike the goal posts on a football field. Between the two goal posts exists God's good and perfect will. When we aim to stay within those posts, we find happiness, security, well-being, joy, peace, and the freedom to be who God intends us to be. To live outside these goal posts opens us up to every manner of distress, fear, and harm. We become much more vulnerable to the temptations of the world. We slip into sin because we slip out of bounds.

One of the great evangelists in the Indian world is Richard Pickup, a Cherokee from eastern Oklahoma. Many years ago I had the chance to spend some personal time with him and heard him say, "Your sin will find you out." He's right—that feeling of guilt is evidence that we have strayed, and the burden of that realization can be crushing. However, Psalm 32 offers a word of hope: relief comes from confession and healing comes from forgiveness.

Thank you, God, for the forgiveness that comes to us through your gracious love. Amen.

I was a supervisor for several years in an agency within the Department of Health and Human Services, so I can attest to the complexities of that work. Policies, guidelines, regulations, and job descriptions are carefully defined. However, on any given day, any number of things can go haywire. At those moments, a supervisor must assert her authority and implement corrective action.

Reading Paul's second letter to the Corinthians, it seems as if things were going haywire at the church in Corinth. Certain abuses were taking place that could endanger the health of the congregation. Paul responds by asserting his authority as Christ's apostle. He calls for "a ministry of reconciliation" from those he defines as "ambassadors of Christ."

I don't consider myself in possession of great authority, spiritual or otherwise; but as chair of the Staff/Parish Relations Committee in my local church, I do have some influence over our small church staff. I have had to confront a staff person in a way that called for corrective action. If a church member takes issue with our pastor, I am responsible for helping to resolve the problem. On these occasions, I do become an ambassador of reconciliation.

The larger implication of Paul's words in these scriptures is the promise of reconciliation for all of us, made possible through Christ. How often have we fallen short? How great are our sins? But our God is not a vindictive God. God doesn't keep track of our sins, or remember all the times we have fallen short. Instead, God forgives us. And this forgiveness allows us to become reconciled ambassadors. Our lives in the world are changed—we now carry God in Christ with us.

Gracious God, help me be reconciled to you so that I may be an ambassador of Christ. Amen.

As I wrote this meditation, Hurricane Gustav was plowing into the Gulf Coast. Nearly two million people evacuated coastal towns and cities. Bumper-to-bumper traffic stretched for miles. Meanwhile, India was dealing with its worst flooding in fifty years. Events like these call to mind the film *An Inconvenient Truth* and its warnings about ice caps melting, oceans rising, shorelines vanishing, and whole species of living creatures disappearing. If I let my imagination run wild, I can imagine a scenario like this:

> Humankind has acted too late, and at last the earth is dying. In a final act of desperation, all the governments of the world have called the greatest convocation in history. The world's leaders decide that someone must be sacrificed in order to save the world. My son Matthew, a filmmaker, is there to witness this convocation and to record what will take place. World leaders announce that there is no time to search for a candidate. The choice must be made here and now. My son is the closest person, the first one they see. They turn to my son. I protest. I scream out, "No way! Not my boy!" I refuse to allow my son to pay the price for the sins of the world and as a result, the earth and all its inhabitants are destroyed.

I love my son too much to allow him to be killed by a bunch of fools who brought the world down on their own heads. But wait. Isn't that exactly what God has done for us, given God's only begotten son for our salvation? Yes, we have sinned and fallen short of the mark. But for our sake, God "made him to be sin who knew no sin," and in so doing, he has given us a way to be redeemed.

God, we praise you for the work you have done in our lives and in the life of the world. Amen.

The scene at the opening of Luke 15 features Jesus and a crowd of people—publicans and sinners. Jesus is welcoming them and even eating with them! Pharisee tongues begin to wag. They grumble. They are outraged. But Jesus was not deterred by the reactions of the religious authorities.

A Kiowa friend of mine named Gus reminded me of something one day while we were driving around town. He said that when the Kiowa were a nomadic people, they considered sharing food with visitors and travelers a sacred act, because to share food is literally a life-sustaining act. Apparently Jesus thought the same thing.

Several years ago, the little Indian church I was attending decided to make a mission trip to my dad's reservation in northeastern South Dakota, a place characterized by racial strife and socioeconomic problems. Among those in the group were my brother and one of my closest friends, Kyle. I was keen to go with the group because I had just returned to the reservation a changed man—I no longer was a part of the alcohol scene. Kyle and I decided to team up to spread the word of the mission trip and the revival services taking place that week at the Indian Baptist church. We had prayed hard prior to our trip.

We walked around, talking to people about our faith. We ran in to an old street person I knew. He was obviously addled by liquor. Even so, he remembered who I was and said he was glad to see me. Kyle and I invited him to church, and then we both spontaneously kissed him on his cheek. Tears began to stream down his face. To us he was no longer a street person; he was someone Jesus himself would have welcomed to his table.

Forgive us, Lord, when we see other people through the eyes of the Pharisee rather than through the eyes of Jesus. Amen.

FOURTH SUNDAY IN LENT

The story of the prodigal son is a great story. There is a protagonist and an antagonist. Jealousy, family strife, resentment, loss, and, finally, redemption feature prominently. The only thing missing is a real ending.

I first heard the story of the prodigal son when I was six or seven. My Sunday school teacher made the story come alive for me, just as Jesus must have done for his listeners. The teacher even took the time to bring to class an example of the husks that the prodigal son had to eat. To this day, that particular Sunday school lesson stands out to me. Why? Because someone made the extra effort to make a story come alive.

Obviously Jesus did not intend his parable to teach his listeners about the value of being a good teller of parables. Yet his method of using the everyday event, the common occurrence, the simple object, helped his listeners pay attention to his message. His method is a call to take seriously our own opportunities to forgive, love, and encourage others.

Every so often I notice youngsters, riding a bike or walking across the street. I think of all the things this world will throw at them, things infinitely more disturbing and potentially more harmful than what I experienced growing up. I long to intervene in some way. I want to get their attention somehow. And then I realize what I'm hearing is God's call to take the time to love and care for others—no matter who they are.

But there remains in this parable the unhappy older brother. He complains to his father about the way the father had welcomed his lost son. The father, still acting out of love, tells this son—the one who became lost even though he never left home—that he, too, is deeply loved and desperately wanted.

God, let me remember today that you love me and that you care for me. Amen.

To Restore the Fortunes of Zion

MARCH 15–21, 2010 • LOUISE STOWE-JOHNS

MONDAY, MARCH 15 ～ *Read John 11:45-55; 12:1-13*

Martha, Lazarus, and Mary give Jesus a dinner party. This dinner begins in the safety of the home of friends. After Jesus raised Lazarus from the dead, Jesus' fame is increasing along with fears of the chief priests and Pharisees. The high priest for the year, Caiaphas, speaks parentally to the council, "You don't know anything! You apparently don't understand that it is better for one person to die than to have an entire nation destroyed!" Caiaphas's prophesying seals the deal, and the plan is set: Jesus has to die.

It's not long before the curious crowds are clamoring to see Lazarus. The plan to kill Jesus widens to kill Lazarus. As crowds gather in Jerusalem for the Passover, they hear Jesus is coming into Jerusalem; a welcoming committee with palm branches turns Jesus' arrival into a parade. In despair or resignation, some Pharisees state, "There is nothing that can be done. The entire world has gone after Jesus" (11:19, NIV).

Between the raising of Lazarus and the parade is the story of Jesus' being sheltered and nurtured. In the home of dear friends, Mary, Martha, and Lazarus, Jesus gets a brief respite.

The forces coming at Jesus are gaining in persistence. Jesus needs solace—not by being alone but by receiving the care of others: a meal, fellowship, anointing.

How do you find solace in the midst of turmoil? For you, does that solace come in time apart or time with persons whose presence is healing?

Pastor, New York Conference of the United Methodist Church, serving First United Methodist Church in Amityville, NY

Jesus is in the home of close friends. There is a deep friendship between Jesus and the family of Lazarus, Mary, and Martha. But there is not peace among the disciples. We can imagine a conversation among disciples huddled away from Jesus—and Judas.

Peter asks, "Why are we ignoring Judas's behavior? He leaves for hours on end. Does anyone know what he's doing?"

"What are you getting at, Peter?" Philip asks. "Judas is a good man. Jesus wouldn't have chosen him if he didn't know that."

Peter is adamant, "I don't trust him. You've heard the talk. The chief priests are looking for any opportunity to haul Jesus before the council. "

Nathanael is incredulous. "Are you suggesting that Judas will tell the chief priests Jesus' whereabouts?"

Peter responds, "He is a thief and would do it if the price were right! Judas likes the jingle of coins. When Mary was anointing Jesus' feet, all Judas could think about was how much the perfume cost. He lamely protested by talking about how that money could have helped the poor."

Judas is one of the most perplexing of the twelve disciples. If we load blame on Judas for Jesus' death, it makes a neat, manageable package. It wasn't the Jews or the Romans; it wasn't the "crowd." It was Judas. At the Last Supper, Jesus reveals that Judas will betray him, because the devil had put it into his heart (John 13:2, 26). Does that relieve Judas of responsibility? Some believe Judas was a pawn of God, carrying out God's direction: Jesus had to die. That is an unsettling viewpoint of God's methods. Scripture tells us that Judas was the one who led authorities to Jesus. We are left with the whys.

What do you believe about Judas? What questions would you like to ask Judas?

E*xegesis*. That was a new word for my theological vocabulary when I learned it—maybe the second day of seminary. Exegesis is a process of study to begin to understand a biblical passage. Bible students use various tools and resources to get a fuller meaning, allowing the Bible's message to emerge. It was awhile before I got to its polar opposite: *eisogesis*. When we think we are exegeting, we may be eisogeting. Eisogesis occurs when we read into a passage what is not there. That happens when we go to scripture to make the point we already believe.

Judas protested the cost of the perfume Mary poured over Jesus' feet. She used so much perfume that the fragrance filled the entire house. Jesus tells Judas to leave Mary alone.

Then comes Jesus' further statement, "You always have the poor with you." Jesus said it. It must be true. Therefore, we shouldn't do anything about poor people, because no matter what we do, there will always be poor people? Good-bye, exegesis. Hello, eisogesis!

Context matters. The full sentence matters. In its entirety Jesus said, "You always have the poor with you, but you do not always have me."

One of the best correctives to eisogesis is to study scripture in community with others. Seeking the guidance of the faith community to understand scripture grants a richness and an authenticity to the Bible's words.

God, you know how hard it is for me to stay tuned to your words. Help me hold the scripture in sacred trust. Restrain my impulse to find in the Bible confirmation of my prejudices and desires. Lead me to uncover your Word's greater depths of meaning. Amen.

We can treasure the old, but there is something energizing about having a new thing. If we grow up with "hand-me-downs," a new outfit can be exciting. Walking into a home in which no one else has ever lived gives us the opportunity to put our stamp on it. The latest car with its new car smell may make our heart race. New is beautiful!

When Isaiah tells of God's prophecy, "I am about to do a new thing, now it springs forth, do you not perceive it?" (43:19*a*), we feel a surge of joy. There are some who are comfortable in old shoes or a beat-up car, but most of us get excited about new things.

I hear this passage quoted often. It raises my antennae to question what's behind the words. Does the person want to inspire me with a vision from God, or is it a plan that has little to do with God and a lot to do with the person saying it? I suspect it is more often the latter than the former.

We have to keep our attention on who is doing the sea-parting and the springing up of water in the desert. When something amazing happens, our thoughts and thanks may go straight to God. We know we didn't do it. But the further we go along the dry path or by the abundant streams, the more forgetful we become of God's doings. And then we start thinking that we are the ones holding back the waters. That has claimed the fall of many gifted people who forgot about the giver.

Changeless God, your love remains constant. Changing God, you are full of surprises and are nimble in breaking in with the new. May I not confuse the unchanging with the changing, staying alert both to new directions and familiar paths. Amen.

RÉSUMÉ

Career goals: To be a partner in suffering with Christ

To become like Christ in death by sharing in the resurrection

Education: Yeshiva School of Tarsus

Studied under Rabbi Gamaliel

Graduated top of class

Employment:

Itinerant rabbi

Job responsibilities: uphold the law; find persons dabbling in teachings of Jesus, arrest them, and escort them to Jerusalem for trial

Evangelist

Job responsibilities: going town to town preaching and teaching about Christ, church planting, letter writing

Am willing to relocate. No incentive to make money. Persons traveling with me may suffer beatings, arrests, shipwrecks, and quick escapes.

My ideal job would give me the opportunity to preach in any congregation at a moment's notice. I am good at giving advice and will write follow-up letters to your congregation and visit if possible to keep members on track. Although presently under the watchful eye of the imperial guard, I anticipate availability in the near future.

Would you invite someone with this resume, someone like Paul, to your congregation to preach or teach? Why do you respond as you do? How do you think others in the congregation would react?

I was walking down the long, barren hall of a women's prison when a woman yelled to me, "Chaplain, did Moses kill someone?" I was delighted that anyone would ask a question about something in the Bible. The background story behind the inmate's question was a theological assertion. "It doesn't matter how big your sin—God will forgive you. Right?" She wanted a simple yes.

In a prison filled with people whose crimes are petty to those who have committed crimes of horror, an unequivocal "yes" would not suffice. Yes, our worst acts can be forgiven. And, yes, it does matter what we do.

Paul, a primary leader of the early church, persecuted and colluded in the death of at least one Christian. Yet he was forgiven. What a riveting testimony he had! Paul had a fine bloodline. He was an educated believer of Judaism. His relationship with God was intact as an observant Jew. He gave himself completely to aligning people's behavior to the laws of God. He had no chits with God.

Through his conversion, Paul began to realize that his formerly flawless observation of the law was secondary to his faith. He understood that people don't attain a right relationship with God completely on their own. By moving out with faith and in faith, folks can become more like Christ. God reaches toward us as we reach toward God.

When I think of people dragged down by guilt, I feel sorrow. Of course, there is harm we can never erase when we have sinned. But there is enough love in Jesus to forgive Paul, even though he played a critical role in the persecution of the very people who became his sisters and brothers in Christ.

Loving God, your care for me is beyond my understanding. I give you thanks for your steadfast and unconditional love. As I extend forgiveness to others, may I receive your forgiveness. Amen.

FIFTH SUNDAY IN LENT

D o you know people who like to suffer? There are a few such folks around. They drag us down. Watch out! The dark cloud perched inches from their head might shift and come rest on you.

Do Christians suffer more than nonbelievers? People of faith seem to have a heightened sensitivity to the needs of humans and do suffer on their behalf. I have heard of studies that say Christians are generally healthier and live longer. I can see how that might be true, but physical suffering visits each of us, Christian or not.

When the psalmist sings of Zion's fortunes being restored, there is laughter and the music of joy. Midway in the psalm after talking about restoration "for them" the writer changes one word in the next sentence. Now it becomes personal: "The Lord has done great things for us and we rejoiced." Realization of the blessing erupts into joy.

The psalm concludes with the affirmation that the people who have within them the dormant seeds for joy will experience a bountiful harvest, giving rise to exuberant joy. During darker days it's hard for me to read that psalm and not be filled with a sense of God's continuing care and hope for the future.

If you are feeling joy today, thank God. If you are around those whose energy and hope seem depleted, do not be pulled down by them but be compassionate. If joy seems to have eluded you, know that your welfare is of concern to God. Remember that in your weeping you bear the seeds for sowing. May your harvest be abundant.

Holy Friendship

MARCH 22–28, 2010 • PAMELA D. HAWKINS

MONDAY, MARCH 22 ~ *Read Isaiah 50:4-9a*

As we approach the end of Lent, I am stopped at verse 7 of this chapter from Isaiah: "I have set my face like flint. . . . " Through the prophet's imagery, I imagine the face of Jesus, jaw jutting forward and eyes strong, as the time draws near to complete the journey begun earlier, when he first "set his face to go to Jerusalem" (Luke 9:51). I wonder if Isaiah's words cross the Lord's mind. Do they inspire courage? Can they settle his heart?

Our reading spreads before us words of untainted confidence in God. At other times the prophet laments the suffering and humiliation that fall upon God's servant, but not now. Here, Isaiah draws upon all that stirs his rock-hard confidence in God's presence, even while in the hands of hard-hearted enemies.

And so, I imagine Jesus setting his face "like flint" toward Jerusalem. He knows what stretches before him, that he will be scorned and spat upon. He knows that some of his friends will be threatened, and some will become a threat. It is enough to harden anyone else's heart; but instead he will only harden his face, compelled to move forward by an unflinching confidence in God.

In any circumstance or struggle, whether personal or global, we have the promise of God's presence with us. Yet most of us have faced circumstances where God has seemed absent. But if we, like Jesus, will make a home for God's word in our hearts, our confidence in God can be strengthened for whatever waits ahead.

God of north, south, east, and west, point our lives this day in the direction that you desire for us. Amen.

Managing editor of *Weavings*, a journal of the spiritual life; author of *Simply Wait: Cultivating Silence in the Season of Advent*; living in Nashville, TN

It is a stark absence. Not once in the forty-nine verses describing Jesus' trial before Pilate will Jesus' disciples stand out in the crowd. They will all but vanish, disappear into the nameless sea of faces until the worst is over. The ones closest to him will distance themselves. His best friends will huddle in the shadows or feign disinterest in anything other than just being one of the crowd. To do anything more, especially in the days and hours leading up to the Cross, will be too risky.

Friendship marks us. We know this. We notice to whom our children are drawn. We worry about whom our youth will want to date. We decide, even strategize, about whom we will invite into our communities or to our homes or to our tables. And if the ones we have called friends begin to struggle with some issue— if they are accused or suspected, if they are addicted or rejected, if they begin to be seen as different from most or to seem dangerous to some—we have to choose all over again whether or not we still will be their friend.

It is telling that in these same verses of scripture where Jesus' best friends will become invisible, the only friendship we see is between his accusers. "That same day Herod and Pilate became friends with each other; before this they had been enemies."

Friendship marks us. We know this. And we know that claiming to be a Christian friend will lead us to be present with many whom others will not choose, will not stay with, and will not stand up for. May we, this Lent, become true friends in the way that Jesus calls us.

O God, guide and friend, deepen our love for you and for each other today and every day. Amen.

I guess it's in God's hands now, isn't it, pastor?" It was a mother's question—half plea, half statement. She was seated on a worn-out sofa in the back of the house as far away from the front-room television as she could get. That way she could not hear the latest news report about her son's pending execution. Imprisoned for murder, her son was out of appeals; his final clock was set.

"I guess it's in God's hands now," the woman said again, not really to anybody in particular; but I heard her, as did my son who had gone with me to share food and presence with this woman and the few friends who had stuck by her through the day-by-day loss of her son. A pretty thin crowd gathered behind pulled blinds. Humiliation by association had worn them down over the years; you could see it in their eyes. They had heard the whispers and seen the jeering looks from other neighbors. And yet, there they were, holding on to thin threads of friendship and a thick trust in God as if their future depended on it.

"My future is in your hand," writes the psalmist, voicing the same thick trust in God as had the heartbroken mother, while strength and hope thin away in misery.

In Luke's account of Jesus' passion and death, words from this psalm are on the Lord's lips as he breathes his last. In the life of the church, words from this psalm most often find their way into liturgies for remembering the dead. But let us not forget that this psalm is also for remembering the living, especially those who live in deep anguish or sorrow. This psalm is for any of our friends who need to find refuge in God. May we bear God's trustworthy word to someone who needs to be remembered today.

O God, may we find refuge in your steadfast love and call upon your name. Amen.

She would slip into the back pew right after the service began. She must have stood just outside the doors listening for that first note of music, entering when she would not have to speak to anyone. She simply came to be present for the Lord's Supper.

And then, right before the service ended, she would slip out again. Her timing was perfect; it never failed. Week after week she would slip in, sit in the back, come forward to share the bread and cup, and then slip out into the night.

When she did approach the table, hands ready for the broken bread, she did not look down but instead always looked right at me. For all of her desire to be anonymous in coming and going, she revealed a vulnerability to be known at the table. Up close, I saw evidence of a hard-lived life—her eyes and face revealed a scarred, haunted presence. But in the dim lighting of the back pew, no one could see it.

Then one night at service's end, she was still there. I saw her smiling in my direction, so I excused myself from a conversation and went to her. All she said was, "I love it here. Something happens." She then told me her first name and said, "See you next week" as she slipped out the doors.

"When the hour came, he took his place at the table," begins Luke's account of the Last Supper. "Then he took a loaf of bread, and when he had given thanks, he broke it and gave it to them," and something happened. From that night on, when any gather at the Lord's table, something happens. Often we fail to remember this. May we be reminded that something happens in the gifts of bread and cup.

Lord Jesus Christ, may we accept the invitation to your table and greet all who come to receive. Amen.

Let the same mind be in you that was in Christ Jesus," Paul writes to the church at Philippi—a deceptively simple invitation into the Christian spiritual life. How hard can it be to begin to think like Jesus? After all, simply through his thinking Christ brought good things to life.

The mind of Christ was compassionate—he cared for the vulnerable and the lost, drawing people to him like lambs to a loving shepherd. The mind of Christ was quick—quick with simple parables, pregnant pauses, and perfect comebacks, causing even the hardest hearts to look at situations in new ways. The mind of Christ was wise at an early age, seasoned before his time, and clear in the middle of chaos. And the mind of Christ recognized the unjust, untrue, and unacceptable, shifting the eyes of many to see what had been overlooked. How can we not desire to have this same mind?

But if we stay close to the rest of Paul's text and stay close to Jesus on the road to Jerusalem, we will discover that God takes an interest in far more than our minds. Soon, verse by verse, this beautiful hymn from the early church reminds us that to become imitators of Christ requires that we use all aspects of ourselves.

God desires our minds and our attitudes to be Christlike, yes; but also our actions. God attends to our feet and our knees, our hearts and our hands. God takes interest in the words on our tongues and the prayers of our lives. But God also longs for us to step out in faith, dismantle injustice, and put sweat equity into peacemaking. This God, known to us in Christ Jesus, is our all-and-everything God—our God who desires that all and everything about us reveal to the world that we are the body of Christ.

O God, may we learn to love you and all of creation with our whole selves. Amen.

It has taken my whole life to notice the beauty of broken seashells. For years my beachcombing routine has been predictable. As the surf rolls back, I search around my feet for a shiny edge of something lovely, something partially revealed between sand and sea that I can quickly pinch before it disappears again. And with just a moment in my hands, I decide whether the shell is worth keeping. Imperfect, broken ones I usually reject— returning them to the sand with a disappointed toss.

But lately I have begun to notice a different beauty in broken shells. My eyes are being caught by the color of a fragment or the shape of a fractured edge. For some reason I am drawn toward wonder about the life created for the shell's intricate space—what did it look like? Where, in the depths of the sea, had been its home? I cannot say why, after all these years, I can no longer walk past what I have been rejecting, except to say that something has changed the way I see.

As I read from Psalm 118, my eye is drawn to verse 22 and my imagination to those tossed-back shells of earlier years. What had appeared unappealing and imperfect to me, have been, in the eyes of God, treasures not to be rejected. So too, this text reminds us, is the treasure and gift of Jesus, the cornerstone of our faith. He was set down in the tides of power, poverty, and politics; but many could not see him for what he was. And so, he was tossed back—rejected—at least, so it seemed, until a few days later he appeared again to some whose eyes were opened to see in new ways. May the light of God illuminate our journey with Christ in new ways this season.

O God of light, pour out your mercy on us that we might see with new vision any whom we have cast aside. Amen.

SUNDAY, MARCH 28 ~ *Read Luke 19:28-40*

PALM/PASSION SUNDAY

It is a most intimate moment in the text, one almost hidden in the comings and goings before Jesus' final entry into Jerusalem. As a young colt nervously stamps the dust and jerks against the lead, cloaks are quickly thrown onto his back. And then, the strong arms of the disciples set Jesus on the colt. Jesus does not climb up alone, according to Luke; he places his life in the hands of his friends as he faces the road into Jerusalem.

For the disciples to set Jesus on the colt requires getting close to the Teacher, to grasp an arm or brace a shoulder. It means being close enough to feel Jesus' breath on their skin, close enough to smell the sweat on his cloak. At least one friend will be to Jesus' back; others will be eye-level, looking him square in the face. Jesus could have found a nearby wall to stand on without leaning toward his friends, but Luke describes a different kind of friendship.

For Jesus, once he enters the city, there will be many intimate moments of discipleship. There will be bread-breaking and wine-sharing. There will be foot-washing and truth-telling. And at what would appear to many as the end of the road, there will be time once again for a few to put their hands under his arms and their faces to his face as they set him down from the Cross. Intimate moments, all.

The Christian's journey to Jerusalem and beyond calls for extraordinary acts of intimacy. Discipleship requires vulnerability, closeness, and a willingness to lean in the direction of others. In this Lent, may we give thanks to God for those who stand ready to love us.

O Christ, may we lean toward you this day, as you lean toward us; may we rest, strengthened for the journey. Amen.

A Holy Incredibility

MARCH 29–APRIL 4, 2010 • MAX LUCADO

MONDAY, MARCH 29 ~ *Read Hebrews 9:11-15*

In the world's history, there was one man who, though he had the appearance of a human, claimed to have the origin of God. There was one who, while wearing the face of a Jew, had the image of the Creator.

Those who saw him—really saw him—knew there was something different. At his touch blind beggars saw. At his command crippled legs walked. At his embrace empty lives filled with vision.

During his final week Jesus asked his disciples, "What do you think about the Christ? Whose son is he?"

Note Jesus didn't ask, "What do you think about the Christ and his teachings?" or, "What do you think about the Christ and his opinions on social issues?"

After three years of ministry, hundreds of miles, thousands of miracles, innumerable teachings, Jesus bids the people to ponder not what he has done but who he is.

It's the ultimate question of the Christ: Whose son is he?

Is he the son of God or the sum of our dreams? Is he the force of creation or a figment of our imagination?

The notion that God would don a scalp and toes and two eyes—we would never create such a Savior. We aren't that daring.

But God did what we wouldn't dare dream. God did what we couldn't imagine. God became human—a man who defeated death so we could follow.

It defies logic. It is a divine insanity. A holy incredibility.

Jesus, son of God, hear my prayer: I am overcome by the depth of your love. Amen.

Best-selling author who serves as Minister of Preaching at Oak Hills Church in San Antonio, TX

We all make choices—sometimes wisely, sometimes not. You've made some bad choices in life, haven't you? You've chosen the wrong friends, maybe the wrong career, even the wrong spouse. You look back over your life and say, "If only . . . if only I could make up for those bad choices." You can. One good choice for eternity offsets a thousand bad ones on earth. The choice is yours.

That's what happened at the cross. Choices were made. There were two other crosses on the hill that day, the day that Jesus died. Two criminals, suffering the same death. And those two crosses remind us of one of God's greatest gifts: the gift of choice. One chose Jesus, the other merely mocked him. Scripture reveals a compelling part of the story:

> One of the criminals on a cross began to shout insults at Jesus: "Aren't you the king of the Jews? Then save yourself and us." But the other criminal stopped him and said, "You should fear God! We are punished justly, getting what we deserve for what we did. But this man has done nothing wrong." Then he said, "Jesus, remember me when you come into your kingdom." Jesus said to him, "I tell you the truth, today you will be with me in paradise" (Luke 23:39-43, NIV).

When one dying criminal prayed, Jesus loved him enough to save him. And when the other mocked, Jesus loved him enough to let him.

He allowed each of them their choice.

He does the same for you.

Jesus, be gracious to me and guide me as I make choices today. Amen.

His final prayer was about you. His final pain was for you. His final passion was you.

Before he went to the cross, Jesus went to the garden. Never had he felt so alone. What had to be done, only he could do. An angel couldn't do it. A man couldn't do it. No force on earth can face the force of evil and win—except God.

And Jesus couldn't turn his back on you. He couldn't because he saw you, and one look at you was all it took to convince him. Right there in the middle of a world that isn't fair. He saw you cast into a river of life you didn't request. He saw you betrayed by those you love. He saw you with a body that gets sick and a heart that grows weak.

He saw you in your own garden of gnarled trees and sleeping friends. He saw you staring into the pit of your own failures and the mouth of your own grave. He saw you in your Garden of Gethsemane—and he didn't want you to be alone.

He wanted you to know that he has been there too. He knows what it's like to be plotted against. He knows what it's like to smell the stench of Satan. And, perhaps most of all, he knows what it's like to beg God to change course at the last minute and to hear God say so gently, but firmly, "No."

At some moment during that midnight hour an angel of mercy came over the weary body of the man in the garden. Jesus stood, the anguish gone from his eyes. His heart will fight no more.

The battle has already been won. Jesus is at peace in the olive trees.

On the eve of the cross, Jesus made his decision. He would rather go to hell for you than go to heaven without you.

Jesus, may I follow you in all the choices that come before me. Amen.

A Holy Incredibility

HOLY THURSDAY

It is a stark scene. Jesus praying in Gethsemane, saying "My heart is ready to break with grief . . ." Does this look like the picture of a saintly Jesus resting in the palm of God? Hardly. We see an agonizing, straining, and struggling Jesus. We see a "man of sorrows." We see a man struggling with fear, wrestling with commitments, and yearning for relief.

We see Jesus in the fog of a broken heart.

My, what a portrait! Jesus is in pain. Jesus is on the stage of fear. Jesus is cloaked, not in sainthood, but in humanity.

The next time the fog finds you, remember Jesus in the garden. The next time you think that no one understands, reread the fourteenth chapter of Mark. The next time your self-pity convinces you that no one cares, pay a visit to Gethsemane. And the next time you wonder if God really perceives the pain that prevails on this dusty planet, listen to the pleading among the twisted trees.

Seeing God like this does wonders for our own suffering. God was never more human than at this hour. God was never nearer to us than when God hurt. The Incarnation was never so fulfilled as in the garden.

Time spent in the fog of pain could be God's greatest gift. It could be the hour when we finally see our Maker. If it is true that in suffering God is most like us, maybe in our suffering we can see God like never before.

Watch closely. It could very well be that the hand that extends itself to lead you out of the fog is a pierced one.

Jesus, may I watch with you in your pain and so come to understand that you watch me in mine. Amen.

GOOD FRIDAY

"Woman, behold your son."

Mary is older now. The hair at her temples is gray. Wrinkles have replaced her youthful skin. Her hands are calloused. She has raised a houseful of children. And now she beholds the crucifixion of her firstborn.

Mary wasn't the first one to be called to say good-bye to loved ones for sake of the kingdom. Joseph was called to be an orphan in Egypt. Jonah was called to be a foreigner in Nineveh. Hannah sent her firstborn son away to serve in the temple. Daniel was sent from Jerusalem to Babylon. Nehemiah was sent from Susa to Jerusalem. Abraham was sent to sacrifice his own son. Paul had to say good-bye to his heritage. The Bible is bound together with good-bye trails and stained with farewell tears.

What kind of God would put people through such agony? What kind of God would give you families and then ask you to leave them? What kind of God would give you friends and then ask you to say good-bye?

The answer to that question is clear but not easy: A God who knows that the deepest love is built not on passion and romance but on a common mission and sacrifice would do that. A God who knows that we are only pilgrims and that eternity is so close that any "Good-bye" is in reality a "See you tomorrow."

And finally, a God who bade the ultimate good-bye: "Woman, behold your son."

Jesus, help us to say good-bye, to let people go. And show us the way to move on when you call us forward. Amen.

All need to be made right with God by his grace, which is a free gift. . . . God gave [Jesus] as a way to forgive sin through faith in the blood of Jesus' death. (Rom. 3:24-25, NCV)

Christ came to earth for one reason: to give his life as a ransom for you, for me, for all of us. He sacrificed himself to give us a second chance. He would have gone to any lengths to do so. And he did. He went to the cross; and in that moment when God's great gift was complete, the compassionate Christ showed the world the cost of his gift.

Trace the path of this Savior, the God who swapped heavenly royalty for earthly poverty. His bed became, at best, a borrowed pallet—and usually the hard earth. He was dependent on handouts for his income. He knew what it meant to have no home. He was ridiculed. His neighbors tried to lynch him. Some called him a lunatic. His family tried to confine him to their house. His friends weren't always faithful to him.

He was accused of a crime he never committed. Witnesses were hired to lie. The jury was rigged. A judge swayed by politics handed down the death penalty.

They killed him.

And why? Because of the gift that only he could give.

Jesus was "not guilty, but he suffered for those who are guilty to bring you to God" (1 Pet. 3:18). As a result, God's children are forgiven.

"My God, my God, why have you forsaken me? Why are you so far from helping me?" (22:1) This is our Lord's cry. This is the cry of redemption.

God, help me to stand strong as Jesus makes his sacrifice for me and for all the world. In thanksgiving, I will sing your praise. Amen.

SUNDAY, APRIL 4 ～ *Read Philippians 2:5-11*

EASTER

The message of Easter is clear—the story's not over yet. We haven't heard the punchline, and we haven't finished the battle. Don't be premature in your judgments or too final in your opinion. The Judge hasn't returned, and the jury isn't in yet.

The story isn't over yet. All that needs to be said hasn't been said. And all that will be seen hasn't been seen.

That's good news. If your eyes have ever moistened at the newsreels of the hungry, remember the story's not over yet. If you've ever been bewildered as you beheld pain triumph over peace—keep the Easter story in mind. The story's not over yet.

If you've ever found your fists clenched in rage at the atrocities at Auschwitz, I've got something to show you. If you've stood distraught as you hear stories of yet another hijacking . . . another serial murderer . . .

Or perhaps your feelings are more personal . . . Maybe the one who promised to love you forever loved you for only as long as it was convenient.

If any of this is true for you, then know that one thing more is true: the Land of Promise, says Jesus, awaits those who endure. The Land of Promise, the place of Jesus' resurrection, is the promise that God really does love us—no matter what. Not just on Easter Sunday when our shoes are shined and our hair is fixed. But what about when we act like jerks, when our tongue is sharp enough to slice a rock and we snap at anything that moves?

The word this Easter Sunday is grace. Grace to cover all our sins. Grace to cover all our needs. Grace to cover the world in its broken places. Grace. Pure and simple. The grace of Jesus' resurrection.

All praise to our risen Christ! All praise to the God who made us. All praise to the Holy Spirit, who goes with us, now and forever more. Amen.

Peace for a Fearful World

APRIL 5–11, 2010 • BEAUTY MAENZANISE

MONDAY, APRIL 5 ~ Read Acts 5:27-28

Abuse does terrible things—to the abused and to the abuser. I'm reminded of a couple whose misunderstandings finally led to a hurtful divorce. During the legal process the husband did everything he could to tarnish his soon-to-be ex-wife's name. Yet in spite of the husband's onslaught of false accusations, the wife picked up the pieces of her life and started over, stronger than before. The same could not be said of the abusive ex-husband.

After Jesus' resurrection, those who had supported Jesus' crucifixion were now fearful. The high priest said, "We gave you strict orders not to teach in this name, yet here you have filled Jerusalem with your teaching." Imagine how angry the chief priests and scribes felt. After doing everything they could to defame, discredit, and destroy Jesus, there were still people loyal to him.

These eyewitnesses to the Resurrection were speaking out. And people were listening to their story! The only thing left for the high priests to do was to silence the "Jesus talk." As the rest of the book of Acts tells us, their attempt was unsuccessful.

We in the church must witness to the crucified and resurrected Christ. Let us start afresh this Easter. Let us bear witness to our risen Lord.

Lord Jesus, help us to be bold and strong in our witness to your presence in our world. Amen!

Ordained elder in the Zimbabwe East Annual Conference of the United Methodist Church; first female dean of the Faculty of Theology at Africa University

A young girl of primary school age was visiting her grandparents soon after the Zimbabwe liberation struggle. While she was with them, she noticed there was no United Methodist Church in their area. Without fear of what adults might say, this little child organized a worship service at her grandparents' homestead. Many Christians in Zimbabwe were still hiding for fear of being discovered and persecuted for their faith affiliation. But such fear found no place in the heart of this young girl. Today a flourishing parish exists precisely because of this young girl. Christ is risen! Christ is risen indeed!

Today's text gives us a glimpse into the hearts of Peter and the other apostles. They were not fearful, discouraged, or ashamed to declare the gospel of Christ's death and resurrection. They openly proclaimed to the chief priests and all who would hear that Jesus was the mediator between God and humanity. They knew the truth of the gospel. And in spite of all the difficulties they experienced as witnesses to this gospel, their courage never waned. Like the young child who began a church in her grandparents' home, the early disciples had hearts too full of the gospel to be contained.

The free gift of life we possess through Christ Jesus' resurrection was not bought by money and price but by his precious blood. His resurrection and presence among the living was witnessed by many. Paul had to remind King Agrippa of Christ's resurrection saying: "This was not done in a corner" (Acts 26:26). Because we are among many who have received Christ as our Lord and Savior, it is our duty to introduce Christ to those who are still in doubt of his resurrection. May our hearts be full of courage to witness to that good news.

Lord, the world around us discourages us from proclaiming your presence among us. Help us this day to take courage from your resurrection and know that we are never alone. Amen.

Every year on the last Sunday in July, all the local congregations in the Zimbabwe United Methodist Church come together to celebrate Harvest Thanksgiving. Prayer groups come one by one, singing their favorite songs, showcasing the new songs emerging in the church. Worshipers use traditional and modern instruments on this celebratory occasion. Individually and collectively, the church praises God with body, soul, and mind, sharing gifts of thanksgiving for the blessings God has given to the community throughout the year.

Likewise, the psalmist knew that some of the deepest praise of God could come through singing, playing instruments, and dancing. When the holy flame starts burning in us, the only way to express our praise to God is in worshiping with our whole being. The psalmist's gratitude for divine blessings found expression in the yearning for a deeper experience of God's grace. Those of us redeemed by the blood of Jesus have a similar yearning: to celebrate our salvation made possible through Christ's sacrifice.

What does the Lord require of followers? The Lord requires gratitude. And for those of us in the Christian tradition, Jesus wants our gratitude to increase more and more until, like a holy flame, it burns within us and we burst into songs and deeds of thankfulness to God and neighbor. To express genuine gratitude to God, our deeds must demonstrate our love, trust, and service. We should be doing good works and singing songs of praise out of the thanksgiving of our hearts.

Lord, help us remember to express our gratitude every day to you with praise for your many mercies. Amen.

In a world that constantly tempts us to give over our allegiances to worldly powers, the text today reminds us that Christ is the Alpha and Omega, the beginning and the end of our lives. Christ is our only allegiance because he is the only real power that is from the beginning and will still be here in the end. Many titles are attributed to Christ, but none is so expressive as ruler and controller of all earthly kings. His reign is universal and perpetual and cause for the multitudes to sing, "Praise him for his mighty deeds; praise him according to his surpassing greatness!" (Ps. 150:2). There is no other ruler on earth who has the power as king of all creation but Jesus.

In the prologue to the Revelation of John, Christ the cosmic ruler is also portrayed as "Prince of Peace." The wondrous irony of Jesus' kingship is that he rules not to wield power or wage war but to bring peace, the peace no worldly power is able to offer. While our hearts thrill at this notion of Christ as "King of kings" and "Prince of peace" the crucial question remains: Have you crowned him king of your life?

It is one thing to talk about what others say and what you yourself believe. But consider this: when your life is in great turmoil, do you know the peace that passes all understanding and maintain balance and calm, even while the people around are worrying for you? If so, when people ask your secret, the only answer you can give is that, as one redeemed through the life and death of Jesus, you meet tribulation in the world with the assurance of Christ's peace. This peace comes directly from Jesus through the word and by the Spirit. This peace is the kind that can never be taken away and never destroyed.

Crucified and risen Christ, grant us your peace so that no other powers can have dominion over us. Amen.

I'm sure all of us have found ourselves at one time or another wishing we hadn't done something. We may feel heartsick or depressed or simply regretful; but we know deep down in our heart that we made a wrong choice. And when we realize the damage our action may have done to another, we want to hide under a rock and never show our face again.

Place yourself with the disciples on that first Easter morning. Recall the meal that previous Thursday evening when each disciple had given his word to stand by Jesus no matter what.

But then Judas walked away; he betrayed Jesus in the garden. Peter acted no better. Ultimately, they all failed Jesus. The one they celebrated on Palm Sunday was arrested, mocked, and crucified; they were left watching helplessly from the shadows. Don't you think they were angry that Jesus did not prove to be the hero they thought he was? Then perhaps they became angry with themselves for failing to stand up for their master. Certainly they felt confused.

In the midst of the disciples' anger and confusion, something unexpected happens: Jesus appears. The Gospel tells us that Jesus appeared when the disciples least expected him but precisely where they needed him: in the midst of their fear and disappointment. Yet Jesus did not come to them with words of anger; he came with words of peace. His words of peace told them that he understood what they had gone through. His words were given without ill will or hurt feelings. His words were balm not blame.

Have we not failed our Lord in many ways? Have we not found ourselves saying, "I wish I hadn't done that"? For all those times, be still and listen for the words of peace from the risen Christ.

Merciful God, thank you for your unfailing love and promise of peace. Amen.

Some of us have a hard time accepting secondhand information. We prefer to believe only what we see or hear ourselves. And every once in a while, we even have a hard time believing what the Lord wants us to believe.

Our reading today highlights how fear and uncertainty can lead even a follower of Jesus to doubt what was once believed. Thomas was one of Jesus' chosen inner circle of disciples. And yet, after Jesus' death, when Thomas heard his friends say that they had seen Jesus alive (just as Jesus himself predicted they would), Thomas refused to believe them. Unless he could see for himself the prints of the nails in Jesus' hands, he would not believe. So only after Thomas hears Jesus' invitation to look at the wounded hands and touch the pierced side does the one-time doubter acknowledge Jesus' suffering and resurrection to proclaim: "My Lord and my God!"

We may not be able to touch Jesus' pierced side, but the prints of the nails in Jesus' hands are real for those of us who believe. The marks Christ bore for our sake bear witness to his resurrection, promising eternal salvation. They remind us that Christ still comes among us, even when we are hiding, afraid, or doubting, with outstretched hands and grace that is sufficient for our needs. We only have to believe.

Gracious Lord, thank you for the gift of the cross and your resurrection. Thank you for the promise of your grace and your mercy. Thank you for extending to us your nail-scarred hands that our faith might be as bold and strong as your sacrifice. Amen.

In 1988, as a new pastor straight from seminary, I dreaded opening the door to start a new day. I was serving a rural five-point charge, the Chiduku Circuit in Zimbabwe. I was naïve, with no pastoral experience. I trusted the people who were telling me what to do more than the One who called me. This brought stress and confusion to my life. One day, standing in the middle of my house, I heard a voice saying, "Beauty, Jesus is right there with you, not as a visitor but as One who wants to guide you."

That was my "aha!" moment. Immediately I felt a sense of peace. I truly believed that the risen Christ was there with me and would never leave me. With the hymn writer I sang: "My hope is built on nothing less than Jesus' blood and righteousness."

Today's scripture encourages Christians to stand firm in their faith in Jesus. Christ has already promised that he will support us, sustain us, and bring us through to victory. As those who believe in the resurrected Christ, we must go about our daily living with the intention of leading others to Christ. We have to be careful of every step we take because the tempter is watching. We live in a hostile world and are surrounded by temptations. For this reason, we must keep close to Jesus.

From today's verses we learn that even those who have not seen can believe. Those who came after Jesus' time—you and me and the rest of today's faith community—can believe because we have the written record of the disciples and other believers, of what they have seen and done. This Bible of ours—this story of God—is a great and mighty gift. It is a strong anchor for us in times of trouble and a strong witness to the entire world.

O Lord, grant us the strength to minister in your name. And may your peace reside within us so that the world can see you through us. Amen.

Transformed by Grace

APRIL 12–18, 2010 • YONG HUI V. MCDONALD

MONDAY, APRIL 12 ～ *Read Acts 9:1-6*

By God's grace Paul was transformed from a fearless persecutor of Christians to a fearless messenger of God. His story of transformation encourages many people, especially helping those who have committed horrendous crimes, to know that God can shower them with mercy.

Several years ago, I began work as a chaplain at the Adams County Detention Facility, a facility with 1,300 inmates. Here, I learned about God's transforming power and grace. Just as God did with Paul, God's grace is changing many of these inmates from violent offenders to kind but fearless messengers of hope.

One of those inmates, Corey Dean Wagner, received life without parole for the murder he committed. Through God's transforming grace and Wagner's acceptance of Christ, his life has now become a positive influence on many others. In fact, Corey's ministry has transformed the lives of inmates and police officers alike. He has shared his life's story in the book *Maximum Saints Ordained by God*. Corey's story is being told in jails and prisons nationwide, reaching out with the message of Christ beyond his own confines, just as Paul did through his many travels and letters.

Use your gifts to reach out to others. Discover your talents and lend them to building up the kingdom of God. If you have a big empty heart that is not filled, ask yourself if you are using your gifts to the maximum to serve God.

Lord Jesus, what can I do to inspire others to get to know you? Show me how to use my gifts. Amen.

United Methodist chaplain serving at Adams County Detention Facility in Colorado, spiritual director and author

When the Lord asked Ananias to visit Paul, he protested because Paul had persecuted Christians. The Lord convinced Ananias to go by telling him that Paul was God's chosen instrument for bringing many people to Christ. When Ananias obeyed, Paul was healed from his blindness. Ananias likely had little inkling that he had just baptized one of the most famously effective Christian missionaries the world would ever know. Sometimes our understanding of others is clouded by our own preconceptions, and God must give us eyes to see what God sees.

In my ministry in the prison community, God spoke to me about two inmates, Timothy Garcia and Monica Valdez. I was led to interview them for a newspaper article. Before becoming a Christian, Timothy had been a Satanist. Monica lost her left leg in a car accident, but later she experienced a spiritual transformation. Both were growing in faith and helping others to grow. At first, I was hesitant to interview them because they were new converts. But as they shared their testimonies with the newspaper reporter, I felt strongly the presence of the Lord. They honored God with their powerful testimonies, and it was a privilege for me to listen to their stories of transformation and commitment to serve God. Praise God!

If you have never visited a jail or prison to witness what God is doing with the incarcerated, I encourage you to make the effort to do so. You will be blessed beyond your expectations. God's treasures can be found in jails and prisons.

Lord Jesus, open my heart to reach out to the undervalued, underserved, underprivileged, and the poor with the message of your love and power. Amen.

Weeping may remain for a night, but rejoicing comes in the morning.

On July 9, 2008, Keith, my husband of thirty years and also a United Methodist pastor, and I were invited to an Adams County Special Olympics fund-raising dinner. I was to lead the opening prayer, so we drove separately to ensure that I would arrive on time. But Keith never made it to that dinner; he died in a car accident on the way. I could never fully describe the grief and despair that filled my heart, and I cannot adequately describe the overwhelming support I received from my friends. God truly brought me healing in several ways.

First, God assured me that my husband had lived a full life. Then, three nights after Keith died, God told me in a dream that my husband was being well cared for. Then Keith appeared to me in my dream. He stood in front of me, bowed, and said, "Thank you," and disappeared. I was so comforted.

Three weeks after Keith's death, I still wasn't ready to return to work, so I visited my daughter. Driving home, I was listening to one of Keith's favorite songs "God of Wonders." Suddenly, I had a vision of Keith smiling and dancing in the sky. God gave me such joy that I was able to go back to work the next day.

Finally, God spoke to me, saying I needed to let go of my husband, and to let go of the grieving that was hindering my prayer life. So, I gave Keith to God, along with my wishes, desires, self-pity and expectations, and asked God to heal my mind and heart. I believe God did that for me. Today I am filled with joy because God healed my broken heart.

Ask God to bring healing in your heart today for whatever you have lost.

Have you ever wondered how Paul felt after he encountered the risen Christ on the road to Damascus? Blinded and unable to walk without assistance, Paul must have felt helpless, even powerless. "For three days he was without sight, and neither ate nor drank" (Acts 9:9). I believe his vigil of prayer and fasting was repentance for his sins and preparation for hearing a fresh word from God. And that word from God came to Paul in the person Ananias, who restored to him his vision and, in fact, gave him new eyes to see how to serve God.

God's grace can free us from our sin and guilt as well. Randy Palmer came crying, lamenting over not being able to stop someone from committing suicide. The night before, Randy had spoken to the man and had a feeling he was suicidal. "You're not going to kill yourself, are you?" Randy asked. The man replied, "No, I am not going to kill myself." But that very night the man hanged himself in his room. Randy had no way of knowing this man's intentions but felt nonetheless that he could have done something to prevent it. Randy couldn't sleep at night and suffered under the heavy weight of self-imposed guilt.

A couple of days later, Randy shared with me that he'd had a dream. In this dream, the man who had committed suicide appeared and said, "I am sorry that I lied to you. Please forgive me." Randy forgave the man. Randy believed God gave him that dream so that he would no longer have to suffer from guilt. God can free us from our guilt and shame if we only ask for that fresh word of grace.

Lord, Jesus, free me from guilt and shame. Amen.

John had a vision of a heavenly worship service. He wrote, "In a loud voice they sang: 'Worthy is the Lamb, who was slain, to receive power and wealth and wisdom and strength and honor and glory and praise!'" (Revelation 5:12). This vision teaches us the importance of worship. We can worship God once or twice a week in our church's worship services, but it is also important to worship God everyday.

Even though I lead twelve worship services at the Adams County Detention Facility (ACDF) every week, I know I cannot neglect my daily worship of God. I know God is present in those regular worship services at ACDF, and I am extremely blessed by them. However, they constitute my ministry in the world, and cannot take the place of my devotion to God. Until recently, I held the misconception that loving my ministry was the same as loving God. Now I understand those two activities as separate yet related in the life of faith. I must choose to love God and love others.

After my husband passed away I spent a lot of time mourning that loss. After a while, God asked me to spend five hours every day with God. At first, I thought that would be impossible. In fact, I had been trying to live up to that standard of devotion for several years. Sometimes I succeeded; but most of the time, I neglected to spend that many hours with God because I was spending so many hours in ministry with others. Thankfully, the Holy Spirit started helping me organize my life so that I could eliminate distractions and simplify my life. As a result, I was able to focus on spending more time with God.

Reflect on how you spend your time. Focus on eliminating distractions and simplifying your life so that you may spend more time with God.

Today's text from John makes it clear that Peter's assignment was to take care of God's business with the help of the Holy Spirit. Our spiritual assignments also become clear when we listen to God.

One of the inmates at the Adams County Detention Facility, Greg Lisco, learned to listen to the Holy Spirit. He began reaching out to others by preaching at the chaplain's worship services and in his own housing unit.

"The people that fill our jails and prisons," he said, "are there because Satan figured out what God wanted to do with them before they figured out what God wanted them to do. Somehow the devil kept them from hearing God's voice speaking to them. It makes me sad."

Greg plans to attend a Bible college and enter the ministry. He is listening to God's voice and understands that following his calling is crucial for his spiritual growth.

If we want to hear God's calling, we must first listen. But—and this is critical—if we listen for God's call, and we respond, there are no guarantees about where God's call will lead us. Peter's decision to feed the flock and to follow Jesus results, eventually, in his seizure and death. God's call can lead to risk and loss of control. And yet, if it is God's voice that we hear, we have the sure promise that God will be with us. God doesn't promise us safety; God does promise faithfulness.

Lord Jesus, speak to me; I am listening. Holy Spirit, guide my path. Help me recognize your voice so that I have the heart to respond to it. Amen.

The Adams County Detention Facility has an exciting Hispanic ministry, in large part because of the bilingual Hispanic leaders' passion to reach out to the lost and their love for the people. When I started working as a chaplain in 2003, there was no Hispanic ministry at the facility. I noticed there were no Spanish Bibles available. I called a friend; she donated $500 to purchase several Spanish Bibles.

That was just the beginning. Many more donations followed, and our facility provides Spanish Bibles to those inmates who need one. One day, several Hispanic inmate leaders approached me and told me that they needed worship services and a Bible study in Spanish for those who did not speak or read English. Since no chaplain could speak Spanish at the facility, I started five Spanish-speaking prayer circles in different units and eventually was able to recruit Hispanic pastors from outside the facility to lead worship. Now there are seven Spanish worship services held every week at ACDF! In 2007, more than 2,000 Hispanic inmates attended worship services. In addition, a group of inmates initiated a project to have my book, *Journey with Jesus*, translated into Spanish. The vision of these leaders resulted in funding from the General Board of Higher Education and Ministry that will help pay to finish translating into Spanish two books: *Journey with Jesus* and *Maximum Saints Ordained by God*.

Because we, as a community and as individuals, were willing to listen to God's call, we were led in directions we could never have foreseen. And, in all the places God has led us, we have found God already there, waiting for us.

God, lead us where you need us. Give us the gift of discerning your will in our lives. Amen.

We Lambs Are God's Children

APRIL 19–25, 2010 • CHRISTOPHER MILLER

MONDAY, APRIL 19 ～ *Read Psalm 23*

Take a few moments and read Psalm 23 slowly and silently.

God's love for us mirrors the love of a parent for a child. God is proud of our accomplishments. God weeps when we stumble. God gets angry when we break the rules. God sees in us who we might become. God is our Creator, and the love of God feels very much like the love my wife and I share for our daughter.

Why else would God deliver us from evil? Or lead us away from temptation? Why else should God send goodness and mercy chasing after us? And why do we not stop to receive them? Are we too busy for our own salvation?

Our faith in the Lord demands that we separate ourselves from the speed of our lives. When we slow down, we find still waters and a deeper connection with each other and with God. When we slow down we hear the voice of King David in the psalm.

We feel calm and secure and protected. We find that the paths of righteousness lie before us. The power of prayer, the power of silence, the power of God overwhelms us. And as God's people, we find our cup overflows with God's love.

God embraces us with love so that we may live without fear, and the calm inspiration of the Psalms sounds to us like a lullaby. The cadence of the Psalm 23 soothes and reassures us. We open ourselves to God's word and allow it to flow freely through us.

Holy God, me free me from the chains that bind me to my daily routines. Help me to hear your voice. Let me rest in you. Amen.

Husband, father, estate attorney, and member of First United Methodist Church in Alpharetta, GA

Today read Psalm 23 aloud. Listen for the sounds of God's love. See, in your mind's eye, the greatness of God's care for us. God's love reflects itself to us through the prism of a shepherd's devotion to the flock. God creates green pastures and still waters as food and nourishment to us who are God's sheep. Psalm 23 illuminates a picturesque source of strength and endurance for God's people.

Yet in Psalm 23, the table God prepares before us is laid in the presence of our enemies. The enemies that usually pursue us are harmless. They are present, but not to harm us. Might this be a way for God to help us bring disputes to an end? Perhaps God anoints us with oil to bless us with the wisdom, the endurance, and the strength to find peace with one another. We simply have to use these skills.

As a lawyer who works with trusts and estates, I sometimes find clients deeply at odds with members of their own families. I too have found myself spiritually and physically far away from my parents. God calls us to the table, to the center, to a place where we may find joy and love everlasting. But if God puts us in the right place, we must do the right things. We must open our hearts and share our love and lives with one another.

Coming together in this way is what it means to dwell in the house of the Lord. We are learning to love God as our parent, learning to act as God's servant, learning to love each other and to seek peace.

Dear God, my Creator, you are the source of my strength and thought. Guide me with your hand and show me how to love. Call me to the table with my brothers and sisters. Help me to share your love with others, so that we all can be the fulfillment of your work. Amen.

Comparing people and sheep, Jesus the Rabbi helps us in this passage to distinguish God's place in our heart from among the many other influences in our lives. In the passages leading up to this showdown between Jesus and some Jews of Jerusalem, Jesus speaks again and again in a metaphor that seemingly flies over the heads of those listening to him. He calls himself the Good Shepherd. He explains to them that he came in through "the gate," and plans to lead his followers out through "the gate."

This gate marks the way through which we must pass to go into Jesus' fold. And, from this passage, it is clear that we sheep must be led through the gate. Some of us bound through that gate without hesitation. Some of us halt, bleating against the flock's momentum. Once through that gate, however, we are sheep of Jesus' flock. His sheep follow him and live by his teachings. Under the care of our Shepherd's staff, we shall not be lost. Once nurtured into disciples, we go back out into the world to be shepherds in our own right, nurturing Jesus' many flocks.

Jesus' audience in Jerusalem is struggling to categorize him either as the Messiah they are waiting for or just another smooth-talking magician. They are eager to pigeonhole him. Their inability to understand and their demands that he "tell us plainly" clearly expose them as unwilling to step out and follow Jesus. Being a disciple is about following whether or not the way is clear. It means having faith without rational support.

We believe in Jesus the Teacher. We embrace Jesus as our Shepherd. We join the flock of God's children willingly. We profess our faith openly, and we become Jesus' sheep.

Jesus, my Good Shepherd, let me hear your call today. Help me to follow you, for in your care I am safe. Amen.

The disciple Peter shows us through his actions that in carrying the light of Jesus into the world, we too can work miracles and inspire other believers. Peter's healing of Tabitha is but one in a series of stories in which the disciples restore people to health and carry divine rewards to those who carry out God's will.

Here, Tabitha is identified in two ways. First, she is called a disciple in the village of Joppa, and second, she is known as a woman "devoted to good works and acts of charity." Tabitha had thus earned her place in the canon. Presumably, her reputation also preceded her in biblical times, as we read that Peter left his work in a village ten miles distant to attend to her needs and give her a second life. The saints and widows had given her up for dead.

Indeed, don't we all wish to be remembered as one devoted to good works and acts of charity? Such works embody the most meaningful of God's edicts: Do justice, love kindness, and walk humbly with your God. (See Micah 6:8.)

Thus, through Christ's teachings, we find ourselves pulled toward the practice of philanthropy. Tabitha had sewn tunics and shared her company with widows as her ministry, and upon her passing, they wept for their loss. What is it that we can give to our community? Do we have the gift of compassion? Or the skills to build and repair? Are we good at speaking? Do we excel in writing or advocacy? And beyond that, can we lead others to share their gifts? Tabitha sets a high standard, but she lives again so that we might strive for such blessings.

Dear God of heaven and earth, set my hands to work for others. Give me the strength to provide not just for my family but also for those around me, that I might join Tabitha in being faithful to you. Amen.

Figuring out God's message in the Revelation to John is far from easy. We in the twenty-first century are removed from the original oral tradition and the audiences for whom Revelation was written. And yet the images described in this passage from Revelation are still powerful. We can see them in our mind's eye as clearly as if they were directed and staged by Cecil B. DeMille himself.

In his book *The Throne, the Lamb & the Dragon*, the Canadian professor Paul Spilsbury describes an almost extinct form of literature called an *apocalypse*. He shows how the dreamy sequences of Revelation's passages are meant more as symbolic metaphor and less as a retelling of history. Thus we gain a new perspective on this story of a crowd giving praise to God. Rather than treating it as a literal prediction of the future events of Armageddon, we can instead read it as a persuasive closing argument that encourages the reader to believe in God's power, in God's wisdom and in God's generosity.

Just before this passage, John counts out 144,000 descendants from the original twelve tribes of Israel who presumably are among those chosen for God's eternal grace. But then he suddenly calls the people too many to count and takes pains to explain that these come from every nation, from all tribes and peoples and languages. His message is that God's love stretches toward all of humankind—we are all God's children.

John allows us to claim a connection to God not through our ancestry but through our profession of faith. So it is well within our reach to join that joyful multitude and participate in worshiping God. In doing so, we will be sheltered. We will hunger and thirst no more. And we can receive for ourselves the salvation and inner peace that God provides those who believe.

Amen! Blessing and glory and wisdom and thanksgiving and honor and power and might be to you, our God, forever and ever! Amen.

We Lambs Are God's Children   125

Who can withstand God's wrath? The scripture says that the faithful can. But *how* are the faithful able to stand? They are able to stand because God and Jesus, God's lamb, sustain them.

To be faithful to God—to worship God and to follow God—is a lifelong challenge for us. To worship God is to nurture our connection with God. And, in spending time with God, in nurturing that connection, we find for ourselves the truest form of worship.

To follow God is to set out on high adventure, for God is in all places: beautiful and desolate, lush and parched, postmodern and rustic. God is present in the midst of war, and serves to comfort those in the deepest poverty. To follow God is to carry God's works with us to all of those places. How much easier it is to stay at home to pray than to meet God's challenge to enter into the bleakest corners of society and to see the light of God's hand there, quietly beckoning us forward as God's agent of change!

In today's passage, we get a sense of the people's struggle both to follow and to worship God. The elder recognizes the difficulty of the spiritual journey taken by a true believer, and he commends them for their successes. God rewards those who continuously follow God, those who worship day and night and invite God nearer to them. This bounty of spiritual fullness can infuse us. It can quench our thirst, ease our hunger, and shade us from the blinding desert sun.

More than that, the peace we find within ourselves when we are connected with God sets into perspective our mortal sufferings. God gives us the strength to overcome illness and death, to transform our lives into acts of God.

Lamb of God, show me how to be your true follower. Lead me today, and make my life an act of love. Amen.

Throughout the week, we have drawn parallels between our experience as people living in God's embrace, and a flock of sheep tended to and guided by its shepherd. Looking back, then, what do we affirm?

We start with a simple statement: "The Lord is my shepherd." We are God's sheep. We think independently, but we are indisputably part of a group led by God and collectively subject to God's will. At different times in the Bible, God gets angry when we as a flock scatter or we sacrifice ourselves to self-centeredness. God's love for us strengthens us when we freely give ourselves to God and when we tend to the other members of our flock. As faithful people, our call is to follow God and to worship God.

Jesus our Shepherd lived his life as both example and Savior. He encourages us to recognize the love that God showers on us. He tells us to follow in the steps of Tabitha, who wove clothing for the widows. He shows us by his example how to find God's truth in the world. We recognize that we are beloved sheep of God—we are God's children. Jesus the Shepherd is also Jesus the Lamb. He was, like us, a follower and worshiper of God. He gave his life for us, that we might believe in God's power and love. So we turn to each other, and guide one another, living as Christ taught us to live.

God, give me shelter today. Strengthen me to worship you and to follow you. Guide me to the places you are, that I may live in your love. Amen.

Tending to the Holy

APRIL 26–MAY 2, 2010 • AMELIA CHUA

MONDAY, APRIL 26 ～ *Read Acts 11:1-18*

Over the ages, believers have been called to defend their faith. Persons offer this defense as often for the community of faith itself as for those beyond it. Sometimes this defense flows into a treatise supported by a climate of tolerance. Any challenge to inclusivity within the church requires defense—even today.

Acts 11:1-18 includes Peter's defense. The passage opens with criticism of Peter from the apostles and believers in Judea. They demand an explanation of his actions. Rather than accusing him of baptizing people upon whom the Holy Spirit fell, they chastise Peter for going to uncircumcised men and eating with them. Six circumcised brothers who witnessed to the coming of the Holy Spirit among the Gentiles could not dispel the prejudice against the unclean.

There comes a time when a believer is called to challenge the prejudice of the faith community. Institutions do not change easily, and yet God calls us to be the agents that bring in the new wind of the Spirit with new paradigms of love in fulfilling God's plan for the reconciliation of all peoples. As disciples of Christ we know our defense may be costly, and repentance by the community may or may not be forthcoming as it was with Peter. Yet we follow in the great tradition of the saints who understood the unity of wisdom, courage, and love for neighbor.

We thank you for choosing us to be agents of love, O God. Help us to live out our calling. Amen.

Clergy member of the California–Nevada Conference of the United Methodist Church; spiritual director; Pacific Grove, CA

I ardently believe that the God we worship is one who actively tries to reach us. Often, however, our frame of mind causes us to miss the revelation. This frame of mind includes incessant busyness, lack of attention, fatigue, and sometimes a sophistication that doubts forms of grace that do not fall within the ordinary.

The worldwide resurgence in the ministry of spiritual direction arises out of a desire to tend the holy in our lives. People of faith are awakening and listening to what God has to say. Often the primary task in spiritual direction is to create a space that helps the faithful remember and listen deeply. To remember is to collect the pieces and put them into a whole that one can understand and appreciate. This remembering and collecting often entails our retelling our experience.

This passage basically retells Peter's experience as recorded in Chapter 10. Generally Peter is accepted as the apostle who held closely to the Jewish Christian tradition. In reviewing his story step-by-step with a group of believers, Peter has the opportunity to understand a vision and integrate it with his experience in Cornelius's household. His challenge in growth is to understand that God's grace extends to all people, far above and beyond what Peter has ever imagined. To Peter's credit, he moves forward to be an instrument of that grace.

God is actively working to extend our horizons of belief and understanding. In pausing to remember those moments when the Mystery touched our lives, we savor the Holy in our midst. As a result, our faith increases, our joy abounds, and we are empowered to follow God more closely.

May I remember your goodness, O loving God. Let me pause to savor your presence with me. In Christ's name. Amen.

Sometimes living in the modern world gets to me. Last Thursday it was the traffic jam that started at 2:47 in the afternoon. On Saturday it was the computer that froze halfway through the writing of this meditation. Today it was being bounced along an advanced technological phone system for twenty-five minutes, waiting for a real person who could do something to answer my call. I accessed the "Express Service Line" with a monitor for quality control.

Though telling the stars, the snow, and the trees to praise the Lord may seem like an unusual perspective, I can relate to the author of Psalm 148. More and more, it is when I turn to nature that I feel grounded and keep a perspective on what is real. Looking up at the stars late at night, I experience the depths of the universe and remember what "big" means. Catching a snowflake on my tongue, I marvel at the cold and the seasons. It is a cycle of providence, of seeding and harvesting, of using and recycling. Arching my back to look up at the tip of a sequoia tree, I wonder at what it has seen over its lifetime, what visions lie embedded in its rings of age.

Human beings create technology, utility, and complex systems. Often these systems now determine our day-to-day reality. However, there is a vast difference between what will stand the test of time and what will not. God and our relationship to our Creator is still the ground of reality on which we stand. As the world swirls at ever greater speed around us, it is often nature that reminds us of what will remain.

May your beautiful creation ground me, O God, for you are the Rock of my Salvation. Amen.

As we approached the turn of the millennium, the media was promoting images that sought to capture the spirit of a certain age, like the Ming dynasty in China or the postmodern era in Europe. Some are still pictures; others are fast-forwarded in a time sequence to project them into the future. Some of the "Brave New World" projections I have seen have been rather bleak: They depict scarcity of world resources, authoritarian rule, violence, darkness, and weary masses.

The vision of the new heaven and new earth in Revelation 21 is very different—full of light, hope, and joy. As we juxtapose this vision of the future with a hard look at the world in the present, what surfaces is the deep, deep longing in our hearts for all creation to live in the harmony (shalom) planned by its Creator. Our hearts yearn for the time when everyone will have an adequate share of daily bread and hunger will be no more. We long for healing and wholeness, a time when tears will not reveal hearts shattered by pain. We dream of the earth's people living truly as neighbors in peace because justice prevails.

As people of faith, we hold the tension of the present with our hope for the future. In the most troubled spots in the world, a spark will ignite and maintain a steady glow. Each spark of love for neighbor as self adds harmony; each spark of justice adds peace; and each spark of love for God adds glory. Many people of faith and people of many faiths share the vision of the new heaven and earth. In their time, these sparks will burst into bright light.

God of all ages, let me live in the new heaven and earth today.
In Christ's name. Amen.

The minister turned to her and said, "Julie, repeat after me." Julie glanced at the minister, nodded slightly, looked at Jonathan shyly, and resolutely repeated each phrase: "I, Julie Mei-Ling, take you, Jonathan Wei-Ang, to be my wedded husband, to have and to hold, from this day forward, for better, for worse, for richer, for poorer, in sickness and in health." Julie paused and her eyes brimmed. Jonathan squeezed her hands to pass her his energy.

The minister picked up and Julie followed, "to love and to cherish . . . " Her tears overflowed, she lowered her head, and a tear dropped to her glove. Jonathan smiled, reached into his trouser pocket, and took out a linen handkerchief. He reached out, brushed aside a wisp of her hair, and lifted her chin. She smiled, closed her eyes, and offered her cheeks. He gently dabbed her cheeks and wiped the traces of her teardrops. The congregation held its breath.

We all recognize those moments of holiness when a scene of love takes our breath away, and we too stand on holy ground. The beauty both captivates us and inspires fear in us. In that moment, we too believe that all will be well and all hopes will find fulfillment.

The new Jerusalem, the holy city, will be prepared as a bride adorned for her husband. God will lead her forth and dwell with her. God's home will be with mortals, and God will wipe every tear from our eyes. I can imagine no more tender scene of love than this. With a touch of God's hand, we can leave behind the past and walk into a new future. We will not look back, for the picture of love we see ahead will transform our history.

Come, my Beloved, and tenderly lead me forward in my walk with you. In Christ's name. Amen.

When I hear of so-and-so being at the height of his or her glory, I visualize someone at the pinnacle of success, in robust health and vitality, having accomplished something so outstanding as to be recognized by the community as having made a significant contribution. This person has power, prestige, and influence.

When Jesus talks about God's having glorified him, he refers to the culmination of a long, hard road of meeting resistance; fighting the religious, economic, and political establishment; back-breaking work, misunderstanding, and betrayal by friends; and impending death. The contrast stuns me.

Each step of the way to his glory, Jesus had a choice. It was within his power to turn away, if not to downscale or slightly distort the gospel. He read people's hearts; he knew that the consequence of each decision led him closer to a final confrontation with death-dealing powers. Having a God-consciousness of good and evil embodied in a human self made the choice for God's glory a very painful one indeed.

We praise Jesus for his faithfulness. In choosing obedience to a death he freely accepted, he redefined glory for all believers. Just as we continue to face choices for good or evil and battle death-dealing forces, we have a Savior of the world who we know has won our glory for us.

Praise to you, Lord Jesus Christ. May I be glorified in you. Amen.

As a young girl, I loved new things. I couldn't wait to tear off the wrappings and put on whatever new thing I received. I loved to put on new shoes and go out somewhere, anywhere. When I planted my first narcissus bulb, I got up at night hoping to catch its flowers coming out. When I got my first pair of goldfish, I paid them so much attention and fed them so much that they floated on the surface the next morning.

Though impatience has diminished with age, I still delight in new things. New things catch our attention because they are unsoiled by use and dirt. Newness brings a sense of not being weighted down: a fresh perspective, an excitement of something not tried before, a hope of something better.

The essence of Jesus' teaching was actually familiar to the disciples. For centuries God had tried repeatedly to convey the message. Jesus' message of forgiveness and hope, his actions of healing and providing for needs, his embrace of his disciples as friends actually recall an old, old message: God's faithfulness through the ages.

Yet by leaving what he calls a new commandment, Jesus wraps up his message and presents it to us in a memorable way. He tells us that loving one another as he has loved us will become the distinguishing mark of those who bear his name. Stated this way, it is new and it is easy to remember. This new commandment not only embodies teachings of the past, it is an invitation to look for and create new opportunities for love.

May your love, O God, find new forms and expressions within me. Amen.

God's Vision for Us

MAY 3–9, 2010 • KEN R. HAYDEN

MONDAY, MAY 3 ~ *Read Acts 16:9-12*

During childhood, we value our freedom to play. As we grow older, someone will invariably ask the question, "What do you want to be when you grow up?" That can bring us up short, leaving us bewildered imagining all the possibilities. We sometimes talk with a family member or a trusted friend. Occasionally, some of us receive an answer to that question in a dream or a vision. This happened to me when I was a teenager. I heard a voice in a vision calling me to be a minister.

Such visions and voices are not easily dismissed. But they can be difficult to respond to. It was not until my mid-twenties that I sought the counsel of two United Methodist pastors about how to make sense of the voice. Both pastors said to me, "You had a vision and a call to ministry."

In Acts 16, Paul has a vision that called him to a new mission. He saw a Macedonian man asking him to leave Asia Minor and go for the first time into the Roman provinces of Europe. Such areas were unknown to Paul, and he may have been a bit anxious.

Visions and voices can be daunting when they call us to leave our comfort zones. But I learned from both Christian and Delaware (Lenape) Indian teachings to fully experience the moment and vision of God as Creator. Being open allows the Holy Spirit to work in our lives, to direct us and give us courage to respond to God's voice and vision for our work in ministry.

Most gracious God, we give thanks for the many ways you offer us, your people, a vision for our life's work. Amen.

Chaplain and tribal member of the Eastern Delaware Nation; ordained elder in the Illinois Great Rivers Conference of the United Methodist Church

Our lifestyle demands that we act quickly to complete assigned tasks. We live in a fast-paced, globally connected world.

The Lenape words, *elan kumankw*, mean "we are all related." It is an important spiritual principle. It describes the connection between animate and inanimate things; it celebrates the natural way of our mother earth. "We are all related" taught me this was the way the world was meant to be. We often think that new life, new insights, and new relationships are our doing, something we do that is unrelated to the rest of the world. But in truth, our relationships are always more complex than movies or social networking sites would have us believe.

The apostle Paul had many friends among the churches he established. Often those relationships bore fruit, and Paul's words opened the hearts of the people who heard him. In Acts 16, Lydia, the dealer in purple cloth, is moved by Paul's words to open up not only her heart but also her home. She becomes a model of New Testament hospitality—making of space for the holy other, a gift from the Creator God.

When I was a teenager, aunts, uncles, and cousins from far away places often came to visit us in our home. My mother and father, regardless of time of day or season of the year, offered them hospitality of shelter, rest, food, and fellowship, and an opportunity to tell their stories of hope and trouble. Such relationships took time, required a slower pace, and had no need of electronic equipment. Such relationships are more difficult to establish precisely because they call us to "disconnect" from one world in order to connect with God and with those others who come across our path.

God of hospitality, we give thanks for the times and seasons of our lives in which you have offered kindness, truth, and faithfulness to us. Amen.

In some American Indian tribes, a vision quest is a part of a person's discerning his or her life purpose. The Delaware (Lenape) people honor all those—young and old, male and female—who request to go on a vision quest.

Many people think that those who seek a vision must do so alone. They do not. Those who decide to take the vision quest have family, friends, and other spiritual people support them with prayers and encouragement throughout their spiritual journey. The whole process involves a community action of prayer and deep discernment. This journey to a solitary place is the work of the Creator God who fulfills the purpose of the process.

In our modern society, when we want to "get away from it all," we go on a vacation or perhaps take a brief retreat. We hope simply getting away from the routine on our own will renew our heart and our vision.

The vision quest, however, is different. It is a journey one takes with the support of a community and the guidance of God. Unlike the individualistic perspective of doing something solo, the Lenape "vision quester" does not take the retreat or ascend the mountain alone. The renewal sought is a renewal inspired by the Holy Spirit. The blessing of a vision comes as a consequence of searching for that vision among a community of hope.

God of vision, God of the mountain, let us hear your voice clearly on our journey to renewal. Amen.

History books tell us that Hernando deSoto was a conquistador whose goal was to find a lost city of gold. Unfortunately, deSoto's search was unsuccessful; there was no city of gold to be found. He had been looking for great wealth in order to feel important and significant. But in the end, his obsession with earthly treasure caused him and the soldiers who followed him to be disappointed.

The Bible tells us that there is a city whose streets are made of pure gold—a New Jerusalem. But that city is neither found on earth nor found by people looking for earthly treasure. Rather this city belongs to God and is offered as a gift to those who seek God's glory before their own.

Recently, my wife and I were in British Colombia to celebrate our son's marriage and our fortieth wedding anniversary. As we stood on the beach, we were illuminated by the brilliant yellow-white sunshine, blazing in a clear blue sky, with soft white clouds floating along a light ocean breeze. We stood there, listening to the sounds of the waves, surrounded by a sacred circle of our children and their spouses, our grandchildren, and our dearest friends, beneath the shade of a totem pole. Overhead, a golden eagle soared. For a moment, I felt completely uninterested in the world's riches, unburdened by all the things that people accumulate. I felt as John must have felt as he saw the vision of "the holy city Jerusalem coming down out of heaven," a place without need of artificial lighting because "the glory of the Lord is its light." In that moment, I was not disappointed by what I'd found—I was transfixed.

Gracious God, creator of all heaven and earth, help us live this day in your image and with a vision of your Holy City. Amen.

Craftsmanship is a common characteristic of many American Indian peoples. According to the teachings of the Delaware (Lenape) people, a teenager (or even someone older) who desires to learn some skill or craft must go with a gift for an elder and ask for help in learning that particular elder's craft.

One of the first lessons an elder taught me was always to leave a mistake in whatever you create. In this way, you will know you are not the Creator God but are instead a creature that imparts the Creator's spirit for the benefit of the craft. Because God has made us and loved us first, we can then impart to others that spirit of God's love.

When Jesus spoke to his disciples about the relationship of the believer to God, he assured them that they had been given God's Holy Spirit as both a reminder of Jesus' teachings and as a conduit for Jesus' peace. In them dwelled a Spirit given for their benefit but also for the benefit of others. By learning from the Holy Spirit, believers can have the assurance of Christ's presence and the confidence and skill to bear witness to the world of that presence.

By holding close to the gift of the Spirit, we all can be protected, encouraged, and transformed by that Spirit. This is Jesus' gift to us.

O Holy One, we give you thanks for the gift of the Holy Spirit who comes to us by your mercy and grace. Amen.

My wife is a strong Chickamauga Cherokee woman. She was born in Thousandsticks, Kentucky, located in the Redbird Missionary Conference. As a child she loved to sing the old church hymns in her grandma's porch swing. In 2004 she was diagnosed with breast cancer and as she began her treatments, she recalled the story of my eighty-one-year-old mother. In the 1950s my mother underwent cancer radiation treatment as part of an ongoing research project. Thankfully, she survived.

As the weeks of treatments passed for my wife, Evelyn, she could feel her physical energy slowly diminishing. And as her body weakened, so did her spirit. She became discouraged. She yearned to sing again. So finally she decided that, during each radiation session, she would visualize being in her grandma's swing—rhythmically swaying back and forth, back and forth. With each session, she began to feel more and more embraced by the loving presence of God. She was no longer sitting alone behind locked doors. God was there with her, rocking her in that porch swing.

After two months, Evelyn's energy began to increase, and her health returned. She is now a four-year cancer survivor and bears witness to God's healing grace. We continue the legacy of remembering and telling our faithful family stories as a means to celebrate God's continuing graciousness to us. "Let the peoples praise you. O God; let all the peoples praise you."

O God, you are with us. You are with us in small locked rooms of our hearts and minds. You are with us on swaying porch swings. You are with us when we least expect you. Thank you for new beginnings every day. Amen.

God's sense of timing is often quite different than our own. The up side, though, is that it is in God's time that we often experience God's most amazing grace.

Our daughter and son-in-law thought their family was complete. They had two children, a daughter of fifteen and a son almost ten. Then—surprise!—our daughter found out she was pregnant. A third child was on the way! She and her husband scrambled to make a new plan of action since their three-bedroom home was not going to be adequate for a family of five. Time was short, but after several months of negotiating in a troubled mortgage market, they finally purchased a new home. They were relieved to have one more month to move and prepare for the birth.

On the weekend of our fortieth wedding anniversary, my wife and I celebrated the arrival of our new granddaughter, Isabella Grace. Amazing grace. God's timing—perfect timing.

Weeks later, while visiting a very fussy Isabella Grace, my wife tried to soothe her by singing the familiar hymn, "Amazing Grace." Almost immediately, the hymn became a lullaby and Isabella Grace grew calm and fell asleep. When we think we have all things planned and have brought everything under our control, God surprises us with gifts and grace that exceeds our greatest imagination. All we can do is join the psalmist and sing: "God, our God, has blessed us."

O Lord, we give you thanks for the unexpected. May we celebrate the surprises of your grace. Amen.

The Mystery of the Ascension

MAY 10–16, 2010 • SAM PURUSHOTHAM

MONDAY, MAY 10 ~ *Read Luke 24:44-53; Acts:1-11*

The death of Jesus utterly devastated the apostles and his other disciples, even though he had told them of the impending event. To add to their discomfort, his body was missing from the tomb—but then Jesus appeared to some of them.

While the apostles were trying to make sense of what was happening, Jesus again appeared to them. He admonished them for their bewilderment. He showed them his wounds and assured them that they were witnessing the fulfillment of the prophecies. They were excited to see him, yet still wondering and uncertain.

Jesus made clear what was going on—he reminded them of their post-Resurrection mission. He urged them to get prepared to be witnesses to his Resurrection. He appeared to them repeatedly and spoke to them about the kingdom of God. And after he was carried into heaven, his small band of followers began to witness with new energy and joy.

Jesus promised the apostles then and he promises us today that God will supply all the resources we need. As disciples of Christ we must live lives that will draw persons near to him.

I have a need to be convinced of the authenticity of that which I read or observe; nevertheless, when I recite the words from the creed, "He ascended into heaven, and sitteth at the right hand of God," I find myself moved by the mystery of the ascension.

Gracious God, give us faith that we may discern your presence in our lives. Amen.

Director, the United Methodist General Commission of Christian Unity and Inter-religious Concerns

Appropriately, this reading follows yesterday's Ascension story. This psalm celebrates God as the "great king over all the earth" and "king over the nations." The psalm draws on ancient Israel's enthronement liturgy. Here, God was elevated as the most powerful sovereign. The psalmist uses the word *Elyon* for God. It means "God most high," and it guides us to a new understanding of the festival of Ascension.

Just as witnessing God ascend to the throne is a world-changing event, so too the dramatic festival of the Ascension is less about getting the body of Jesus off the earth and more about the dramatic moment when Jesus' presence becomes the rule of mercy and law over all the earth.

So when Jesus' ascension is celebrated, we know that our God rules over everything that is and was and shall be. It is our job now to proclaim it.

I am a second-generation Christian. My grandfather was a Hindu convert. In an age of such pluralism, it can become more difficult to talk about our own binding truth. But while we remain deeply committed to Jesus Christ and carry in our hearts the mandate to witness to our faith, still one thing remains: Our belief in Jesus' ascension is shared with others out of mutual respect—not imposed.

We are called to be witnesses to the ascension. God continues to be the ruler and Lord of all. Finding faithful ways to proclaim our convictions, while respecting others' beliefs is our God-given task.

God of all peoples and nations, races and faiths, help us to respect all our neighbors, wherever they may be and whatever their faith. Amen.

This is another psalm about God's power and authority. Clearly this God does not use authority tyrannically. This God spreads righteousness and justice by exercising power and authority. God's destructive power destroys falsehood, superstition, unbelief, indifference, and hardness of heart. God clears pathways through insurmountable obstacles.

God's powerful presence fills us with warmth of grace that in turn softens us to humility and obedience like wax softens in the presence of fire. This wonderful power was revealed to humankind as the Messiah. Let us pray that all nations may see the glory of God for the furtherance of peace on earth. We need strength from God to do this.

God's light is always available to us. But we need to open the drapes and let that light come and fill our beings. We need to rejoice in the Lord and share the gifts that we have received from God with those around us. We have the chance to let others know how we have been blessed. We can help our neighbors and friends experience the grace and peace of God that passes all understanding.

Even with all the power and love of God available to us, we are not promised an easy way. The hardest I have prayed in all my life was when my wife developed a blood clot after routine surgery. I waited, agonizing in prayer. Along with me were several other people praying for her, including my pastor. Despite their best efforts, the doctors were unable to save her. But those prayers yielded a strength that enabled me to withstand the weight of shock and grief. I can attest to this fact without a doubt.

Almighty God, you never fail those who seek you. Be with us, and give us strength this day. Amen.

ASCENSION DAY

Paul and Silas were going to the place of prayer when they met and cured a slave girl who was disturbed by a spirit. Because her owners had been using her disturbed spirit to make money, they were angry and had Paul and Silas put in prison.

That night there was an earthquake. The walls shook and the chains of Paul and Silas broke. Terrified the prison guard ran back to see if they had escaped. Had Paul and Silas escaped, the he faced certain and terrible punishment.

But the guard found that his two prisoners had made no attempt to escape. The prison guard was so impressed and grateful that they did not escape, he decided on the spot to follow their God from that day on.

Our lives are filled with times when we experience God's grace when we least deserve it. I had a friend in India who was a poet. A few of us got together once a month for dinner, and we would sing her poems.

One of those days we were to meet for dinner, my friend had gone out, and another of our friends was driving her. Neither of them remembered to check the gas in the car. The car stalled; the friend borrowed a bicycle and traveled several miles to get a can of gas. My friends were hours late for dinner, with a house full of guests waiting.

When the hostess and friend finally arrived, they threw themselves on the couch and affirmed, "It is so difficult to be Christian. But we managed not to get angry with each other!" They had given each other the gift of unexpected grace in the middle of unexpected circumstances. May we also today give someone a word of unexpected grace.

God of love and God of power, pour your grace on us. May we share that grace with those that enter our realm and in doing so may we serve you always. Amen.

As Christians we believe that Jesus was born around 2000 years ago. He was sent by God to redeem the world. As far as we know he did not have a formal advanced education. But he was wise and had a good grasp of the prophets' writings.

Jesus had a faithful band of followers, twelve of whom were close to him, eleven of them until the very end. They were mostly small business people, at least four of whom were fishermen. Jesus was God's messenger and preached a simple message of hope and salvation. He summoned people to help the needy, feed the hungry, clothe the naked, heal the sick, and comfort the sorrowful and dying. At the end of his mission on earth, he was crucified and buried. He rose from the dead and ascended into heaven. Today, amazingly, his followers are spread all over the earth.

It is for these followers that Jesus prays. He imagines a long line of believers who will share in a deeply profound relationship with Jesus and with God. His is the prayer that will bring past followers and future believers together before the throne of God.

Sometimes, it seems the church may never be one. Doctrinal differences, conflicting understandings of salvation, and differences and disagreements about money—all these things can tear the church apart. Still, Jesus' words in John are a strong testament, a sure promise that God's church is bigger than any of us, and that the love of God can bridge all differences.

Teach us, Good Lord to serve Thee as Thou deservest; to give and not to count the cost; To fight and not to heed the wounds; To labor and not to ask for any reward, save that of knowing that we do Thy will. Through Jesus Christ Our Lord, Amen. (Ignatius Loyola)

The writer of this letter gives praise and thanks to God for the believers in Ephesus. Nevertheless he prays that they may come to know more fully God's power, to be aware of the hope to which Jesus is calling them.

God's power has been wonderfully made known to us through the resurrection of Jesus Christ. God was able to accomplish many mighty deeds on earth through his (Jesus) life. There are many powers on this earth that we confront every day. But the power of God as manifested in the life, death and resurrection of Jesus Christ is above all other powers.

God bestows on us power to do good. But the writer of this letter says that such power is to be exercised only in the name of and in obedience to God. Yet the temptation is there: How can we do good on this earth and not be tempted to think that we did it with our own strength, our own wisdom, and our own power? As Paul says in 2 Corinthians 4:7, "But we have this treasure in clay jars, so that it may be made clear that this extraordinary power belongs to God and does not come from us." We must keep this thought in the forefront of our prayer lives.

We also sometimes try to understand Christ by defining him in narrow terms. This passage calls us to move beyond our narrow comprehension and into new realms of discipleship. We would do well to love our neighbors by engaging in social action. In this way, both love and faithfulness are served. By acting together we strengthen our means to serve God. Let us so act with the power God has granted to us.

Gracious God, fill me with your love, and show me how to serve the people whose paths I cross today. Amen.

I've been thinking lately about retributive justice (punishment meted out by the state) and restorative judgment (justice centered on the one who has committed the crime and the victim of that crime). It's a big shift in focus, and whether one pursues retributive justice or restorative justice makes a big difference in our society.

In the middle of this debate with myself, I think of my mother. One thing I learned early on from her was the capacity to forgive. I still strive to reach the level of forgiveness that she was able to practice; I do recall, time and again, her forgiving me.

Elisabeth Kübler-Ross tells the story of a woman who was seen standing in silence daily in front of the prison at Auschwitz. When asked why she did it, she told of her entire family having been killed within those walls. A small child, she had escaped simply because there was no room in that chamber. Her daily visit was to enable her to forgive the people who had committed those atrocities a little at a time so that one day she would be able to forgive them completely.

It's a powerful story, and one that the writers of the apocalyptic books of the Bible would not find foreign. As hard as that story is, as tough as the tribulations were in the early church, as difficult as we today find it is to walk in faith—in spite of all this, the apocalyptic writers are certain of one thing. It is God who stands before us, beside us, behind us. It is God who goes before us and beckons us to follow. It is God—and not evil—that will finally win out. No matter how dark the night or how frightening the day, God is with us. God is victorious. God will win the day.

Kind and gracious God, we your children receive your grace and mercy. May we show mercy all through this day. In your name. Amen.

Feeding the Spirit

MAY 17–23, 2010 • JEANETTE STOKES

MONDAY, MAY 17 ~ *Read Acts 2:14-20*

I spent a week at Koinonia Farms in the early 1970s. This intentional Christian community in Georgia was founded by Clarence Jordon and Will Whitcamper in the 1940s as a way to work with and support struggling African Americans in southern Georgia.

By the time I visited there in the early 1970s, Clarence Jordon had died and Will Whitcamper was an old man. Will had flowing white hair, wore simple work clothes, and did odd jobs around the farm.

One afternoon while Will was sorting metal from paper garbage, I asked him when he prayed. "All the time," he answered. He explained that he talked with God and listened to God all day long. His main job, indeed his calling on the farm, was being the trash collector.

I couldn't believe that someone had figured out how to pray while picking through trash. I thought communication with God had to be at a church with a Bible reading. Will and God had worked out a language between them that was compatible with collecting trash and recycling.

In Jerusalem, people were gathered "from every nation under heaven," going about their daily business in Jerusalem when God's Spirit broke in. As it was for Will, so it can be for us—the Spirit can, and will, break in at the most ordinary and mundane of times.

As you go through your day, remember Will and his commitment to be present to God's spirit throughout his day.

Presbyterian minister, founder and director of The Resource Center for Women and Ministry in the South, living in Durham, NC

I have a well-established garden, if not a well kept one. The oregano is as big as a doghouse. I used to plant vegetables, but they did so poorly that I felt incompetent. I prefer hardy plants that take care of themselves and come back each year on their own.

The plants multiply. I make a habit of letting flower stalks stand long after they have bloomed. I figure the birds like the seeds. Each year I find daisies and lamb's ear growing in surprising new places. I pull coreopsis out like weeds. There is just too much of everything.

In a well-established garden like mine, gardening is mostly about removing things, clearing out, making space so that what is there can breathe and grow.

I've decided that weeding, writing and spiritual practice are alike. They are all about clearing out. Generating words on paper has never been the problem for me. It's editing. The hard work is making choices, deciding what to leave out. I always want to say everything I've ever thought in a short essay.

Spiritual practice is also like that. There simply are not enough hours in the day. In order to make space for the Spirit to get my attention, I have to choose thoughtfully what I will do. The passage from Romans is a good reminder to me. If I want to be led by the Spirit, to be called a child of God, I must leave some places open and welcoming for the Spirit of God to break into my life.

How is your "garden"? What do you need to clear out in order to invite the Spirit in?

I am afflicted with the cultural plague of busy-ness. Trying to find time each day to write, walk, meditate, or make art and work makes it painfully obvious how busy I am. While I would not call myself a workaholic, I do tend to keep moving and I keep busy.

Spirituality is the experience of the presence of God. Spiritual practices are those attitudes or activities that open a person to the experience of the presence of God. The ones that come first to mind are prayers, meditation, reading the Bible and attending church. In recent years many Christians have been adding to the list so that we now think of a walk in the woods, sitting in a sunny window with a cup of tea, or even knitting as spiritual practices. Anything that allows us to be still or to focus our attention on the Holy One can be a spiritual practice. Anything we come back to day after day, anything to which we give our attention can be a spiritual practice. Washing dishes, walking the dog, even taking out the trash.

My biggest spiritual problem is forgetting. I forget that God is right there beside me all the time. In ancient Hebrew times, scribes tied big floppy tassels to the hems of their long robes. The tassels got in their way many times during the day, and each time it happened, the scribe was reminded to stop and think of God.

Pentecost was an immensely lavish reminder to the early believers about God's presence and power. This extravagant gift of the Spirit nourishes us and enables us to be nourished in the faith by others. When we forget that God is right here, the Spirit shows up with wind and power to remind us just how close God keeps us.

The early church's experience of God's presence was loud, showy, extravagant. When has God has crashed into your life? When was God's presence more subtle and muted?

One Saturday morning in mid-May, I was sitting in the back-yard under the pecan tree listening to the chatter of birds overhead and the squeak of a swing in the park next to my house. I was tired and so happy to be still. There was a soft breeze. A storm earlier that week had cleared the air and lowered the temperature. It was a perfect morning.

I was watching a small bird feeder in the garden. I had put it out of commission the previous year after losing a struggle with squirrels, but having acquired a large bag of seed from a neighbor who moved away, I decided to get the feeder out and try it again. The squirrels had not yet attacked it, the birds seemed to enjoy it, and I was happily watching them fly back and forth, eat the seed, or perch on the tall wrought-iron crook that holds the feeder.

I had been too busy that spring and knew there is no one to blame for the shape of my life but myself. If I take on too many commitments, set my standards for my garden too high, answer the phone every time it rings, or answer all the e-mail when it arrives, only I am to blame.

So, I resolved to begin again at the beginning, to write in my journal for thirty minutes every morning instead of checking my email first thing, and to make art, even if it is bad art, because those are the things that feed my soul. And I promised to sit in my backyard more while the breeze danced through tall flowers and the birds threw empty hulls from their feeder.

How can taking on fewer commitments, not answering the phone sometimes, or waiting an hour before responding to the morning's e-mail make you more available to the gift of the Spirit at Pentecost? The psalm reminds us that we all look to God for our food "in due season." Reflect on how clearing some space in your life can prepare you to receive "in due season" what God has in mind for you.

Several years ago, I attended a meditation retreat at the beach. I learned to eat in silence and to chew my food slowly. I watched the sunset and the full moon rise over the ocean. I wandered silently, peacefully, aimlessly on the beach with twenty-five other people. But what taught me the most about gratitude was my chair.

We spent a lot of time meditating in a seated position. Some limber people sat on cushions on the floor. I sat in a chair. I had a lot of discomfort because I am a short person and the chair was too big for me. I was so uncomfortable that I kept thinking to myself, "I'm going to give up in two minutes." Two minutes later I'd still be there, so I'd think, "In two more minutes, I'm really going to leave." I didn't leave, I just continued to be irritated with the chair.

After the retreat ended, I realized that my experience with the chair was like my experience with other difficult situations. Sometimes I find myself in uncomfortable or even painful situations. I have the feeling that I have to do something to make the situation better. Sometimes there is nothing anyone can do. Sitting still with the uneasy feelings and remembering that God is present in the midst of the discomfort may be the best thing to do.

This was certainly true for the early believers. Jesus was about ascend to heaven. And that fact made them uncomfortable. Actually, they were beyond uncomfortable. They were facing the prospect of Jesus leaving them, and they were worried. But Jesus seems to say, "Sit still and wait. God will send the Advocate, the Spirit, and you will no longer be alone."

Do you recall a time when you were alone or bereft and God's Spirit came to you? How did the Spirit make itself present to you? Spend time in prayer offering yourself to the Spirit's power.

I stopped one June morning on the way from the house to the garage—pocketbook in hand, briefcase on my shoulder—to look at the garden. I set the briefcase down and said to myself, I'll pull just a handful of weeds. Twenty minutes later, I had pulled a couple of grocery bags full of weeds and had broken off the remaining dead flower stalks from the year before.

I feel like an unreliable friend to my garden. I look out the back windows of the house and think to myself, "Why are you still blooming?" I've let the grass grow up among the irises. I forget to fertilize.

This morning instead of berating myself, I stopped to notice. The apricot rose bush was blooming its head off. The irises seem not to be concerned at all about the grass at their feet and are stretching happily towards the sun. The big summer flowers in the middle of the garden had huge green leaves. The butterfly bush I planted in January was doing fine. The peonies were covered with huge buds about to burst.

I got it. The garden is like a relationship with God. A garden is not something you grow in an afternoon. A friendship is not something you can make in a day. A spiritual practice is not something developed in a week. Love is not something you can go get. And your relationship with God needs attention over time. But even when we don't tend it, God is always right there.

God's gift of the Spirit is like that, too—giving and forgiving, always at hand and ready to break in. I am grateful for the grace of God and the gift of the Spirit because I am a dedicated, if sometimes forgetful, spiritual seeker.

It is good to know that God does not neglect us, even when we neglect God. How might you make yourself more available and open to the Spirit?

PENTECOST

Because my art supplies and my office are in the same building, I am never far from my paints, but days and days can go by without my ever picking up a brush. One particular day, I went to my painting table and made marks all over a big sheet of paper with green, orange, and purple crayons. I then painted big swaths of watercolors over them. I love watching the paint pool and flee from the wax.

When I was a child, my mother would pack me up with an art project and take me to my grandmother's in Texas for a couple of weeks in the summer. I loved being in my grandmother's small-town world, and I loved making stuff. When we weren't visiting elderly relatives or buying bushels of peaches or corn, I'd sit at my grandmother's big dark dining room table and paint by number, make tile coasters, or weave cotton potholders.

I knit and crocheted my way through college, did some quilting and made a couple of hooked rugs in seminary, sewed curtains for my first apartment after seminary. After that, I got too busy making a nonprofit organization to make things.

But I'm happier when I'm making stuff. In my forties, I fell in love with painting with watercolors. Now, if a week goes by without my painting, cutting paper into cards, or stitching up handmade books, I am not happy.

Meinrad Craighead, a spiritual artist in New Mexico, says that when she paints, she is praying with images. If she did not paint she would lose track of herself, lose track of her relationship with the Holy. It is a form of praise.

Psalm 104 asserts in a most extravagant voice that praise—extravagant praise—is a the way to respond to God and God's gifts. The creativity of our hands and hearts is fitting praise.

How do you praise to God? Do you write, paint, garden, sing, spend time in solitude?

Each Face of God a Gift

MAY 24–30, 2010 • ALICE KNOTTS

MONDAY, MAY 24 ~ *Read Proverbs 8:1-4*

It was so simple. I shut the doors, rounded up the stuff that goes in my bag to work, locked the front door and left. Three hours later I came home and discovered that I had left the back door unlocked. I spent fifteen minutes checking the house. Nothing was missing; but the next day, the local news reported that a burglar in town was entering unlocked homes.

Consequences of burglary are more than loss: they are a fracturing of trust, safety, and security. These could have impacted my work, my life, and people around me. I saved a few seconds in my rush to get out the door, but my lack of attentiveness could have had a very high price.

It is too easy to be hurrying on to the next thing or have too many things that need to be remembered to take the extra time that can make all the difference. In our hurry-up culture, some important things can't be rushed. Wisdom is one of those things.

"You who are simple, gain prudence," says Proverbs 8:5 (NIV).

The writer of Proverbs says that divine wisdom calls to us, seeking to meet us precisely where life is the busiest and where our work and business bring us. Divine wisdom meets us "beside the gates leading into the city," the place of traffic, trade, work, decision making, judgment, and people.

Wisdom calls to us.

Dear God, help me to receive your wisdom in the busiest, most stressful moments in life. Give me prudence, wisdom, and understanding. Amen.

United Methodist pastor, teacher and writer working with campus ministry development of low-income student housing at San Diego State University in California

We climbed aboard a bus in San Diego and took a winding, narrow road to the top of Mount Palomar where guides immersed in astronomy showed us giant telescopes. In a great unheated room with a telescope ten stories high, we stood on a platform that gracefully turned tons of machinery so that the telescope could peer into dark reaches of the heavens in any direction. Our guide talked about amazing discoveries far beyond our solar system. It was one of the most incredible experiences that I ever had as tourist.

As I struggled to stay awake late at night when the lights were dim, I heard the experts declare in scientific terms what the author of Proverbs said so long ago: "The LORD created me at the beginning." No matter where scientists look, they find that the fundamental elements of all creation are the same. Particles emitted from an ancient creative explosion are the same as those that compose the earth and us.

This text from Proverbs is part of a poem about God creating wisdom and wisdom being present before the heavens and the earth. In the greatness of God's creation, we were there, too. God is in us. Wisdom is in us waiting to be tapped. God's wisdom in us is a gift, and it brings another gift. "I was filled with delight day after day, rejoicing" (NIV). The gift of delight in God's presence, in the created world, and in the human race—these come from a God who loves us very much.

I was euphoric coming down from that mountaintop experience. I left Mount Palomar certain that I had been in the presence of God. God gives us fresh perspective. Wisdom waits for us to discover the big picture and experience the gift of delight in God.

Awesome God, may we see your wisdom in creation, in its intricacy and connectedness. Open us to the delight of praising your name. Amen.

Each Face of God a Gift   157

Melody lived under the scrutiny of experts: a public health services doctor treated her medical conditions, a social worker helped her find housing, a foster parent took care of her son, a counselor assessed her mental and emotional state, a case worker decided what assistance she could and could not receive. Each expert saw only one piece of the picture. These overworked civil servants whisked her in and out of their offices. But Melody needed an identity, a way to be a whole person rather than being seen in part.

Who are you? Not, "What do you do?" or "What is your role?" but "Who are you?" You are you in relation to others and the world around you. You are a compilation of your genetics, culture, environment, faith, and character. So when it comes to understanding the identity of God and our identity as humans, it isn't surprising that the psalmist uses some of these measurements.

The psalmist describes God as "majestic," "glory above the heavens," and "the moon and the stars that you have established." Metaphorically, God's genetics are the elements of space. God's character and scope is as vast as we can imagine. God's power can "silence the foe and the avenger." God's identity is confirmed in relationship to human beings who are the object of God's care. It boggles the mind to think that the creator of earth and space would care for you and me. Psalm 8 declares that God has crowned human beings "with glory and honor," assigning us responsibility over creation.

Melody needed to be treated as and become a whole person. I believe God can provide that. It happened for Melody. It can happen for us.

O God, when we experience uncertainties and when we only see in part, give us a sure identity in you. Amen.

Jason lay on his back in a hospital bed with his head bandaged, his right arm in a sling and his right leg raised in traction. His girlfriend and mother sat by the bed. "Motorcycle accident," he explained. It had been a close brush with death. "Have you been thinking about what it means?" I asked. Yes, he had, and it was changing the way he thought about everything. There were several things in his life that he planned to change.

Susan wanted desperately to make a change in her life. Her second husband, who gave her a second chance in life, was experiencing confusion and memory loss during recovery from rotater cuff surgery. She was in crisis, losing the man who filled her life with joy, even as she sat by his bed and cared for him. He regained some memory but finally lost it again.

Each of us has a story. It's not a simple thing to fix lives. There's no super glue or duct tape for this. How, then, do we come to have an experience of peace?

The face of God in Jesus helps us. Jesus genuinely loved people into being at peace with themselves, others, and God. Jesus showed us the breadth of God's love, the meaning of forgiveness, and the power of grace. If his answers to tough religious questions seem ambiguous, it's because he wanted people to experience God for themselves. Jesus didn't succumb to fear; he proclaimed God's message of love that reverses ordinary expectations.

Paul wrote that we have peace with God through Jesus Christ. Love, forgiveness, and grace triumph over judgment and brokenness. By faith we accept this gift of love, and, with it, brokenness can be mended.

God, make me a new creation. Give me courage to seek your help and find the life of joy and peace you intend for me. Amen.

Each Face of God a Gift

Melody planned to jump off the high bridge with weights tied to her legs. The image was so clear that I went with it. "If you do that," I said, "you'll be like a lump stuck in the mud on the river bottom. Your son will not have his mother, and you will never be the artist you were born to become. You have to make the choice to live."

That was the last I heard of Melody. I had no telephone number or address for her. My life went on, and I didn't know about hers until she called four months later. "I really hit bottom, but I kept coming back to what you said. I didn't want to end up as a lump in the mud. God has something for me to do, and my son needs a mother."

God has something for us too. We may have to work the Twelve Steps or go through tough challenges, but the prize of life lived in God's love is worth it.

Paul suffered in the cause of preaching the message of Jesus Christ—there were beatings, imprisonment, even shipwreck. Yet he discovered this pattern: "Suffering produces endurance, and endurance produces character, and character produces hope, and hope does not disappoint us."

Paul found new life in Jesus who gave him an unshakeable fresh faith. Paul stopped imposing his views of right and wrong on others. Turning away from being a man on a punishing crusade, he became a man of hope. Instead of being a persecutor he became a compassionate preacher. He preached Jesus' message of new life and hope.

And Melody? Melody became an attentive mother, an artist, and a church member.

Thank you, God, for the gift of hope. Give me hope so that I can endure and thrive. Amen.

As Jesus says good-bye to his disciples, he promises that the Spirit will guide them into truth. The disciples haven't learned everything there is to know. The relationship between God and Jesus and the Spirit is a close one, so that what the Spirit reveals is consistent with God and with the teachings of Jesus.

Each of this week's scripture passages describes how one of these ways of knowing God holds gifts for us. Wisdom gives us prudence and delight. The creator gives us identity. Jesus' love gives us peace, hope, and new life. Today we consider the Holy Spirit's gift of truth.

Sarah's life had been difficult and broken. To celebrate her birthday, we drove to a beautiful waterfall and sat down for a picnic by the creek. Sarah noticed a twisted tree growing out of a high rock cliff. This image gave her hope that she could endure. With hope, she was able to thrive.

The change point for Sarah was an inner experience. It did not alter her circumstances, but it made her aware of another truth that was deep inside her. The Holy Spirit enabled her to reach the resources that God had given her. Sarah experienced delight as she saw God's creation. She discovered her own identity. She shared bread in that beautiful setting. The love of Jesus gave her peace. The tenacious tree that put roots in rock crevasses inspired her sense of endurance, bringing out her best character and giving her hope.

Now Sarah had a new truth, one that enabled her to be open to God's work in her everyday setting. By the grace of God, Sarah could embrace the truth of God's love.

Holy Spirit, when we fail to see God's work in us and get discouraged, keep us open to your gift of truth. Amen.

TRINITY SUNDAY

For hundreds of years and many generations, for Jews and for Christians, Psalm 8 has been an important text of the worshiping community. This first hymn in the book of Psalms begins, "O LORD, our Lord, how majestic is your name in all the earth!" (NIV). This cadence repeats in praise of God. Even children and infants praise God. Then the psalm extols God's creative acts and God's care for us. "When I look at your heavens, the work of your fingers, . . . what are human beings that you are mindful of them?"

Reading the text again, hearing the rhythms, listening to the poetry brings memories of times and places where these very words have been used in my community—a church of my childhood, one my grandparents attended, one in a new community, and still another in a country far away. Today people of faith who are part of our far-flung community—Rhoda, Elizabeth, Ross, Marge, Kiyoshi, Kazuko and a host of others—share these words, wherever they are.

Many summers ago, my family and I sat in our little motor boat on a lake with its view of forests and mountains, and this scripture was part of our Sunday church service on the water. When we canoed down Colorado River canyons, red rock cliffs representing millions of years towering over us, we remembered God and repeated, "What are human beings that you are mindful of them?"

Today we celebrate the gift of God present in a faithful community. This is a great gift, and one that calls us to rejoice.

Dear God, we praise you and give thanks for bringing people together in faith through your holy word. O Lord, our Lord, how majestic is your name in all the earth! Amen.

Open to Receive

MONDAY, MAY 31 ~ *Read 1 Kings 17:8-16*

These lines are filled with the mystical and the miraculous. But today, as I come out of my morning prayer, something else about this story fills me with wonder. I notice how attentively Elijah listened to the Lord and how obediently the widow listened to Elijah. The words they heard resonated in their souls. But just as remarkably, both Elijah and the widow acted on the guidance of their hearts with faith and courage.

I wonder how many mystical signs and miraculous events I have missed because I wasn't listening. But I know that on the days when I *can* be relatively still, I hear how much God loves me and how I might best serve.

It can be hard for me to put into words what I experience. Some of the difficulty might be in translating the language of stillness into the language of the world. But I think it's more than just a matter of translation. It has to do with the loving intimacy that exists between our Lord and us. It is not so much secret as it is sacred—that which passes from one heart to another.

So, today when I read how Elijah and the widow listened carefully to what they heard, I am left to marvel at how they took that holy word and boldly carried it out into the world to do the work that needed to be done.

Lord, help me to listen. Help me to take your words to heart. Show me what I need to do today. Amen.

A convinced Quaker for over thirty years, working for the city of Philadelphia, PA, mediating neighborhood and racial tension disputes

From the woman whose son has just died comes an outpouring of questions and blame. Her loss is great. Her sorrow is real and, for that moment, inconsolable. We can hear her crying out to Elijah, "Why have you done this to me?" And Elijah asks God the same thing. This woman took him in and shared what little food she had. And this is her reward? What has she done to deserve this?

Who among us has never posed the question: "Why it is that bad things keep happening even when I'm trying so hard to be good?" Do we not tend to judge unwanted events as negative? When we say that bad things happen, don't we often mean that we didn't expect them to happen that way or were hoping for something else to happen? In truth, we are the ones who label things "good" and "bad."

Is it possible to expect nothing and accept everything as God's grace? Or do we expect God to act like Santa and bring us something from our personal wish list as a reward for effort? Perhaps our struggle earns us the next lesson for our spiritual growth. The bitter-tasting pill could be our next opportunity to shake loose unhealthy habits, quick temper, or false pride. The best gift of all might be that we get to look back with a little wisdom and see how the Lord's perfect plan was played out.

There is more to the woman's good news than having her son returned to her arms. She has witnessed the power of Elijah's faith in God and by it, her faith is awakened, her joy is made full. She has seen the hand of God at work in her life. What price would you pay for such a treasure?

Lord, open my eyes. Help me to see your grace at work in my life. Amen.

I was watching the news as a tornado survivor was being interviewed. Every house on the block was flattened but hers. She said: "The Lord was with me today." I thought about that statement. I felt her gratitude and her relief, and I probably would have said the same thing. Still, I asked myself if there is ever a day when God is not with us. Wouldn't the Lord have been with her even if the tornado hit her house and missed every other property in town? But, who among us can peer through the haze of fresh pain, fear, and loss to see God's wise hand at work in all things? If a tornado carried away my home, I don't know if I could praise the Lord right away.

Years ago, I heard a church elder talk about prayer. He said that the way most folks pray, you'd think God was the Great Bellhop in the Sky:

"Lord, make this person love me the way I want them to love me."

"Lord, I haven't studied all semester so help me with the answers to this test."

After hearing prayers like these, God must long for the good old days when people sent God psalms. But like most loving parents, I'm sure God is happy whenever the kids call. Love is like that.

If we believe that the Lord knows our hearts and minds, knows our needs even before we do, and always has our best interests at heart, then there is no better way to pray than in a spirit of simple faith and gratitude. We can ask and know that God will help us in a way that is always for our highest good. Today's psalm confirms it, "The LORD will reign forever, your God, O Zion, for all generations."

Thank you, Lord, for everything. Thy will be done now and forever. Amen.

Psalm 146 warns us not to put our trust in princes or mortals. Today, instead of princes, there are movie and television celebrities, rock stars and professional athletes, all set before us as if they were gods worthy of our worship and adulation. They are placed on pedestals not because of their wisdom, purity or goodness, but because their media handlers and the supermarket tabloids proclaim it. Their celebrity is a shiny thing that catches and holds our attention much longer than is deserved. Beware of false (American) idols, says the Lord.

Those who rule the nations have demonstrated throughout history that power can lead people astray. Our leaders are no better or worse than the rest of us in this. "They" are all of us and each of us—people joined by agreements that are tenuous at best. And so we render unto Caesar the things that are Caesar's but are careful not to put too much of our trust in these political "princes."

Our religious institutions point us toward the Lord and bring us together in worship but they are not God. Because they are populated, managed and maintained by mortals, these organizations are not exempt from the imperfections of this world. Priests, imams and rabbis, after all, are only as human as the rest of us, and they can fall prey to every human flaw and failing. God bless them, for their burden can be great.

All of our endeavors from the greatest to the silliest are susceptible to frailties, corruption and decay. They are not for us to worship. Only God is God and worthy of our worship and trust. We must put our trust in God and find our hope with God.

God, help us keep you forever before us. Let us be happy to have our trust in you. Amen.

Many times I've gone into my daily prayer and contemplation with these verses. They always leave me feeling somewhere between grateful and giddy. I imagine the power of Paul's radical transformation born of mysteries revealed. I think of the good works he performed in ministry while on fire in the risen Christ.

And then I think back to times when I've witnessed the look on people's faces when they, too, are opened and born anew in the Lord. They beam with a lovely light and their faces tell of some blessed gift received. They may not have been blinded by a bright light on the way to Damascus, but their first acknowledged embrace of the Messiah is no less a miraculous experience for them. In that moment, and many times after that, they are filled with a love that awakens them into divine communion.

If you have been blessed with an awakening into Christ's love, and I pray that you have, then you already know that he can fix anything, can change anyone, can make all paths clear. To those who have been touched in this way, Paul's transformation is awesome but not so unbelievable.

Referring to his own experience of divine revelation in his letter to the Ephesians, Paul tells his readers that the mystery now being revealed had not previously been available to humankind. It is as though Jesus, in his perfect love, pulled down an unattainable tree branch so that all of us could reach up, pick and taste of this precious fruit. It is because of the good news, "the gospel not of human origin," that all of us, in covenant with Christ, can have a direct experience of the Lord's eternal love and living Word. It is no less than the promise of and the key to eternal salvation.

Lord, reveal yourself to me. Let me have eyes to see and ears to hear. Amen.

A few verses in Galatians 1 make me smile at Paul's expense. In verses 22-24, Paul says that when the Christians found out he was now preaching the faith he once tried to destroy "they glorified God because of me." I can't help but wonder if those early church members were glorifying God because Paul was saved or if it was, very practically, because he had stopped dragging them away to prison. The enemy had become a friend. The zealous "other" was now one of them.

The "us versus them" mentality strikes as a sickness within us and in our communities. It makes brotherly and sisterly love seem like an impossible or even undesirable goal. Saddest is that such a mind-set creates and maintains the very disease that separates us.

I take public transportation to and from my job. One morning after enjoying my tea and prayer time, I found myself, as usual, on a crowded train filled with "strangers." Cell phone screamers, chattering school kids, fussing babies and all manner of humanity were crammed into a speeding tube. It was all just too much for me after my silent, morning devotions. I became irritable and judgmental and began some inward rant about the demise of civilization, etc.

I didn't want to feel that way. So, I prayed to experience a communion of souls, to know that all are one in the Lord. A few minutes later, to my surprise (I don't know why I'm still surprised when this stuff happens), I looked up at this sardine can full of commuters with a strange, new tenderness. Then, I heard these words: "We are all in this together." For the briefest of moments, I could feel no separation between myself and anyone else on that dirty old train . . . and I glorified God because of them.

God, turn my heart the way you turned Paul's. May I live my life today as a Christian. Amen.

The words and gestures Jesus used were tender. In the city of Nain he had come across the funeral procession of a man who had died. He approaches the procession, and to the grieving mother he says only: "Do not weep." He touches the bier. Just three words and a touch. After he brings the deceased son back to life, Jesus presents this only son to his mother without a word. This is the Good Shepherd tending to his flock, gently, compassionately.

Years ago, a few words and a simple gesture moved me in a way I will never forget.

After my grandfather died, all the members of his large extended family were in attendance at the funeral home. The viewing was ending and people began heading to their cars to drive to the cemetery.

I stayed a while longer with my newly widowed grandmother. The funeral home staff went briskly about their practiced drill. One of the men reached into the coffin to fold in a pale yellow comforter over the body. My grandmother moved in and instinctively tucked in the corner of the comforter herself and said simply: "Good-bye, John." She had made his bed every day of their sixty-four years of marriage and now for the last time she tucked in the corner of this bed covering. I could only imagine all the conversations those two shared over the years; yet now, just three little words seemed sufficient. No drama, no eulogy, no grand show of affection.

Even in the midst of fulfilling prophecy and raising the dead, Christ was fully appreciative of the widow's grief and the solemnity of the occasion. A few words and a simple gesture were sufficient. When God is in the moment, it is enough to let the moment speak for itself.

Be with me today, God. Show me how best to serve you. Amen.

The Welcome Table

JUNE 7–13, 2010 • MARIAN WRIGHT EDELMAN

MONDAY, JUNE 7 ~ *Read 1 Kings 21:1-16*

What happens when those in power don't defend the powerless—when, in fact, they are the source of the threat to those they are meant to defend? Our passage today paints a dramatic picture. The ruler wants the vineyard of an ordinary citizen, Naboth. When King Ahab doesn't get what he wants, he sulks and then allows his wife, Jezebel, to take charge in a merciless plot to falsely accuse, have killed and seize the land of the innocent Naboth. Using the power at her disposal, the deed is done. Naboth is stoned to death and his land taken.

Dr. Choon-Leong Seow points out that Naboth was only the most obvious victim; the very foundations of society also took a blow. Ahab and Jezebel made a mockery of the principles that the society held dear, of justice and care for the vulnerable.

Who are our Naboths today? Who is powerless and dependent on the justice and compassion of the powerful? Children are. They don't vote, lobby or make campaign contributions; their needs are easily ignored by our elected officials. They can't provide for their own food, shelter, health care or education. They can't withstand the injustice of the powerful.

It is our job as adults, and most especially as people of faith, to nurture and protect children, to ensure that power is not abused and the vulnerable don't suffer injustice. God expects no less of us.

Dear God, my sure and strong defender, help me to defend children. Make me a bold voice for the voiceless and powerful advocate for the powerless. Amen.

Lifelong advocate for disadvantaged Americans and the President of the Children's Defense Fund

There ought to be a run on sackcloth, if we were honest with ourselves, if we as a nation fully appreciated the violence we are responsible for—through what we have done and what we have left undone.

Our elected officials might be among the first to put on the sackcloth. How else to show they recognize their guilt or complicity in failing to provide health coverage for all of our nation's children, resulting in children's needless deaths from preventable illness? As children put on emergency room gowns (their last resort for health care) and as children's lifeless bodies are dressed for burial, perhaps Congress and our governors might put on sackcloth.

Those profiting from the prison industrial complex should put on sackcloth, in penance for preferring to build lucrative prison cells rather than promoting school investments that would help every child stay on track and succeed in life. Right now, the odds are better that a Black or Latino boy will end up wearing a prison uniform than a college graduation robe.

We as citizens and members of the faith community might put on sackcloth too. Are our doors closed during the week when children need safe places to go? Do we focus on compassionate service, yet stay silent when our faithful voices are needed to demand justice? How have we failed to vote for leaders who put children first and to hold all leaders of every party accountable for every decision they make that affects the lives of children?

Let us act to protect children so that we can put on clothing befitting our best intentions to be followers of the Christ. Let Christ's binding love be demonstrated in how we care for and seek justice for children.

Dear God, make me bold to confess my shortcomings. Cleanse me from all unrighteousness and renew me to live out your mercy and justice for all your beloved children. Amen.

They forgot we were there." That's how one young boy tried to make sense of a senseless, interminable wait on the hard benches of an intake center for homeless families where he and his siblings and grandmother waited to learn where they could sleep that night. The overwhelmed workers at the intake center may have forgotten he was there. The comfortably housed residents of his city may have forgotten he was there. All across our nation we may have been unaware that he was there. But God didn't forget.

God gives ear to the despairing words of our nation's 13.3 million poor children. God heeds the sighs of our nation's more than 200,000 children who are homeless each night. God hears the cries of our nation's nearly 9 million children without health insurance who may not be able to see a doctor or dentist when they need to. Isn't it time for us, God's people, to do the same? Dr. David Davis, pastor of Nassau Presbyterian Church in Princeton, New Jersey, preached about the ritual of baptism, "We should never be able to dip our hands in that water without hearing the cries . . . not the cry of the baby being baptized . . . but of the forgotten ones."

The psalmist trusts in God for deliverance from enemies. Our children need us, as God's hands and feet on earth, to deliver them from the enemies of hunger, poverty, lack of health care, gun violence, and all of the other dangers that lurk and stalk and hunt and haunt them. Will we, with determination and by God's grace, help to make their way straight, a path toward the promise of life abundant?

Dear God, I turn to you in prayer confident that you hear me—even that you know my thoughts before they are spoken. Unstop my ears and attune my heart to hear the cries of the children and, hearing, to respond with the love and justice you desire. Amen.

H ere, we find the first use in the Psalms of the Hebrew word *hesed*. What an awesome word! Often it is translated "steadfast love" or "unfailing love." J. Clinton McCann notes that *hesed*, of all Hebrew words, best describes God's character because its meaning touches on God's compassion, fidelity, mercy, love and grace.

What has been your experience of God's *hesed*? When have you known God's faithful love and mercy, compassion and patience, loyalty and grace?

Think, now, of a person in your life who has most embodied *hesed* for you. Was it your mother or father? A grandparent? A spouse? Whose steadfast love nurtures and nourishes you?

Think, now, of our nation's children who may never have known *hesed*: the children who are reported abused or neglected every 36 seconds, the 500,000 children in foster care, the 127,000 children who long to be adopted, or the children across the economic spectrum who try to fill an emptiness by turning to drugs or alcohol, too much food or too early sexual activity.

How can we ensure that every child has someone in their life that surrounds them with love and grace, who teaches them of God's love? I think of young college-age servant leaders in the Children's Defense Fund's Freedom Schools, who spend the summer with young children in the rich world of books and songs and cooperative play. I picture Geoff Canada's Harlem Children's Zone where everyone from babies to teens to parents finds a safe haven. I think of the congregations that have partnered with the juvenile justice system to provide caring guidance to children who might otherwise be lost forever in the system. We who have known the abundance of God's *hesed* have so much to offer.

God, I am so blessed by your hesed. *Help me to share with others the amazing truth of your* hesed *through my words and my actions. Amen.*

Bible commentators note that this passage was written as Paul guided a new church struggling with the question of whether there should be two "separate but equal" churches segregated along Jewish Christian and Gentile Christian lines, or whether they were meant to be one. Paul sought to remind the church that in Christ we are made one—we are all justified by faith in Christ and no one needs to "earn" their forgiveness.

I have been blessed by a new experience of church introduced to me by the Church of the Savior in Washington, D.C. Small "churches" of about twenty people are carefully brought together so that there are equal numbers of financially secure persons and of those living in financially precarious circumstances. Some of us are professionals and some are parolees; some addicted to drugs and others addicted to work or consumerism or the culture. Some of us are Black and some of us are White.

What unites us is the recognition that each of us stands in need of the healing love and grace of our Lord Jesus Christ. We meet that Christ in powerful new ways in our communion with each other.

When our churches, despite their best intentions, grow comfortable in separate enclaves—clustering with those most like us in income, race, ethnicity, education—we lose out on the experience of church that Jesus invites us to and Paul encouraged.

Insulated from the lives, loves, and losses of those unlike us, unaware of the hopes and dreams, challenges and struggles of others, we miss a multitude of opportunities to be the one body of Christ. What can you do to reach out, in mutual ministry, to those most unlike yourself?

Gracious God, help me to build relationships with those unlike myself that I may discover that together we are your beloved community. Amen.

I'm gonna sit at the welcome table," begins a spiritual. Jesus' table was always marked by the radical inclusivity that was the foundation of his ministry. Jesus is at dinner with a religious leader of high standing and they are "interrupted" by a lowly woman. Jesus doesn't decline to break bread with the powerful and privileged, but he also welcomes the less powerful, defending their value and place.

What if our national "table" was marked by that same radical inclusivity? When will we welcome those of our national family who have been excluded? What if we extended Jesus' warm welcome to others—toward immigrants, hard-working poor families, single parents struggling to do the work of two, or young people who've gotten off track?

What if we stand up for these people the way Jesus did? Could it be that the most vulnerable, like the woman who lovingly welcomed Jesus, often recognize their reliance on God more quickly than do those who are more financially secure, who may imagine that they "deserve" all that they have? What might we learn from those we usually exclude?

A colleague, Barbara, visited a woman in Honduras who worked hard to provide for her family by making beautiful flowers out of hand-dyed corn husks. When Barbara asked the woman if she kept any to adorn her own home, the woman brought out the sole, exquisite bouquet she had for herself. She placed it into Barbara's hands. After admiring it, Barbara reached out to return the bouquet. But the woman refused; it was for Barbara to keep. The woman's one beautiful possession was given, without expectation, as an openhearted expression of love.

Dear God, help me to open my heart and home to the powerless as well as the powerful. Strengthen me to work always toward hospitality and radical inclusion in my community, my congregation and my nation. Amen.

Who are the women you know who belonged right up there with the twelve and "some women" in their devotion to following Jesus and helping proclaim the good news of the kingdom of God?

The first woman who comes to my mind is my mother, Maggie Leola Wright. Her devotion wasn't just the sit-down-and-pray kind (although prayer and worship were an important and integral part of her life); her devotion was also expressed in an active, following-in-Jesus'-footsteps way. She, with my father, the Rev. Arthur Jerome Wright, welcomed twelve foster children into our home, created and ran a home for the aged, loved the left-out, and bound up the brokenhearted. In the segregated South of my childhood, they worked hard so that every child knew himself or herself to be a beloved child of God.

At my mother's funeral, someone asked me what I do for a living. In a flash, I realized that in my work as the founder and president of the Children's Defense Fund, I do exactly what my parents did—just on a different scale. My brother preached a wonderful sermon at Mama's funeral, but the best tribute was the presence in the back pew of the town drunk, whom an observer said he could not remember coming to church in many years.

Her life was a picture of what it looks like when you really live out the inclusive, enormously loving, always forgiving good news of Christ with faithfulness and generosity. Think of those you celebrate who, like her, have lived lives in faithful response to that call. And then ponder how you can evermore faithfully follow Jesus, like the twelve and "some women."

Dear God, help me to follow you not in word alone but also in deed. Guide me to help you bring the good news, especially to children and families in need. Amen.

Divine Communion, Divine Community

JUNE 14–20, 2010 • KARLA KINCANNON

MONDAY, JUNE 14 ~ *Read 1 Kings 19:1-15a*

Poor Elijah! He's a hunted animal hiding in the wilderness, fearful of losing his life to murderously angry Queen Jezebel. In a righteous frenzy, Elijah had killed all the Canaanite prophets from the queen's religion. Thirsty for revenge, she is out to get Elijah.

Carried away from the murder scene by adrenalin, Elijah finds himself in the wilderness, examining his own appalling behavior. The wilderness is a place of introspection where individuals confront their own vulnerabilities. Under a broom tree Elijah faces his demons of self-disgust and self-pity. He asks God to end his miserable life. He felt like a failure.

When things go wrong in our lives and ease turns to *dis*-ease, we can blame ourselves, feeling self-pity or self-loathing. We may have trouble discerning God's presence. Elijah must have felt this way as he stood on the mountain waiting to experience the presence of God.

This wind-and-fire political activist expected to meet God in nature's sound and fury. Imagine Elijah's surprise. Instead of appearing in the dramatic wind, fire, or earthquake, God came to Elijah in the sound of "sheer silence."

When times are tough, we too hope God will show up in some dramatic fashion to rescue us. At times like these, we need to find our own wilderness. We need to listen to the sound of sheer silence.

Where do you find your wilderness for reflection and prayer?
Where do you go to listen to God?

United Methodist minister, artist, speaker and retreat leader; author of *Creativity and Divine Surprise: Finding the Place of Your Resurrection*

My friend once said, "God can't do anything with me if I'm tired." Yet, in our 24/7 world we sacrifice the gift of sleep for productivity. Our priorities are askew. Elijah's story says God cares about our human needs. God does not ask anything more of Elijah until his physical need is met. Only after Elijah has rested deeply and been fed by an angel of the Lord does God ask, "What are you doing here, Elijah?" God desires that we care for our bodies. Resting when we are weary, eating a healthy diet, and exercising are things God desires for us because we matter to God.

God's query of Elijah implies that it's time for Elijah to get back to work in the political arena. Elijah is in the business of making and breaking kings, and God needs his help. Yet, Elijah hesitates. I can almost hear a self-pitying whimper in Elijah's response: I was just doing what you told me to and now they want to kill me. Elijah needs more than food and drink for his body; he needs nourishment for his soul, a renewal of spirit. God arranges a rendezvous. A caring God makes a house call.

After Elijah's personal encounter with God, the Divine poses the question again, "what are you doing here, Elijah?" Elijah still doesn't understand the implied expectation: it's time to get back to work. Elijah whines the same answer, but God doesn't buy it. The Divine believes Elijah is ready to make history, even if Elijah doesn't. God has provided for all of Elijah's needs—both physical and spiritual. God knows Elijah is ready to be a divine servant once again.

All our needs matter to God who gives us what we need to be kingdom builders. Thy kingdom come.

Pray the Lord's Prayer. Remain open to the ways you can co-create God's kingdom on earth.

When the doctor tells you it's terminal, when the bank fore-closes on your home, or when life turns upside down and God seems inaccessible, allow these psalms to be your companion. The psalmist agonizes over God's absence. Exiled in a foreign land, cut off from all that is familiar, he poignantly remembers experiencing the joy of the Lord in the Temple. His former life has vanished and he is like a thirsty man without water.

Contemporary readers may not understand the importance of the Temple to the author of these psalms. We worship God in many ways: in churches, in private prayer, in nature. When these psalms were written, communion with God was focused on the Temple. The Temple held the ark of the covenant that was believed to contain the very presence of God. Nowhere else could one experience the *face of God*. Furthermore, the altar in the Jerusalem Temple held loaves of bread called the *bread of presence*, signifying God's unremitting nourishment for God's people. With no access to the Temple, the psalmist was limited to his own tears as nourishment. Exiled in a foreign land, he despaired of experiencing God's presence ever again.

Yet, hope in God is exactly what the psalmist proclaims. What a powerful affirmation of faith! In the midst of great despair this psalmist holds fast to God. Acknowledging relationship with God is more than a deep desire. It is as necessary to existence as air or water. This psalmist's life depends on his relationship with God, as all our lives do. He places his hope in the One he knew in the Temple, trusting he will again commune with God. Where do you place your hope when times are uncertain?

Pray the Lord's Prayer again today. When you pray, "Give us this day our daily bread," give thanks for those things that nourish you in the world.

THURSDAY, JUNE 17 ~ *Read Galatians 3:23-29*

Some behaviors stifle our freedom. Perfectionism, guilt, or the incessant need to please others can dominate our actions, making us forget the abundant life Christ offers. Perfectionism causes us to experience life as trying to *get it right*, fearful of making mistakes. If we are dominated by guilt, our actions may be an attempt to *make up for* the initial guilt-causing event. If we are people pleasers, we may be unable to say "no" to another's request, fearing we won't be liked. People pleasers are always trying to win the favor of others! When these traits become habits they affect our spiritual life; we behave as if we are trying to earn God's favor. We may feel powerless to change.

Paul says that for God's people, the law is like those things that inhibit our freedom. He uses the metaphor of "disciplinarian" to talk about the law. The English word "disciplinarian" lacks the nuance of the original language and we miss an important point. In both Hebrew and Greek, "disciplinarian" connotes a slave who guards the young children of the slave owner, making sure the children behave. A disciplinarian is not free; it is his or her job to make the slave owner's children aware of their bad behavior.

Paul offers an alternative to the law and all things that bind us. Whether we are people pleasers, ridden with guilt, or perfectionists stuck in a never-ending cycle of trying to get it right, we need not dwell on our mistakes or bad habits. Christ offers us a new way to live. Faith in Christ sets us free to experience forgiveness and a new beginning. God accepts us as we are, and loves us enough to transform us. Celebrate freedom in Christ!

Offer your own stumbling blocks to God this day. Ask Christ to set you free from those things that bind you.

Many years ago I visited a wealthy suburban church for Sunday worship. I witnessed members of the congregation squirm as a solitary homeless person entered the sanctuary and sat in a rear pew. A look of disgust formed on the faces of several congregants who were seated near him; it was evident he had not bathed for quite some time. After the service, no one spoke to him; it was as if he didn't exist. He wasn't asked to join the fellowship; he was not welcome in that congregation.

As early as the first century, the church tried to determine criteria for membership in the body of Christ—who is in and who is out. Or, who has full rights and who has no rights. At various times in its history, church membership has been based on ethnicity, skin color, gender and sexual orientation. Paul says these are not the kinds of criteria upon which to base membership in the body of Christ.

The Galatian church, wrestling with the issue of who belongs in church, treats Greeks as second-class citizens because they are not circumcised. Paul responds to those who do not want Gentiles in church. He upsets the societal power structure. His message is radical! Paul believes faith in Christ demolishes society's pecking order, leveling the playing field. The church becomes a new community of equality—not just spiritual equality, but social parity. In the body of Christ there is no room for social inequalities. Paul says our faith in Christ makes us one; no one can claim to be any better than anyone else. So, rich or poor, black or white, male or female, gay or straight, we can stand on level ground, equally valuable in God's eyes. As believers, we are all welcomed.

God, you teach me through your Word. Help me understand what equality looks like in your church. Amen.

My friend suffers from depression. He has tried different kinds of therapy and many medications. They work for a limited time before depression rears its ugly head, engulfing him in darkness once again. Unlike the Gerasene demoniac, my friend was never in shackles. But the loneliness of depression has him imprisoned nonetheless.

The tormented man in Luke lived in the tombs. The powers of death and darkness had a dominant claim on him. Unable to fit into the normal social order, he sought shelter among the dead where he was under attack by inner demons and isolated from the support of community. He was not living; he merely existed. Perhaps he had given up hope. However, as he met Jesus stepping out of the boat, hope ignited once again. He begged Jesus, "Do not torment me." It was as if he were pleading, "Do not offer me false hope; I cannot bear another disappointment." My depressed friend feels something like this each time his physician introduces a new treatment.

Persons with long-term illnesses report difficulty remaining hopeful for restored health. Those surrounded by community often heal more quickly. When I suffered a serious illness, I felt I would always be sick. The loss of hope was worse than the illness. The encouragement of family saw me through those dark times.

When Jesus healed the crazed man, part of the healing was restoring him to community. Though the man healed of his demons begged to go with Jesus, the Lord sent him back into his community where the rest of his healing took place. God's love has power over depression and illness. It works to make us all healthy and whole, returning us to community.

Spend a little time thinking about what God has done for you and give thanks.

For first century Jewish audiences this story was scandalous. A Jewish rabbi in Gentile territory, in contact with an unclean demoniac who lives among the dead was a terrible defilement. The Gerasene demoniac was considered unclean because of his illness and contact with the dead. Anyone coming into contact with him also was unclean. In Jewish territory, tombs were even painted white so good Jews would not unintentionally come into contact with them.

Jesus avoided neither the unclean man nor the unclean Gentile territory. He responded to the crazed man by ordering the demons to depart into a herd of swine. The irony of demon-possessed swine drowning in a lake was not lost for a Jewish audience. That which makes one unclean is demolished by God's love. The rules of God's kingdom overturn the normal social order and reverse traditional attitudes.

Jesus' presence in Gentile territory opens the door for the conversion of Gentiles to Christianity, once again upsetting the norms for the Jewish band of Christ-followers that made up the early church. Jesus' message is clear; all are welcome in the body of Christ, not just those we believe fit. Whatever or whomever we call "unclean" today is no match for God's inclusive love.

In a prayerful state, think about those with whom you would feel uncomfortable if they were seated next to you in church. Now imagine attending a great banquet with those same folks. See Jesus at the door of the banquet hall, welcoming everyone with a hug. See Jesus presiding over the feast. Imagine Jesus' love flowing from his heart to the hearts of all his guests. Receive Jesus' love for you, uniting you with the other guests. Give thanks for God's amazing, all-welcoming love.

Trust in Times of Trial

JUNE 21–27, 2010 • NEIL T. OOSTHUIZEN

MONDAY, JUNE 21 ~ *Read Galatians 5:1, 13-21*

Focus, Neil, focus! Play the game! Play the game!" the coach shouted from the sideline. Ignoring the pain in my calf and the opposition striker who had just caused it, I drew myself back into the game. Reading the bounce of the soccer ball, I blocked the pass and sent our Number 11 hurtling down the right wing. I rejoiced with the rest of the team as the ball hit the back of the net. The coach had seen me shifting my focus from the ball to the player who had just hurt me and knew that I was about to get myself drawn into a retributive foul, for which I, and my team, would have been punished.

That is what Paul was telling the Christians in Galatia. Having been set free from the power and effects of sin in their lives, they had set out to follow the way of Jesus with enthusiasm and joy. But gradually they had begun to "take their eye off the ball" and were in danger of slipping into the darkness and destructiveness of sin again. As their coach and mentor, Paul warned them to stay in the game. "Live out your love daily as you serve each other," he said. And the way to do this was to keep their focus on the Holy Spirit.

The apostle would speak the same words into our lives today. Committed to living a life of perfect love, we are often tempted to "take our eye off the ball." We need to remain open to the Spirit in our lives as we live out the good news of God's love for us.

Lord, fill me with your Spirit today, so that I may stay focused on my call in life: loving everyone I meet. Amen.

Senior minister at Trinity Methodist Church, Linden Johannesburg, South Africa; race car driver and cyclist

We will be excused if we struggle to understand where the disciples' response to the Samaritan rejection came from! They had walked with Jesus for three years, seen him heal, feed, and forgive. They'd heard him telling them to love their neighbor, to forgive those who had sinned against them, even to love their enemies (especially those who had abused and persecuted them). They had seen him transfigured and talking with Moses and Elijah, and they had struggled to understand his insistence that he would soon be arrested, tried and killed. And now they wanted to burn up their enemies with heavenly fire! How arrogant. Had they not learned a thing from Jesus?

But wait. We need to be careful about judging Jesus' disciples too harshly, for in many ways the thing we condemn in them is alive and flourishing in us. How quickly we get upset and full of righteous anger while watching the evening news on television. Having spent an hour in worship, we so easily find ourselves reacting badly when a fellow worshiper takes the parking spot we were eyeing outside the corner store, or when we discover the store has run out of our favorite sticky bun.

We react just like the disciples did for exactly the same reason: they took their focus off Jesus and allowed their hurt and anger to take center stage. How easily we do the same when problems intrude into our daily lives. But Jesus corrected them—and us. He has a vastly different purpose in life than reacting negatively to what often amounts to petty problems. And he calls us to follow him in the same way.

Lord, I so often react badly when someone steps into the path I am travelling with you. Help me keep my focus on you and consciously take my eyes off the negative things that draw away my attention. Amen.

Unfortunately it isn't just sin and negative external influences that cause us to take our eye off the ball when following Jesus. Often the very things that give us life also tempt us to slow down in response to Jesus' call to follow him. We see this in each of those who respond to the Messiah's call. We also see it in our own lives.

While he never said so, Jesus could see that the first would-be disciple was trapped by his possessions. While everything that he owned contributed to his life, and his enjoyment of it, it had become a snare that would eventually draw his focus away from the One he was committed to following.

Jesus wasn't being insensitive to someone in crisis when he told the second person to "let the dead bury the dead." It was the solemn responsibility in Judaism for a son to bury his father. This man was willing to follow Jesus but wanted to wait until his father was dead and buried, and he had fulfilled this family obligation. Then he would gladly follow Jesus.

The third person wanted to go around to all his family to inform them about his decision to follow Jesus and get their advice and blessing. Jesus reminded him that he needed to keep his focus on the task at hand.

As we thank God for all the relationships and responsibilities that make up our lives— for our home and other possessions, for family and community who give us meaning and purpose, and for our own family—let us be careful not to let even these channels of grace become avenues of diversion from the Way.

Lord, I thank you for all your gifts in my life, for the many people, places and things that add to my life. Help me, today, to be better a steward of them all, for the furtherance of your kingdom. Amen.

How do we "keep our eye on the ball" as we follow Jesus and seek to live out a life of perfect love? Perhaps this strange story will give us guidance.

The young prophet had no doubt followed his mentor for several years and was intent to do so as long as he lived. He wasn't going to let the difficulty and discomfort of travelling get in his way, and so he followed Elijah from Gilgal through Bethel to Jericho, and then down to the Jordan River. No matter where the old prophet went, Elisha was determined to keep him in his sight, for he knew that his call and ministry were closely linked with that of the famous prophet.

But Elisha was also not going to be put off by the talk and "advice" of others, even if they were well-known prophets (this happened at both Bethel and Jericho). He knew what God's call was on his life, and he intended to obey, regardless of what others said.

Because Elisha kept his focus on his master, as God had commanded him, he received the power and grace of Elijah as the old prophet was transported into the heavens. This was proven in dramatic fashion as he parted the Jordan just as his master had.

And the same applies to us today. Despite the difficulty of surviving in the 21st century, and the opposition we often encounter in our walk with Jesus, it is as we constantly keep our eyes fixed on him that we are able to obey his call to "follow me." This we do through spending time with him in prayer (both formally in devotions and conversationally throughout the day), in reading scripture, and in other study and reading.

Lord, help me to stay focused on you and your grace throughout today. Protect me from those things and those people who will tempt me to turn away. Amen.

Say we are keeping our eye on the ball and following Jesus in our daily lives, consciously focusing on him through prayer, Bible study, and other devotional reading. But what do we do when things go so badly for us that we can no longer bring ourselves to pray, or we find the words of the Bible meaningless and empty? The ancient psalmist found the answer centuries ago.

Crying out to God in crisis, a crisis so deep that he didn't experience God even vaguely responding to his groans and prayers, the psalmist cast his mind back to times he had experienced God as a living, life-giving companion. He remembered God's grace and love in this way so that his awareness of the divine presence could grow.

The same experience can happen to us. When we find our lives stressed and burdened, when the crisis seems too deep for even God to plumb, or the darkness of fear and hopelessness seems to extinguish every last ray of the God-light within, we need to take our cue from the ancient poet. We are to take our attention off the darkness and disquiet that paralyzes us and look on the one who can shine eternal light and life into our brokenness. One way to do this is to reflect on our own life, calling to mind the times God has touched us with love and life. This will free our mind to be open to the divine touch that will drive away depression and bring us to a Christ-balanced view of life. This reflection happens when we journal a record of our Jesus-walk and set aside regular times of retreat for reflection, refocusing and rejuvenation.

Lord Jesus, I thank you that you experienced all of life and so understand my life. Help me to reflect more on you in my life, so that I may know your presence more fully in times of darkness and despair. Amen.

Having found himself in the depths of despair and overwhelmed by darkness within, the psalmist began to reflect on God's grace and love in his life. He soon found himself refocusing on his Creator Friend again. He was set free once again to proclaim God as "holy" in his own life. But his reflection and rejoicing didn't stop at his own life experience. The rejuvenated hymnist continued to reflect on God's gracious activity, broadening his focus. His praises got louder and more heart-felt as he remembered God's dealings with the chosen people throughout their history.

We are in that situation today. To refocus ourselves on the One who gives us life, and who calls us to live life in divine love, we need to reflect not only on God in our own lives but also to remember that we are a part of the much larger family of God. As we reflect on God's grace made manifest in the covenant people of the Old Testament, in the new covenant people in the New Testament, in the church throughout its troubled history, and in the church today, we are set free to acknowledge and proclaim Jesus in our own lives.

We reflect on Emmanuel (*God with us*) in the historical and wider church and in our own expression of the body of Christ as we read church history in its wonderful variety and complexity. We share life stories as we gather with other Christ-followers in Bible-centered fellowship each week and encourage one another in our Jesus-walk. Together we celebrate the living God in our lives when we gather in worship and celebration. Once again we are aware that we all follow the Shepherd who lays down his life for the sheep.

Lord, we thank you that we are a part of a worldwide family of faith. May I find you afresh as I journey today with your followers, those still alive and those celebrating in eternity. Amen.

As Christ-followers we must struggle mightily to live a life of perfect love in a world that is horrendously imperfect and tragically short of love. Tempted by sin, overreacting to things happening around us and sidetracked by all those things that give us life, we need to make sure that we constantly focus our eyes on Jesus, who gives us life in abundance (John 10:10).

It is an integral part of the Good News that as we keep our focus on Jesus we walk "in step" with the Spirit, who frees us from all that tempts us from the Jesus-path. The Spirit empowers us to walk together as Christ-followers, encouraging and enabling one another to better live God's perfect love. As this happens, God's love becomes manifest more clearly in our lives, bringing out the *God flavors* and *God colors* (two wonderful terms used in THE MESSAGE) in our homes, communities, countries, and world. We gradually become aware of God's love, joy, peace, and patience increasing in our lives and bubbling over in all the little things that make up our daily life.

When we keep our focus on the One who called us, saying, "Follow me!" we find ourselves walking in God's perfect love, spreading what John Wesley called "scriptural holiness" throughout the land.

Lord Jesus, help us to keep our focus on you so that we may become more aware of your perfect love within. Help us to live your love today that our lives and world will be transformed by your "flavors" and "colors." Amen.

Doing the Right Thing

JUNE 28–JULY 4, 2010 • CHIP HALE

MONDAY, JUNE 28 ~ *Read 2 Kings 5:1-14*

Have you ever had an experience when someone encouraged you to do the *right thing* even though you were angry—and you followed their advice and did it?

Naaman was the successful commander of the army of the King of Aram. Unfortunately he had leprosy. One of the slaves of Naaman's wife mentioned, "If only my lord were with the prophet who is in Samaria! He would cure him of his leprosy." So Naaman journeyed to the prophet Elisha.

As soon as the king of Israel learned of this he tore his robes, and said, "Am I God, to give death or life . . . he is trying to pick a quarrel with me." Elisha had a different response. He said to the king, "Let him come to me . . . " Naaman, with a great entourage and some portable wealth, went to Elisha's house. The prophet sent a messenger to him and said, "Go, wash in the Jordan seven times, and your flesh shall be restored and you shall be clean."

Naaman was furious. He had expected the prophet to come out and wave his hand over him or do some dramatic act of healing. Naaman's pride was offended and he decided to go home. But one of his servants urged him to just do as the prophet spoke. So he dipped himself, "and he was clean."

If the servant had not encouraged Naaman to go ahead and try what Elisha had commanded, he would have never been healed. We too must be ready to set anger and pride aside in order to receive grace and healing.

Dear God, open me to hear what you would have me do today. Amen.

Senior pastor for twenty years at Spanish Fort United Methodist Church in Alabama

In ancient Greek mythology Atlas was condemned to carry the weight of the heavens on his shoulders. He is always pictured bowed under the pressure of this huge task. Many of us feel as though we are Atlas. Our backs are bowed with heavy burdens, and we see no way out of this interminable pose. But we must remember that we are not God—only God is God.

Jesus went into the desert to face the devil's temptation. The Greek verb *tempt* means "to try" or "to test." Testing may bring out our goodness and faithfulness. But testing sometimes ends in disaster. As we make our choices, we must come to rely on God very closely in times of testing.

The psalmist celebrates that God "brought up my soul from Sheol" and "restored me to life." This was a milestone in his life. God wants us to rely on the Divine. This psalm, a song of praise, carries a very important meaning. It says something quite profound about our relationship with God and God's relationship with us. It says that life—*all* of life, even life at its worst—is a good gift of God. Suffering does not necessarily mean God is absent. Temptation does not mean God has abandoned us. And our lives, no matter what our circumstance, are in God's good hands.

The psalmist affirms that all who are alive, in whatever circumstances, are called to the holy tasks of prayer and praise. We, as God's children, can do no other.

Dear God, help me to celebrate life, no matter what my circumstances. Amen.

Jesus sent out seventy people to go and reach the world. "The harvest is plentiful, but the laborers are few," he told them. This admonition also holds for us.

Albert Schweitzer was a Nobel Prize-winning theologian, philosopher, physician, music scholar and writer. He believed that only those who served others would ever be truly happy. He led by example; the greatest leadership style he could identify was to lead by doing.

In his twenties he wrote outstanding works on Bach, Jesus, and the fundamentals of pipe organs. He became an admirable organist, church pastor, and seminary teacher (with a doctorate in philosophy). At age thirty, Schweitzer became aware of the desperate need in Africa for medical care. He entered medical school and devoted the rest of his life to serving the people of Africa. He and his wife opened a hospital in what was then the province of French Equatorial Africa. They provided desperately needed medical care to people in desperate poverty.

Growing from the experience, Schweitzer developed an ethical principle called "reverence for life." This philosophy spoke to the need for humans to respond to others amidst the experience of living. His life embodied that principle.

Integral to this principle was his faith. His faith was a force for motivation and change. He was one of the great leaders of his era. He focused his attention wherever he heard of great need.

Many of us trivialize our lives looking for something more, something better, a quick fix for them. I believe God intends us for service, for leadership, for faithfulness to the values that revere life and give it meaning. Let us respond today to Jesus' call to go out to love and serve the world.

Dear God, show me the places I need to be in service in your name today. Amen.

The psalmist sings of the fullness of a life healed and made right by a God who has been gracious and faithful. Mourning has given over to dancing, and giving thanks has replaced the sackcloth *forever*.

A similar sacrament of gratitude can be seen in the cup that Jesus shares with his disciples, whether in the first century or the twenty-first. The metaphor of the cup stands for the life and experience that God gives to each of us. This is an opportunity to leave what the psalmist calls "the Pit," and to live an abundant, ethical life.

Yet, there *are* risks. Lacking knowledge of what would happen next, the first disciples said "Yes" to that cup. They did not know about the pending events of just a few days hence where the cup of Jesus' life and sacrifice would involve humiliation, torture, agony and death.

What is our destiny if we unite our lives with the life of Christ? What hardship, rejection and tough times might we face if we actually devote our whole selves to God?

One of my friends told me that he believed "a sin is any act that you are ashamed to perform in God's presence. If you have to stop and ask God to turn around before you complete your thought, words, or action, then you are about to commit a sin." If we accept the dance of the psalmist and the cup of Christ, we begin to live lives that are pleasing to the eyes of God. It means that we can live under the constant gaze of God without fear or dread. If we are going to share Christ's cup and baptism, we must be prepared to live in such a way that we are not ashamed of the constant gaze of God.

Dear God, help us to accept Christ's cup and his baptism. Amen.

My granddaddy almost always saw good in everything. But there was one very big exception to his philosophy: kudzu. He even went so far as to call kudzu "a blight on humanity."

Kudzu has an interesting history in the United States. Introduced to America in 1876, kudzu quickly caught on as an ornamental and forage plant. In the 1930s, during the Great Depression, the Soil and Conservation Service promoted kudzu for erosion control. In the 1940s the Civilian Conservation Corps paid farmers $8 an acre to plant the vines. It soon became apparent that the Southeastern United States was an ideal climate for growing this extremely aggressive plant—and it soon became apparent that the plant was extremely aggressive.

My grandfather came across kudzu at one of the houses on his southern farm. Eventually, it took over the yard and threatened the fields beyond. My granddaddy said, "Kudzu is the closest thing I know to sin. If you let it take root in your life, it will destroy everything it touches."

Many times things come into our lives that seem to be beneficial. But sometimes these things can take over our lives. And sometimes that encroachment can cover our hearts and lives until we are lost in treacherous vines.

The good news is that God's grace is even more persistent than kudzu. The good news is that the word from Galatians is that we are accompanied by other members of the faith who have pledged to watch over us in a spirit of love, to help us live the lives God has intended for us.

Kudzu is hard to weed out of places where it has taken root. Sin, too, is hard to root out; but we can, through the grace of God, be renewed for "doing what is right."

Dear God, watch over me in love and gentleness. Show me when I become entangled in destructive things, and lead me into freedom in you. Amen.

There are times in our lives when we meet people who are careless, indiscreet and reckless. They give no thought to consequences. All of us have encountered such people, sometimes to our misfortune.

In F. Scott Fitzgerald's book *The Great Gatsby* two of the main characters, Tom and Daisy Buchanan, are exposed as careless, reckless people. The Buchanans wreak havoc in people's lives and then they retreat to their own lives, leaving other people to clean up the mess. Careless people like these two fictional characters can do great damage.

At times, the disciples could be careless people. Sometimes they failed to look deeply enough into Jesus to understand the true significance of his life. Some in the church at Galatia became careless. They did not tend others in the community the way they had promised. Perhaps we are all sometimes a bit careless. We do not look deeply enough into the hearts of others to see the significance of their lives. But God calls us to turn away from carelessness and become caring people. God, in this passage from Galatians, calls us in the Christian community to be deeply connected with one another. We are called to exercise a spirit of gentleness as we live with one another.

The choice of what kind of people we are going to be is always before us. Do we carelessly walk away from our responsibilities and commitments? Do we strive to treat difficult situations "in a spirit of gentleness?" Are we willing to be careful enough to love as Christ does?

There is great joy in living a life of meaning and purpose. There is great challenge in looking beyond ourselves and doing what needs to be done. May we live lives worthy of a true follower of Christ.

Dear God, help me to learn how to be careful and caring in the way I deal with others. Amen.

I recently painted a picture from an old photograph of my great-great uncle Eli.

This 1895 photograph and my painting show Uncle Eli as a very handsome twenty-three-year-old. It was taken on what was to have been his wedding day. My grandparents told me how much he was in love with Tess, a woman seven years his junior. The night before the wedding, they sat on the front porch planning their life together.

The next day Uncle Eli put on his new suit, pocket watch and boutonnière. But the bride never showed up. No reason was ever given . . . at least not one that I heard.

The couple had already paid the wedding photographer. So Eli told the photographer, "Just take a picture of me." That picture has haunted me all my life. His blue eyes look incredibly sad.

In painting his portrait I started with the eyes, blue and broken. It was though he gave up on life. He moved out of the family farm house into a shanty. He never married. He did not return to church. He never met the expectations of him on the farm with any consistency. Though he lived many years, in truth, he died the day his bride did not show up.

I sometimes wonder what might have happened if, after any period of mourning he deemed necessary, my Uncle Eli had come back to pick up the pieces of his life, to go on with whatever lay before him. I often wonder, but I do not know.

We all have difficulties that cause us great pain—the loss of a love, the loss of a friend, the loss of our health, the loss of our faith. It is hard to pick up and go on. It is hard to decide we want to live. Yet God's promise is there. God's "favor is for a lifetime."

Dear God, please help us to have the courage to face life. Amen.

Are We as Faithful as We Think?

JULY 5–11, 2010 • DEE DEE AZHIKAKATH

MONDAY, JULY 5 ~ *Read Amos 7:7-9*

I hate to clean my house. So I figured out how to cut corners. To clean my tile floor, I would use a flat mop. It was easy, disposable and quick. Over dinner one night my friends confessed that their own floors had become filthy without their knowing it and they were using the same speedy method I'd been using. In my mind, I began to defend my floors. They are not that bad. They still look good. It was not until I got home and began to scrub one tile that I realized the truth.

Amos tried this same rationalization with God twice, before he finally saw what God had been telling him all along. The Israelites did not measure up. Their faithfulness to God had degenerated into lackluster devotion. Amos did not want to see it. He did not want to believe it. How could God be so disappointed in the Israelites? God loved them, created them, saved them. But a plumb line does not lie. It measures precisely how well things are (or are not) constructed. A poor quality wall built quickly and haphazardly cannot be trusted to sustain a house.

Once Amos finally realized the truth, he could not help but speak up to shake the Israelites from their sinful trance. Sometimes ignorance is bliss. We go through the motions of a faithful life, yet overlook our spiritual foundation. Fancy furnishings mean little if the walls that surround them are likely to topple over.

God wants more from us than simply going through the fast and easy motions of a faithful life.

What would a plumb line say about your faithfulness?

Ordained elder in the United Methodist Church, director of the Wesley Foundation Campus Ministry in Tucson, AZ

My mother used to say, "When crossing the street it is important to look both ways, even in a crosswalk. There is right and there is dead-right." While this adage about avoiding confrontation holds true in many incidences, there are times when we must stand up for our convictions even if it risks our life or something we value.

Amos, face to face with Amaziah, knew this was his moment. Amaziah was the highest priest within the King's court, and it was well known that one did not reach that position by being at odds with the King's decisions. He was, for all practical purposes, the King's chief puppet, and Amos' prophecy was threatening his sweet deal. Unfortunately, Amaziah underestimated Amos. For Amos' convictions were not motivated by the hope of personal gain. Amos was not a paid prophet. He was not an apprentice to a prophet or part of a group of prophets that could be found in cities like Bethel. He was a shepherd from a small Judean village. He had no financial incentive to speak the word of God. His only motivation was that he knew his message was from God.

As Christians, we are not called to be shrinking violets when it comes to speaking and doing the word of God. I remember hearing early on from mentors: *if your preaching makes people feel good all the time, then you may not be preaching the gospel.* We all want to be liked. We want the gospel message to be easy. But when we avoid conflict and allow false prophets to speak, we dilute the gospel message. The word of God is worth proclaiming, even if it pushes us out of our comfort zones and challenges our whole being.

Where are you being called to speak the gospel message despite risk or adversary?

We have all been there: recipients of an unjust action. We know the hurt of false accusations being slung in our face. We are all too familiar with the sensation of being cornered, feeling as if we have nowhere to turn. We remember the helplessness that comes when it seems we have no power to change the situation. So we cry out to God, the only one who can save us. We call on the only one who can right this injustice. While we know that God will overturn this wrong, the situation seems unbearable right now. How long? How much longer must we endure?

Asaph, the director of King David's choir, composed this psalm. It was not just an individual's plea for justice but also a people's plea: all Israel declared the desire for justice as worshipers sang this psalm together. These people cried out with the same anguish we experience. It is not right that the poor and the needy go without. It is not right that society rewards wrong, and institutions congratulate the greedy. Do something God, quickly!

Taking his place as head of the divine council, God knows what the gods have done wrong. They have become lax. They have failed to bring down the wicked and raise up the oppressed. God has empowered these so-called gods, and yet they pretend they do not know what responsibilities are entrusted to them. This action had been tolerated, but now the cries of the people have challenged the position of the caretakers. God is now in charge.

Matthew 21:22 says, "Whatever you ask for in prayer with faith, you will receive." No matter how deep the pain, no matter how widespread the injustice, no matter how lowly we are, our just and righteous God listens to our cries and our pleas for justice.

God, let your work be not for me but for all those who need to be rescued, for all those who need justice. Amen.

As I go about my daily activities, I often attribute "divine power" to something or someone I admire—often without realizing it. For instance, there is the "cookie goddess" at church who can bake cookies like no one I have ever known. And I rail against the technology gods who are usually battling against me when I have a deadline. Of course, I cannot forget the parking gods who, while not knowing me personally, offer their spot to me at the perfect time. These titles are, of course, only exaggerated metaphors. But what if we ourselves were somehow charged with doing God's work?

Psalm 82 is a trial of the "other gods" who are accused of being unjust and showing partiality. It is this kind of injustice that will destroy the world. The psalm says that as long as nations do not realize it is God who reigns and that it is God who brings justice to the world, these nations will instead follow other gods. The same is true for us as individuals: if we do not understand the reign of God as the ultimate claim on our life, we will be enslaved to other gods, gods that bring not justice, but sorrow.

The psalm is a call to us. God has entrusted us with the tasks of rescuing the weak and the needy, helping the lowly and the destitute, bringing justice to the weak and the orphan in the name of the Lord. The choice is ours—follow our God, or get lost in the mischief and sorrow of "other gods."

To be the people God created us to be, we must rise up and do the things God desires us to do. It is to this standard God will hold judgment.

God, help me to recognize injustice and pain when it crosses my path today. Give me the grace and courage to respond. Amen.

FRIDAY, JULY 9 ~ *Read Colossians 1:1-14*

Growing up, I spent my summers in the state of Washington. Now and then when my family would drive by the apple orchards, I would stare out the car window, amazed at the splendor of the trees. I was mesmerized by how enormous the orchards were and how perfectly the trees were aligned.

As I got older I realized this beauty was a sign of the labor put into the orchard. Each tree had to be watered, pruned, inspected for insects—and that is just the beginning. Off in the distance I could see younger trees maturing, getting ready one day to be harvested. While these trees were not bearing fruit, they were tended to with as much, if not more, attention than the trees bearing fruit. I realized that none of this beauty, and especially none of the fruit, could occur without care, patience and endurance. For neglected trees wither and eventually die.

Paul first speaks of "fruit of the Spirit" in Galatians 5:22-23 and continues the metaphor again in Colossians. This image of fruitfulness is very appropriate. The gospel message is indeed a living, growing reality for those who receive it. It dwells within us, taking root and maturing as deeply as we care for it. As fruit bears seeds that then spread and germinate, we are able to share and spread the gospel with others so that they may bear fruit as well.

What Paul is commending the Colossians for is not, in this case, the power of the gospel but the believers' patience and endurance to stay faithful. It is not easy to be faithful Christians in this world. Likewise, those with whom we share the gospel will not mature instantly. Disciples are not made overnight. They too need to be cared for with gentleness and patience, so one day they will have a fruitful faith.

How have you helped spread the seed of the gospel in another?

Both the lawyer and Jesus knew well the laws of Torah. So when the lawyer begins what seems like a taunt of rhetorical questions, it is no surprise that the lawyer actually answers those questions himself. It is even less of a surprise when Jesus commends the lawyer for his response. However, what is interesting in Luke's version of this story (compare Matthew 22:36 and Mark 12:28) is that the answer the lawyer makes is not in response to the question, "What commandment in the law is the greatest?" but rather, "What must I do to inherit eternal life?"

Years ago a parishioner and her husband volunteered at a weekend spiritual gathering as prayer partners for the evening worship services. Early on they noticed a man who obviously had been crying. They could tell his spirit was beaten down and, at first glance, they thought he might have been living on the street. As they got to know this man and his prayer needs, they learned he actually had a doctorate in religious studies and was teaching nearby. Physically drained and spiritually thirsty, he shared with them that he knew God's commandments, but he did not know God's love.

According to Jesus, knowledge of the commandments is important but it is not enough. The lawyer must take what he knows and live it out. That is the key to living both now and eternally, Jesus says. In other words, it is never enough simply to know all the plays and rules of the game; playing the game is what counts.

Or to put it another way: Love is an action verb. The apostle Paul reiterates this lesson on more than one occasion, reminding us that the most important thing is to love your neighbor as yourself. (See Romans 13:9 and Galatians 5:14.)

When have you actively loved God and neighbor this week?

The parable of the good Samaritan is one of the most well known stories in the Bible and one most of us have heard many times, either in Sunday school or from the pulpit. And thanks to the marvels of You Tube, you can watch scores and scores of different visual interpretations of this parable. While many of these versions are fabulous and thought provoking, most of them present the Levite and the priest to be the villains of the tale.

Focusing on the generosity of the Samaritan, Jesus does not supply much detail about the moral dilemma the priest and Levite likely experienced. The crowd Jesus addressed may have understood more than we do the predicament faced by the two passersby. They likely knew that neither the Levite nor the priest was concerned very much about being thrown off schedule by stopping to give care. Instead, they were concerned that contact with what may have been a dead body would mean they could not perform their temple responsibilities. They were caught between what they understood as their responsibility to God and their obligation to a fellow human being.

Our daily lives are filled with responsibilities. We have jobs, tasks to accomplish, grocery shopping to do, laundry to fold, meals to cook, not to mention family members to look after and love. People depend on us. On our way to pick up our children from school, would we stop and fish a guy out of the ditch? On our way to catch an airplane for an important meeting out of town, would we stop and tend to an accident victim while dressed in our best suit? Would you risk losing your paycheck by taking time off to swing by a motel and offer to pay for a stranger's care? It's worth considering.

O God, give us the heart, soul, strength and mind to go and love our neighbors. Amen.

Pursuing Righteousness

JULY 12-18, 2010 • STEVEN J. CHRISTOPHER

MONDAY, JULY 12 ~ *Read Amos 8:1-6*

According to scholars, Amos prophesied during the reign of Jeroboam. This period was one of enormous political and economic prosperity for both the Northern and Southern Kingdoms. This economic vitality was, unfortunately, matched by a lack of devotion to Yahweh. Rather than bring economic prosperity to the lower classes, this time period brought instead a widening gap between the wealth of the elite and the lower classes.

Amos was convinced that observance of religious rituals and regulations were meaningless unless they led persons to be just in their relationships with one another. He reveals the unrighteousness of Israel by condemning specific unjust practices, such as practicing deceit with "false balances" and trampling on the needy. For Amos, those who engaged in these practices were not behaving in a manner acceptable to God, even if they faithfully observed all the religious rituals and regulations defined in the Torah.

For people of faith today, there are several principles that we can take from Amos. All of us, whether we are "good religious people" or nonchurchgoers, are called to be just in our economic and political relationships. The mere observance of religious practices will not earn God's favor if we do not act justly with our neighbors in the worlds of business, politics, commerce and the workplace. These are the places where we have the obligation, and the privilege, to be God's people.

Today ask God to give us the wisdom to discern the ways our own culture manifests injustice in political and economic relationships, and for wisdom to address these practices.

Managing attorney of the Legal Aid Society of Middle Tennessee and the Cumberlands in Gallatin, TN

Yesterday's reading from Amos describes the criteria through which we are evaluated by God. Amos reveals that God measures our righteousness according to whether we are just in our political and economic relationships. In today's reading, Amos tells us about the consequences of failing to be just.

Amos describes the consequences of failing to act in conformity with God's desires for justice using the metaphor of a famine. Those who turn away from God will experience a "hunger and thirst" for the Word of Yahweh. Persons stricken with this figurative hunger and thirst will search restlessly and tirelessly for the Word of Yahweh, but will not be able to find it.

It is revealing that the acts of injustice described by Amos mirror acts of injustice committed today in our cultures. It is likely that many "good religious people" who sit in the pews of American churches and sing hymns on Sunday morning are responsible for part of it. It is also likely that those who commit acts of injustice today, despite any pecuniary gain, are left with spiritual emptiness.

In the end, when we choose to turn away from God's agenda of justice and righteousness, we will be left in a spiritual famine. When this happens, the only way that we can satisfy our hunger and thirst is to turn to God with all our hearts. I believe that when we have turned away from God, God is willing to forgive our sins when we turn to God with repentant hearts. I also believe that in those times when we have wandered away from God's plan, God is acting within us through God's grace to bring us back into God's presence.

Today pray that God would fill us with grace so that we can learn to imitate Christ, who came among us as a servant, so that we might reveal God's plan for justice.

This psalm is a "torah liturgy" or "liturgy of entrance." It was used by the faithful in Israel before entering the Temple for worship. Prior to the beginning of worship in the sanctuary in Jerusalem, the faithful gathered outside the sanctuary would collectively ask, "O Yahweh, who may sojourn in your tent, who may dwell on your holy hill?" From the inside of the temple, the priest would then recite the line "only the one who walks blamelessly may enter the Temple of Yahweh." The faithful would then enter the Temple to offer praise and offerings to God.

The entrance into the Temple revealed the nature of Israel's covenant relationship with God. God chose to enter into relationship with Israel, and in return, Israel agreed to show fidelity to Yahweh and Yahweh alone. This fidelity was manifest by observance of proper rituals and regulations, and by acting with righteousness. By entering the Temple, the Israelites were reaffirming their decision to live as God's people and, in conformity with God's standards. Likewise, by entering the Temple, Israel was acknowledging that God was faithful to God's promise to remain in relationship with Israel.

I always think of everything on Sunday morning as representing something that is going on invisibly in our relationship to God and to one another as the body of Christ, the church. The passing of the peace represents the fact that through the presence of Christ, we can find peace within ourselves and in our relationships. Singing hymns represents the adoration that we feel for God in our hearts. In light of this psalm, the very act of entering a sanctuary and gathering in worship represents our promise to recognize God's sovereignty and to live our lives as disciples.

Today give praise to God for God's faithfulness to the covenantal relationship with us and God's continued willingness to bestow grace upon us through the power of the Holy Spirit.

The psalmist, like Amos, indicates that God calls persons to live lives of righteousness. And like Amos, the psalmist differentiates the righteous and the unrighteous based upon an individual's social, economic and political practices. Those who are just to one another are righteous, and those who are unjust are unrighteous. This division of the righteous and the unrighteous is strikingly prosaic.

The psalmist's message is also striking in its specificity about the unjust practices that the psalmist recognized in ancient Israel. The righteous will not lend money with interest. The righteous will also refrain from taking bribes against the innocent.

I am sure that many would have averted their eyes and stared at the floor when hearing these words in the Temple. I think there would be a similar reaction if this psalm were read on Sunday morning to those sitting in the pews of American churches today.

The psalmist's message reveals the need for Christians today to cultivate the spiritual disciplines of discernment and faithfulness. If God wants us to be just in our relationships with one another, then we must be able to discern what justice means in our church, our workplace, and in our government.

Once we decide what is "just," we then need God's grace to remain faithful to our convictions so that we can make the right choices and live lives that manifest God's plan for justice. There will ultimately be times when in retrospect, we realize that we made a decision that was not consistent with God's justice. However, if we continue to turn to God in repentance, God will continue to fill us with the strength to be true to our convictions and to live as God's people.

Today pray that God would lead us to distinguish righteousness and unrighteousness and that God would fill us with grace to follow in the way of righteousness.

Like many of Paul's other letters, the letter to the Colossians was written to address errors in doctrine and practice that had arisen in a local church community. In this case, Paul is addressing the church in Colossae, which was a small city near Ephesus in Asia Minor. We are told in the letter that Paul has been informed that members of the church had engaged in idolatry through worship of "elemental spirits." Paul is writing, at least in part, to remind the community at Colossae of the nature of God and the need to refrain from idolatry.

Paul refers to the creation story in Genesis to remind his listeners that there is only one God, and that the worship or recognition of any other God is thereby idolatry. On this basis, the focus upon any other object of worship, such as elemental spirits, is a denial of God's sovereignty and power.

Paul's Christology in Colossians remains relevant to the church today. On one hand, there are certainly significant differences between the culture of Paul's day and contemporary cultures. In my own American society, I do not encounter persons who worship elemental spirits, and I do not envision having to address this issue at any time in the near future at any administrative council meeting. However, what remains relevant about Paul's comments is the notion of the need for the church to recognize Christ as the instrument through which God brought about reconciliation with the world, and on this basis, Christ must remain the central focus of faith and practice. Like those in ancient Greece, there is always the temptation that other things can become objects of adoration and attention, which detracts from the centrality of Christ.

Today, as you pray, focus on the centrality of Christ in your life and congregation. Consider what obscures that focus.

Paul's theology in Colossians 1:15-20 reveals his understanding of Christ as the instrument through which God brought about reconciliation and salvation to humankind. In Colossians 1:21-28, Paul discusses how the community in Colossae is called to respond to the revelation of God in Christ and Christ's saving work among us, and provides a model of individual discipleship as well.

Paul gives two instructions to the church. First, the church is called to remain steadfast and securely established in the faith. Second, the church is to fulfill the commission to "make the word of God fully known." Paul's instruction creates a model for a faithful church's ministry. A faithful church will gather in prayer, study of the scriptures, and worship in order to remain steadfast in its commitment to live faithfully, and in order to maintain purity of doctrine. A faithful church will practice evangelism in order to fulfill the task of making the "word of God fully known." Faithful churches will also engage in works of piety in order to live lives in imitation of Christ.

Paul's model of individual discipleship reflects his understanding that through Christ, we are transformed and become a new creation. In other letters, Paul uses the image of the "New Adam" and the "Old Adam" to reflect our rebirth in Christ. Through Christ, the "Old Adam" who fell into depravity has been replaced by the "New Adam" that is alive in Christ. Consequently, we take upon ourselves the presence of Christ and live as a servant, as Christ did. We reflect the fact that we have become a new creation in Christ by reflecting the light of Christ through our actions. We also become willing to live and die for others, as Christ did.

Today pray that God's Spirit would be present in your own community of faith, to direct you and your community to remain steadfast in the faith, and to spread the good news through proclamation and by doing good works.

A very wise member at a large membership congregation where I served as the associate minister once told me that "it takes just as much energy to fail as it does to succeed." I think about that statement when I reflect upon the meaning of Jesus' statement to Martha.

As many commentators have noted, we can easily sympathize with Martha. Although not explicit in the text, we can safely assume that she is busying herself with tasks that are virtuous, such as making her home comfortable for Jesus and other guests. Meanwhile, her sister sits at Jesus' feet and listens to his words. Surely we can see in Martha's exasperation reflections of our own experiences of being stressed out with too much to do and too little time.

The lesson of Jesus' response to Martha is that our actions must be grounded in a solid understanding of why we do what we do. If we busy ourselves with a million tasks without reflecting on why we do what we do, much of our work and effort may be in vain. In contrast, if we have a worldview that is clear, we can focus our work in light of that worldview, and our actions will likely be more purposeful and effective.

As disciples of Christ, we are called to sit figuratively at Jesus' feet and absorb Jesus' word, and to discern God's call through prayer, contemplation, and participation in the ministries of the church. With this solid foundation, we can go into the world and live as God's people with direction. Going about the busyness of our lives without being grounded in God's word, even when we claim to act in Jesus' name, can cause us to fail.

Today pray for the strength and diligence to take the time, like Mary, to listen to Jesus' words, to ponder them, and to have the courage to act in conformity with them.

Redemption

JULY 19–25, 2010 • GENE PISTILLI

MONDAY, JULY 19 ～ *Read Hosea 1:2-10*

This is a story of sin and redemption and the infinite power of God's love. It is a true story. It is a story about how even the most punishing challenges can be endured and overcome by God's boundless, unrestrained love . . . and our willing heart.

Garrett (this is not his real name) admits to having brutally murdered two innocent people. He was convicted of these crimes and sent to prison. Prison is where he will spend the rest of his life.

There is only One who could lift the spirits of someone like Garrett. It was a long time in the making (you'll follow Garrett all this week), but he finally came to believe that there is no one God does not forgive and that by helping others even he, a murderer, could find a way to serve the Lord.

Hosea's story is chillingly similar to Garrett's—except that in his case, Hosea is not the perpetrator, but the victim. An unfaithful wife is hurtful enough. But Hosea's wife is unfaithful in dramatic, public ways that must have seared his heart and stirred his anger. The resemblances between Gomer's behavior and the behavior of Israel toward God are strong.

And yet God could not, would not let Israel go. God declares, to Israel and to us, " . . . in the place where it was said to them, 'You are not my people,' it shall be said to them [you are] Children of the living God."

Can there be any better word than this? For Israel, for Garrett, for you and me?

Reflect on God's graciousness. Recall times when you felt God's grace in your life.

Songwriter and founding member of the vocal group Manhattan Transfer; works recorded by artists from Belafonte to Beyonce, living in Nashville, TN

G arrett's earliest memory is one of flying through the air and then violently smashing into a wall. His father had a bad temper, and he took it out on the family. Garrett, the youngest, was not spared. It's no real surprise that he was addicted to alcohol and drugs by his sixteenth birthday.

Will you be angry with us forever?
Will you prolong your anger through all generations?

At nineteen, Garrett was convicted and sentenced to two consecutive life terms in prison for the cold-blooded killing of an elderly couple who surprised him while he was breaking into their home. He confessed to both crimes, although he was too high to remember exactly what happened that night. The only thing he remembers is hearing shots and having a vague notion that it must have been him firing because each time he heard a shot he felt the gun recoil in his hand. For assaulting prisoners and guards alike, Garrett spent much of his early prison time in solitary confinement, alone for days at a time in an eight by ten room with no windows. Deprived of almost all sights and sounds, he began to miss many things he had taken for granted before. But the thing he missed more than anything else was seeing the green grass.

Eventually his behavior began to improve and he started to spend less time in solitude and more time with the general population. It gave him so much pleasure when he caught sight of the sun shining or the rain falling on green grass it could bring him to tears. It still can.

Will you not revive us again, so that your people may rejoice in you?

Reflect on God's pardon of Israel and Israel's wonder at God's goodness in restoring them to life. Had Garrett read that scripture, what do you think his reaction might have been? How do you relate this psalm to your own life?

Let me hear what the LORD God will speak . . . the LORD will give what is good.

G arrett is serving two consecutive life sentences. He managed to keep his sanity after several extended periods of solitary confinement; many don't. At the age of twenty-two he had to face the fact that being allowed to live among his fellow prisoners is as free as he will ever be until the day he dies. But for an addict there is one good thing about prison: it's the easiest place in the world to obtain drugs. And Garrett was still an addict.

To those who live in them, cells are not referred to as such. They are called houses. When permitted to leave their houses, inmates tend to gather in groups by race, religion, or ethnicity which are by nature hostile to inmates outside their group. But Garrett noticed there was one group made up of all kinds of inmates. They appeared more relaxed, less angry. If they got boisterous it was always in a good-natured way. Garrett had been a loner but he was drawn by something about the inmates in this group. The word that came to his mind was "peaceful." Peaceful was a word he understood but a way he had never felt.

He also noticed that on Wednesday evenings these inmates got to leave their houses for an hour to go to a meeting. Two people from the free world came in and ran some sort of meeting about drugs and alcohol and getting sober. The meeting was sanctioned by the warden himself and no guards were ever present. Garrett weighed the cost of a lecture about the dangers of drugs against the opportunity for ninety minutes of unsupervised time out of the house. It was a no-brainer. The following Wednesday night Garrett went to his first AA meeting.

What does it mean for you to hear—not just to listen, but to hear—what God is saying to you?

"Where is this Big Book?" was the first question Garrett asked at an Alcoholics Anonymous meeting. For the life of him couldn't understand why it cracked everybody up. In the beginning, just being out of his house on Wednesday night for almost two hours was reason enough to keep going to the prison's AA meetings. Garrett sat as far back as he could, acting disinterested, but he couldn't help catching bits and pieces of what was going on.

Garrett never talked about his crimes to anyone, yet here were men whose lives and crimes were as bad or worse than his, telling their life stories in front of two dozen inmates. They spoke with a matter-of-fact sincerity about how hurt and abused they had been, but more than that, they didn't hide from the pain and suffering they had caused. They accepted responsibility for their actions. Sometimes they broke down and cried and some parts of their stories were really funny in a way that only men incarcerated for a long time can understand.

Garrett heard certain phrases and words repeated at every meeting that stayed in his mind and made him uncomfortable. Still he kept coming back. By the third or fourth meeting it became obvious to him that these ideas were in something called the Big Book. He resolved to read them for himself. So one Wednesday night he asked where the Big Book was kept. Nate, who was chairing the meeting, picked up a book from the table and held it out for Garrett to see. It was dog-eared and beaten up, but as books go it was not particularly large. "This is what we call the Big Book. If you want to know why we call it that, see me after the meeting."

Reflect on Colossians' claim that nothing should compete with Christ for our loyalty. Twelve step programs emphasize maintaining singleness of focus toward sobriety. How does this idea relate to your faith journey?

Like all addicts and alcoholics, Garrett didn't think he was one. Then he met Nate, and Nate had something Garrett wanted—or maybe needed was more like it. Garrett didn't know exactly what it was, but he knew it was something important.

Like Garrett, Nate was a lifer. Nate was older and had been in prison longer, but in spite of that Nate seemed to be as comfortable in his own skin as Garrett wasn't in his, and Garrett felt he would try just about anything to have what Nate had.

Nate held out his copy of the book *Alcoholics Anonymous* and asked Garrett if he would like to take a look at it. It was well worn. Over the years Nate had written personal comments in the margins of many pages. His notes alone would make a pretty good read for someone who wanted to get clean and sober. Nate told Garrett he was welcome to borrow it on the condition that he read it all the way through from cover to cover.

Nate explained to him that the program in the Big Book was his key to the peace that Garrett seemed to want. "If you want, we could get together a few times and talk about it and see where it goes."

Garrett was skeptical and hesitated. Then he said "OK. I can't see it doing any good but I guess it can't do any harm either, and I would like to talk with you. You seem to know a lot of things, and even if I'm not an addict I think you could teach me a lot."

The disciples asked Jesus to teach them how to pray. Women and men in AA gather to learn how to get and stay sober. As you think of where you are in your faith journey, what do you most need to learn?

Because of his many years in the prison's Alcoholics Anonymous (AA) program, Nate's schedule was as flexible as anyone in prison could have. He arranged it to accommodate Garrett's limited free times and he had access to a private place where they could talk. The only requirement was that for as long as they got together Garrett remain sober. Believing he could he gave word his that he would.

When they got together a few days later the first thing Nate asked was if Garrett had kept his promise. Sheepishly Garrett admitted he'd gotten high. "How many times?" and when Garrett heard himself say "Almost every day" he felt absolutely ashamed for not keeping his promise. But instead of showing anger or disappointment, Nate said "It's OK. I appreciate your being honest. This is only our first meeting so let's start now." Nate's forgiveness made Garrett feel even worse. How could he break his word so easily to someone he respected so much? He swore to himself that he wouldn't let it happen again.

A week passed. They met again and Nate asked him the same question. Garrett gave the same answer. And so it went, week after week after week. Garrett couldn't believe it; from the beginning the only thing Nate asked of him was to stay straight and he was unable to do it.

Garrett decided that at their next meeting he would tell Nate they didn't have to get together anymore. He didn't want to waste Nate's time. But Nate said something very peculiar—something Garrett couldn't remember anyone ever telling him. "I won't give up on you. God's not giving up on you, either. Just keep coming back."

In Hosea, God moves from telling a disobedient Israel "You are not my people" to gathering them back again and tenderly calling them "children of the Living God." When have you had an experience of feeling reclaimed by God?

It took a long time and several relapses, but Garrett was one of those who sought and found the courage and humility to admit that he was powerless over drugs and alcohol, that his life was unmanageable, and that he had to rely on a higher power to regain his life. And then, one day while he was working in the laundry a profound thought hit him like a blow to the solar plexus. Throughout his entire life, Garrett had tried to lie his way out of trouble, to avoid the brutal beatings his father gave him, to avoid taking responsibility, to escape incarceration for the petty, then not so petty, offenses he committed in his youth. He had even tried to lie his way out of murder. He had lied for so long that it was as natural to him as breathing.

It was when he began to acknowledge to Nate—and to himself—the truth about his addiction that he realized it was the first time he could actually remember telling the truth about something so important.

After a long war with his hurt and anger, battles which none of us ever completely stops fighting, Garrett came to believe that God truly cares about him. He understands that beauty and joy do exist, even in his prison world. And he is facing the challenges of chaos and suffering by telling God—and himself—the truth. Garrett never turns down the opportunity to help anyone who asks for it. He will tell you that doing so is how he keeps his own sobriety. And he will also tell you about his peace, which does indeed surpass understanding.

Colossians calls us to remember who we are, and whose we are. Reflect on what your faith journey has in common with Garrett's, and how his journey and yours are different.

Doxology, Theology, and Ethics

JULY 26–AUGUST 1, 2010 • THOMAS R. STEAGALD

MONDAY, JULY 26 ∽ *Read Hosea 11:1-11*

The heavens are telling the glory of God, and the firmament proclaims God's handiwork" (Ps. 19:1).

Creation and the God who created the world are worthy of praise. But it is not only God's world that is worthy of praise; so is the law of God. "The law of the LORD is perfect, reviving the soul . . . the commandment of the LORD is clear, enlightening the eyes" (Ps. 19:7-8). The law reveals not only the power of God but the will of God, that we might bear witness to a faithful life. The Commandments, the Beatitudes, and the Gospels all give substance to the faithful life—how God would have us worship and how God would have us treat others in the world.

In the Hebrew scriptures that same task of leading a faithful life falls in this passage to Hosea, who helps us see divine love, with all its disappointment and triumphs: anguish, anger, longing, memory, relinquishment, faithfulness, and commitment. Hosea shows us what God feels toward a wayward child, for Israel, the chosen people have been wayward.

Today's passage speaks the truth about God's love, and it is a truth that sets us free for authentic worship, spiritual friendship, loving obedience, and faithful service.

God, set us free this week to worship you, to befriend others, and to live in loving and faithful obedience. Amen.

Pastor in the Western North Carolina Conference of the United Methodist Church, spiritual director and adjunct professor

In the Hosea lesson for the week we are privileged to overhear an amazing conversation: God talking with God's self! In the face of Israel's abiding rebellion and sin, God is wrestling with the "available options." And we are there! We are afforded the amazing opportunity to empathize with the Almighty!

The historical circumstances of this passage are complex but crucial. Despite appearances, Israel is in deep trouble both politically and economically. There is terrible economic disparity between rich and poor. Religious activity has replaced authentic acts of faithfulness. Israel's leaders are too "realistic" to entertain the prophet's call to trust God for the welfare of the nation—though it was God who brought Israel out of Egyptian captivity. To the north, long-dormant Assyria is militarizing and mobilizing. Over time, Israel's king comes to believe that the nation's only hope for survival is to submit themselves to Egypt.

The irony is breathtaking—to move from oppression to voluntary submission. And God cannot understand why Israel will not call upon its true Savior and Provider.

The prophet gives voice to God's anger. "Fine!" God seems to shout. "You want Egypt? You can have Egypt, and Egypt can have *you*!" It is a sentiment all angry parents know. But all loving parents also know that hot anger cools, and that compassion, mercy, and longing emerge. God is determined to be faithful to Israel no matter what.

Merciful God, help me this day to understand the strength of your love. Amen.

The Talmud, a compendium of rabbinic commentary on Hebrew scripture, suggests that God prays three hours a day: "May it be my will that my mercy may suppress my anger, and that my compassion may prevail over my other attributes." Perhaps the rabbis had Hosea 11 in mind as they wrote!

Hosea 11 shows us the heart of God—warm remembrance of the early days of the covenant after the Exodus, hot anger regarding the rescued: "the more I called, the more they went from me" (11:2). The Israelites' alliances with other kings (and indeed other gods!) were a kind of apostasy; for God alone was their king. The "marriage" bonds between God and Israel were horribly broken. And yet, as Hosea continued to pursue and rescue faithless Gomer, God continued to beckon faithless Israel—to renew the vows, to reenact the covenant, to love the people, though God's love remained unrequited.

In this week's psalm we see the breadth of God's steadfast love and faithfulness after the Exodus: dramatic rescue inaugurates daily care and provision. God provided a "straight way" as the people journeyed through the wilderness, providing them food and water when they were hungry and thirsty. In that way God "redeemed" them. And not just once; God continually rescued them. God's abiding love gives rise to doxology: "O give thanks to the LORD! Let the redeemed of the LORD say so!"

Innocent or guilty, the needy call upon God and God graciously hears and answers.

We join our prayers to the Almighty's—that God's mercy will always overcome God's anger, that we, the redeemed of the Lord, will give thanks to our God who is so very good.

God, remind us that your mercy is stronger than your anger. Help me to seek to be closer to you today. Amen.

The Anglicans of John Wesley's day maligned him as an *enthusiast*. He dismissed their charge, but in point of fact song and praise were so much at the heart of the Methodist revival that Wesley enjoined his followers not to "bawl." That counsel is no longer as necessary as it was. Many of us, and not just United Methodists, have toned it down considerably. Sadly, some disdain *praise* altogether.

Johann Wolfgang von Goethe (d. 1832) famously stated: "Science arose from poetry . . . when times change the two can meet again on a higher level as friends." For the moment, however, science and poetry view each other with suspicion.

One might say the same thing of theology and doxology. Doxology is difficult for the overly analytical: it is really hard to sing with your fingers crossed. Even a mild case of skepticism affects the vocal cords.

It is safer to reflect on the experiences of others. It is even satisfying, in a way, to consider from a distance the worship of others. Sing praise to God ourselves? We understand praise; we just don't *do* praise—and that protects us in a way. We get it, which means we will not be gotten. Yes, it is all very *interesting* how the psalmists call people to prayer and song; but singing that way ourselves would be, well, gauche.

Genuine praise, though, is the wellspring of any meaningful discipleship. Authentic enthusiasm occasions both hospitality and evangelism. Should we lose our doxology altogether, we also lose the essence of our theology and identity, our source and the substance of who we are.

The Bible seems to evidence a pretty clear pattern in these matters: theology arises from doxology. Perhaps when we ourselves are changed, the two can meet again in our hearts as friends.

God, you are worthy of praise, and by praising you we remember whose we are. Guide us in praise of you. Amen.

Theologians have long debated the *ordo salutis*, the "order of salvation." It is an interesting phrase, usually referring to the sequences and consequences of God's grace in the human soul. Grace is "one thing," but like love, grace has many aspects and effects.

John Wesley spoke of prevenient grace, by which God carves a path for us back to God; convicting grace, by which God convinces the wayward soul of its need to come to God; justifying grace, which unites the human soul to the mercy and love of God; and sanctifying grace, which works in and with the human soul to make it more godly. Wesley also spoke of perfecting grace, or "entire sanctification," whereby God enables the redeemed to love God with all their heart, soul, strength and mind.

In our lesson from Colossians there is yet another "order" to salvation: those who have experienced the grace of God in all its aspects are given, as it were, "orders of salvation," or instructions. The commands in these verses are a good place to begin.

Paul, who believes we are under grace and not under law, expects those who praise God to serve God. He believes those who know God's heart will live out God's purposes in the world.

John Wesley had his own ideas about faithful Christian service. He wrote that [Methodist Christians] should evidence their desire of salvation by doing no harm, doing good and loving God. Wesley's *General Rules* and Paul's "general orders" together guide us in ways of praise and faithful living.

God, lead me in your ways that I may sing your praises and be faithful. Amen.

Books about Jesus are more plentiful than ever today. Not all, but many of these books fall into one of two camps, each corresponding more or less to either of the "two natures" of Christ as proclaimed by the Nicene Creed.

On the one hand there are the books that proclaim Jesus' divinity—his heavenly origins and sacrificial death. These books focus on the spirituality and eternity of his message, how he shows us the way to heaven after we die. On the other hand are those books that explore Jesus' humanity and ethical teaching—his peasant roots and concern for social justice. These books often focus on the political dimensions of Jesus' ministry and how he shows us the way to "heaven on earth."

The Gospel lesson this week—the Parable of the Rich Fool—embraces both "natures" of Jesus. When Jesus asks, "Friend, who made me a judge or arbitrator over you?" he pops the balloon of those who would reduce the gospel's message to economics and politics alone. Jesus also said, "You fool! This very night your life is demanded of you. And the things you have prepared, whose shall they be?" He thereby reminds his disciples that sharing God's blessings (a gesture of neighbor-love) has eternal significance and, if we fail to do so, eternal consequences.

I suspect that our portraits about Jesus say as much or more about us than they do about him. On the day of Jesus' circumcision Simeon said. "This child is destined for the falling and the rising of many in Israel, and to be a sign that will be opposed so that the inner thoughts of many will be revealed . . . " (Luke 2:34-35). Our own prejudices are revealed when we embrace one aspect of Jesus' message and ministry to the exclusion of another. But "beware of *all* forms of greed," Jesus said. That includes even the "greed" to be right.

Christ Jesus, we embrace the mystery of who you are, and we rejoice in the spirit of your love. Amen.

S tatic electricity is an inconvenient build-up of inactive charges that irritate or shock. Everyone knows the hair-raising feeling, the unpleasant pop by which the charges are temporarily neutralized.

Electric *current*, on the other hand, is indispensable. It brings light and heat, powers tools and respirators, preserves food and medicine and, when harnessed, provides work and ways to do it. Electric current can be dangerous, of course, but it is mostly life-giving.

To say the Bible is God's "living word" is to affirm that its message powers believers—individuals, congregations, and traditions. The Bible is never static, though what we read can be hair-raising at times, even uncomfortable. The message never merely shocks us, however, nor is its effect ever neutralized. Rather, it enlightens and warms, delivers spiritual nourishment and healing, provides work for the faithful and the tools to do it.

Those who are "hungry for righteousness" find the scriptures life-giving and indispensable.

We have felt the current, as it were, in our readings for the week, the power that courses through the different kinds of biblical literature: doxology, theology, narrative, and ethical instruction. Hosea shows us the heart of God; Israel praises God for the history of divine mercy; Jesus warns foolish idolaters against their many forms of greed, and Paul takes doxology and theology to fashion a rule for living.

How rich and powerful this book! No wonder John Wesley said, "I want to know one thing: the way to heaven. [God] has written it down in a book. Oh, give me that book! At any price give me the book of God."

Make us disciples, God. Make us disciples as we faithfully study your book. Amen.

What God Requires

MONDAY, AUGUST 2 ~ *Read Isaiah 1:1; 10-17*

According to the opening words of Isaiah, one of God's chief complaints against the people of Judah is that they have neglected to care for others. God takes this neglect as a sign of their faithlessness. As a result, God has grown weary of the people's worship: "Even though you make many prayers, I will not listen."

Those words make me shudder. I would like to think God couldn't tire of seeing me sitting in my same pew each Sunday. But then I see it right here in my Bible, the prophet Isaiah declaring that God has had enough of burnt offerings and cannot even stand the smell of incense anymore.

Showing up at the temple with the proper offering did not automatically count as faithfulness. God saw that on their way to worship, these people hurried right past the blind beggar sitting in the street. They made no time to stand up for the outcast in their community.

Look again at the scripture. After denouncing the people's worship, God provides them with explicit directions for making things right. It is straightforward.

The hand that extends to receive the communion cup from Christ's table must also reach out with a cup of cold water in Christ's name. What God is looking for in our worship is not so much what we do when we get there, but what we've been doing before we arrived.

God of justice, grant us the will, and the power, to act on behalf of our neighbors. Accept what we do as worthy of worship. Amen.

Editor, writer, and member of Christ United Methodist Church, living in Franklin, TN

I like to eat. And I'm especially fond of eating the "good of the land," which in the summer means juicy tomatoes, planted, grown, and vine-ripened in my own vegetable garden. I have the luxury, though, of purchasing tomatoes from a grocery store or from a local grower at the farmer's market. I might even be the beneficiary of a neighbor's generosity and find a box of tomatoes sitting on my back porch. My point is, I don't have to expend much of my own labor to eat the good of the land. I do so out of choice.

The people of Judah during the time Isaiah prophesied were intimately bound to the land, God's promised land. The land was their source of life and livelihood. They farmed the land and made their homes on it; they raised both their children and their livestock there; and they worshiped God there. The land and their collective labors in it were theirs by gift.

That gift, though, was nearly always in danger. Political enemies were a real threat to Judah's promised land. It is in that context God offers words of hope that (one would think) even the most rebellious and faithless people would heed. "Let's work out our problems; I'll clean up your sins; you get back to being obedient, and you'll be planting your grain fields in no time." But the people do not heed God's call. Soon they would be laboring in exile, forced to till another's soil.

The biblical account of the relationship between God and God's people is characterized by God's steadfast offer of all things good, and by the people's stubborn unwillingness to live within the boundaries God attached to that offer.

When I imagine never again tasting fresh tomatoes grown by my own hand on my own land, I find God's call to obedience quite compelling.

God of promises, give us grateful hearts for your gifts and obedient lives to be good stewards of them. Amen.

Some readers of the Bible are completely put off whenever a passage proclaims God's judgment, no matter where the judgment is directed. God as judge is not the picture of God we want to use when we pray. We want the God of mercy and grace when we fall on our knees.

But the book of Psalms preserves the broad range of Israel's faith and the people's struggle to know God and themselves. The writer of Psalm 50 sees God as Cosmic Creator with full authority to judge even those who claim faithfulness but who have forsaken God's commands. According to the psalmist, this same judge can condemn those who "keep company with adulterers" (v. 18) and then promise to show them "the salvation of God" (v. 23). As is often the case in the Psalms, the speaker in the text manages to hold in tension various competing aspects of God's character. The God who condemns also pardons; the God who destroys also creates; the God who rejects also welcomes.

With that in mind, I have come to the conclusion that the most important line in Psalm 50 is contained in verse 7: "I am God, your God."

Your God.

Did you get that? This Righteous Judge of all the earth, who appears in this psalm preceded by a devouring fire and surrounded by storm clouds, who makes us tremble by threatening to tear us apart for our forgetfulness, this God is our God. This God is on our side. This God has even given me permission—how remarkable!—to call when I am in trouble. This God calls us "my people." This God I can pray to.

I'm listening God; even when you judge me, I'm listening for your word of hope and promise. Amen.

One of the inherent purposes of the physicality of worship practices (kneeling, bowing the head, walking down the aisle, reciting a litany, giving an offering) is to assist worshipers in approaching God regularly, regardless of how they feel about themselves or about God or about anything else at the moment.

The Psalms give us remarkable glimpses of the worship rituals of ancient Israel, and in particular, of some of those physical worship practices—taking a pilgrimage to the temple in Jerusalem (Ps. 122:1), singing a praise song (Ps. 84:4), or bringing some kind of animal or grain offering to be sacrificed on the altar (Ps. 50:9). The problem, though, with coming to the altar and actually offering something tangible like a sheaf of barley or a turtledove, is that the object itself, after a while, can be seen as containing one's full measure of thankfulness. So the practice becomes rote and meaningless and eventually even a substitute for the thankfulness that the heart no longer contains or desires to express.

Obviously I don't bring thank offerings of grain to the altar rail at my church. Yet sometimes, I'll have to admit, I need a prompt to remind me of why I should be thankful. There are times I enter the sanctuary and feel like being somewhere else. For me the physicality of getting up and going to church on a weekly basis can become almost as routine an activity as I can imagine bringing sacrifices to the temple was to the Israelites.

So when I read in Psalm 50:22 that God is most honored by a heart full of thankfulness offered with all the intentionality of a sacrifice, I figure I'd best not wait till I get to church to offer it.

Thank you, God, right here and right now. Amen.

Once upon a time, I lost my job quite suddenly and found myself sitting at a makeshift desk in my home trying to manage an unexpected career transition. Because it was my first experience of actually being out of work, I dealt with a number of unfamiliar emotions and thought processes. One emotion was grief; I was acutely aware that I had lost something that I could not retrieve. Attached to that feeling was a sense of imbalance. Nothing seemed in its right place, especially me. There were a couple of times I even thought that I was dreaming and that I would return to my office the next morning. I always woke up, still out of place.

As a person of faith, it is easy to presume how you might respond to hypothetical situations. For instance, I would have thought my natural response to a job loss would have been to appeal to a passage like Romans 8:28 about how all things work together for good, or to one of Jesus' comforting promises, Matthew 11:28, about his offer to carry my burden, or to the oft-quoted text from Hebrews 11:1 describing faith as the assurance of what cannot yet be seen. Well, that was not how I responded. At least not initially. For the first few days of being unemployed, I rushed from one networking activity to another, interested only in trying to reestablish my place in my world somehow.

Then one Sunday, the message of the morning's worship service finally named the particular pain and loss I was experiencing. My faith was affirmed—no, more than that: my faith was released from whatever had kept it hidden away, inert, inaccessible. I was able to admit that all I had really lost was a job. Nothing more. God was still with me. God's promises were still in effect. And whether or not I could see very far ahead of me, I knew with conviction that I would find my place again.

God, grant us the courage to see our lives with eyes of faith. Amen.

I find Abraham fascinating, as much for what the Bible does not say about him as for what it does say. In Genesis 2, God tells Abram to leave all that he has known. And his response reported in Genesis 12:4 is simply: "So Abram went, as the LORD told him." Without a single word Abram takes off for parts unknown. Wait a minute. Really? A man of seventy-five leaves behind all he has ever known to follow a three-verse promise made by a voice that from all I know he has never heard before? No wonder the Bible and the rabbinic writings hold Abraham in such high esteem. No wonder the writer of Hebrews 11 was so impressed.

Abraham's faith is a bar set very high for me. Yet I am drawn to his story. He knew something. I'm only guessing, but I think Abraham knew something about himself, about God, and about the nature of making one of life's major transitions. Leaving home—whatever that means, whether changing addresses, going off to school, being laid off at work, or giving up independence for assisted living—always means setting out not knowing where you're going.

Recently I reread William Bridges' insightful book, *Transitions: Making Sense of Life's Changes*. He believes life is all about transitions and how you negotiate them. Leaving behind the familiar for the unfamiliar is a common human experience; that is not the main problem. The difficulty comes in seeing the potential for growth that change represents. Bridges suggests that many of us do not even find our life's truest calling or direction until later in life. If what he says is true, then perhaps the story—and the faith—of Abraham is not so far beyond my grasp.

Maybe Abraham knew exactly what he was doing. Unsure of the destination, perhaps, Abraham felt sure that the journey was the thing he had to do.

God, when you call, give me feet to move even when the way ahead is unclear. Amen.

In Luke 12, Jesus tries to encourage his followers. He's been "proclaiming and bringing the good news of the kingdom of God" (Luke 8:1) for some time now. This passage is part of the lengthy middle portion of Luke's Gospel where Jesus has set his sights on taking that message to Jerusalem. Along that journey, Jesus sends out advance parties of his followers to prepare the way for him in the villages he will visit. He tells a few parables, casts out some demons, and stops for meals. And all the while he is teaching his followers.

But then Jesus decides to speak out against the Pharisees—while at dinner with them. (It is always risky to invite Jesus for dinner.) At this point, some of Jesus' followers may have become a bit nervous. The Pharisees are not happy with Jesus. So Jesus shares his vision of this kingdom he's been proclaiming in the context of a kind of pep talk to his disciples. He addresses two of their (and our) chief anxieties: how to go about daily living in a world opposed to God's kingdom; and what to be doing until God's kingdom actually arrives.

First, Jesus says, we simply don't worry. By that he does not mean we renounce our responsibilities. Rather, he means for us to free ourselves from our obsession with earthly concerns. Stop fretting over the next new phone or gadget or car or house. They'll all wear out eventually. God's kingdom, no matter how threatened or threatening it is, will never wear out.

Then Jesus delivers a loaded imperative. In the meantime, he says, instead of wringing your hands or looking for signs or predicting the weather, do this: "Be dressed for action and have your lamps lit." That's it? Just be ready? Yep. That's discipleship.

God, turn my worries into readiness and my anxious thoughts into actions that will help bring in your kingdom. Amen.

Wisdom

AUGUST 9–15, 2010 • LAUREN L. CHAFFEE

MONDAY, AUGUST 9 ~ *Read Psalm 80:1-2, 8-19*

This Hebrew song of lament, with its vineyard metaphor, engages our imagination and emotions. Psalm 80 is known as a communal lament. The cry of the people who are cut off from their sacred homeland resonates with the pain and bewilderment of a rejected lover.

One cannot live in California for long without developing an appreciation for vineyards. The histories of the older vineyards tell of vine stock—sections of old vines with their roots intact—being brought to this country from other countries, such as those in Europe or Central America. This kind of history forms the backdrop for the movie *A Walk in the Clouds*. The film tells the story of the Aragons, a family proud of its reputation as vintners. One night, because of anger and jealousy, a careless act causes hundreds of acres to go up in smoke. All seemed lost, until it was discovered that the original vine and its roots were not dead but still green with promise.

Israel believed itself to be born of God's careful planting and nurture. Once a band of homeless slaves, brought from a far-off place to a land specially prepared for them, they had grown into a nation large and powerful. But then, things went terribly wrong. Enemies invaded and their glory days went up in smoke. They believed that Yahweh, their Sovereign and Protector, had abandoned them. Their sorrow ran deeper than words. But still they called on God's name for salvation, for restoration.

When you sing a song of lament, what seed of faith renews your hope?

An ordained elder in the California-Nevada Annual Conference of the United Methodist Church, currently serving as a resident chaplain at the Presbyterian Hospital in Albuquerque, NM

Like a country music love song, this psalm weaves the tale of a spurned lover. Moving from a lament about being mistreated to a plea for the beloved's return, love's paradox appears. "You did us wrong, God! But please come back and make things right." Hear the depth of passion and pain, along with the underlying belief that all will be well . . . if only God will return and love as before.

Anyone whose heart is broken by the demise of a love relationship knows how crazy it can all seem. First you shake your fist; you accuse; you blame. Your former love is the cause of all your pain. Then, without warning, you are conjuring up wild schemes to lure the demon-turned-hero back so that things can be as good as they once were. "If only" is a common phrase that finds its way into these dynamics. If only he or she would apologize and promise to do better from now on, everything would be all right.

Israel's theology assigned to God power and responsibility for everything that happened in their world. When God was pleased with them, they prospered. When God was angry with them, they suffered. To our modern ears, this kind of thinking seems arbitrary and primitive. How can God be a benevolent and kind provider here, and a vindictive and violent judge there?

If we believe that God is ultimately a God of love, then perhaps our real task is to discern God's grace in the midst of the chaos we ourselves create. Rather than asking God to come and fix everything we've destroyed, perhaps our prayer should be for God to help us come to our senses and take responsibility for the gifts we have been given.

Are you suffering from a broken heart? What part will you play in your own healing?

This poetic passage is among the most famous in Isaiah. It is known as a "juridical parable," and is reminiscent of the encounter that took place between Nathan and King David in 2 Samuel 12. The writer draws us in by telling us a story of betrayal. The scene opens in a vineyard, then moves suddenly to a courtroom, where the listeners witness a trial. An agreement or contract has been broken. The vineyard owner has planted, fed, and protected the vines, but they have not done their part. Instead of producing juicy, beautiful fruit, they have only yielded wild grapes—sour and inedible. What should be done?

Quickly, the hearers of the parable turn from being the jury to becoming the defendants, and it is they who have failed to give to the owner what was due. The poem has God playing the part of vineyard owner, while the Israelites play the defendants, the bad vines. Once more, God's beloved children have squandered and abused the gifts of God, leading to their own ruin. This prophetic text, echoing our other lectionary texts, speaks to the theme of broken agreements, broken promises and broken hearts. When God's people choose to live selfishly, without regard for what is just and holy, the fruit of their lives is rotten. God's heart breaks yet again, as the beloved creatures reject the sacred love and life offered them.

How many times have we invested ourselves in some relationship or project that showed great promise, only to be rejected or dismissed? Remember how you felt when all your efforts seemed to be in vain? How might it hurt God when we reject and dismiss God's investment in us? Thankfully, God's mercy is great.

What does it mean to think of yourself as a tender shoot that God has planted and nurtured with love? How will your fruits reflect your gratitude for what God has done?

When we are young, we imagine that love will solve everything. If we could just fall in love, love our neighbors, make love not war, then all would be well. But as we mature, we discover that love also brings pain, anger and conflict, along with joy, meaning, and connection. In this text from Luke, Jesus is showing "tough love" when he declares, "I came to bring fire to the earth." He's sounding a wake-up call, hoping to loosen his followers from the grip of complacency.

The tone here resonates with the Jewish eschatology of the time, conveying a sense of immediacy about the trials to come. Jesus calls for decision, commitment, and integrity. Do we love him? Then let us align our priorities, values, and goals to reflect that love. True love often requires tough choices. And better that we choose sooner, rather than later; for if we wait, the choice might be made for us. That which holds real promise and meaning may slip away, leaving us with only cheap substitutes. God through Christ is pushing us to question our attachments to material possessions, rituals, routines, status, or addictions. These are the cheap substitutes for right relationship with God and God's creation.

Jesus takes hold of us and urges us to "choose life." It is love and a desire for the best that God has to offer that is behind Jesus' words. When our beloved is making poor choices, we can't just look the other way. In that same way, Jesus challenged his followers to live faithfully and choose a life of integrity, authenticity and joy.

God wants only the best for us. Can we love and empower ourselves enough to choose that which is life-affirming?

Living in the San Francisco Bay area for 15 years, I recall one sight that never failed to thrill me—the ocean fog rolling in over the coastal ranges. Hot summer temperatures cause the surface of the ocean to evaporate, creating a massive cloud cover. The ocean breezes then blow the cloud mass ashore, blanketing the area with a moist, cold shadow. It took me a while to figure out the pattern and learn to anticipate both the fog and the return of warmth after the summer sun burned off the fog. People who have lived in the Bay area for a while can tell you when to expect a fair day, and when to dress in layers for protection from the fog and chill. It doesn't even require training as a meteorologist or the use of precise technical instruments. You just know to expect the fog following several hot days.

The words of Jesus, according to Luke, highlight the common sense we humans develop based on observation and experience. We don't need a doctoral degree to learn most of what we know in life. Basically, we just have to show up, pay attention, and connect the dots. We can usually tell whether we are in a promising or dead-end job or relationship. Parents often sense when their children are concealing something that might negatively impact their future.

But what happens to our sensibilities when it comes to recognizing and responding to the activity and presence of God in our midst? We pray fervently for miracles, all the while failing to notice the miracles around us each day. We ask for God to guide us, but tune out the messages and opportunities to act with faith and courage. We pray for comfort, but shut out the people who could offer what we need.

Invite God's Spirit to help open your eyes, heart, and mind to God's path for you.

I don't know of many Christians who do not find this text inspiring. It is hard to read this passage without being swept up by this litany of courage and tenacity. The writer portrays faith in God as a kind of unstoppable power that enables ordinary men and women to accomplish extraordinary feats. Any who are discouraged, who feel like giving up or giving in, will find hope in this recounting of these heroes of faith who faced great odds and fierce enemies.

This was a crucial message for the early followers of Christ, as they struggled to stay faithful and alive in a hostile environment. The stories of those who had preceded them brought them encouragement and assurance. Those first Christians had powerful enemies and modest resources, and so their heritage of faith was something no one could take away.

Contemporary Christians still have battles to fight. We worry about things like war, the economy, our health, our children, and the environment. Some of us hope that God will intervene and solve our problems for us, perhaps through a chosen leader, or through divine intervention. But the message of this passage is that we have it within ourselves to transform our world. We have all we need, and more, if we join with the Spirit of God to do what is needed. Rather than sitting along the sidelines worrying about the condition of our families and the world, we can act for justice, show compassion, or promote peace. We can work for education, healthcare, housing, and nutrition for the world's poor and displaced. We can help a local group build peace in our neighborhood and community.

The saga of faith continues to be written as each decides how to live in this world. What part will you play in the story?

The challenges of this world can only be met with God's spirit of truth and love. How are these embodied in you?

Whether it's the *AIDS Walk*, the *Race for the Cure* or any of the many other altruistic walks or races for raising funds, we live in a time when "running the race" has become a symbol for the fight against disease and death.

This metaphor is a wonderful expression of the courage and strength that is required to remain faithful, alive, and healthy in this world of ours. The early Christians were up against great odds in the hostile environment of Roman rule and staunch Judaism. They were ridiculed, persecuted, and killed. Their faith and lifestyle came under intense scrutiny by the Jewish authorities even as jealousy and conflict brewed within the new communities of faith, and within households divided against themselves. Was following the teachings of Jesus really worth this struggle?

When I was in college, I served as the resident barber for most of the swim team. Before the really big races, many of the swimmers would have their hair cut as short as possible, then go back and shave their entire bodies. They did not want even one hair to slow them down. Beating their opponent would require all the speed, strength, and agility they could muster, as well as the absence of anything that could cause "drag," including body hair. I used to laugh at them: "What possible difference could a few little hairs make?" But they knew.

The writer of the letter to the Hebrews exhorts, "Lay aside every weight . . . and run with perseverance." We are often better at seeing what is causing "drag" in the lives of others than we are at acknowledging what holds us back from compassionate and courageous lives of faith. The "cloud of witnesses" remains as a powerful reminder that it is possible to run the race with vitality and courage, if we let our faith lead us.

Who is part of your cloud of witnesses, living or dead? How do they help you run your race?

Called to Stand Upright

AUGUST 16–22, 2010 • BETH COOPER

MONDAY, AUGUST 16 ~ *Read Jeremiah 1:4-10*

There was a knock at my office door at the Wesley Foundation, and a first-generation college student stood in my doorway. She was nervous and anxious. I invited her to come in.

The student explained that she wanted to run for a student body position but that she didn't think she could do it. She recounted all the reasons she couldn't run for office.

When she finished talking, I asked her how I might help. She paused. She repeated all her excuses. I listened. I asked her how her grades were: they were great! I asked how her family was: they were fine.

The young woman went on to say that she even felt God wanted her to try for this position. As we talked further, she discovered what was preventing her from going forward. It was fear—fear of doing something so big, fear of failing at it, fear of what it would mean if she were elected.

The student did not get the office, but I watched over the next months as she grew in confidence, excelled in extracurricular activities, and became quite a public speaker. This shy young woman has graduated and is working on her law degree.

O God who chose me and knew me before I was born, in my struggles and conflicts, never let me underestimate that you promise to be with me and help me to face my fear. Amen.

Singer, songwriter, and United Methodist pastor serving as United Methodist campus pastor at the Wesley Foundation and executive director of the Wesley House Student Residence program serving San Diego State University in California

"Before I formed you in the womb I knew you."

Jeremiah was a prophet who lived in disruptive times. In this passage, God gives Jeremiah pep talks encouraging him to do the hard things that lie ahead. As a people of faith, we all know that we need times of prayer, revelation moments, and pep talks from God for those things that face us.

When I moved to San Diego, I found it extremely hard to make friends. The culture of southern California doesn't always allow time for "front porch" conversations or talking time to get beyond "Nice weather today!" One incredibly harried day, everything that you could imagine went wrong—the plumbing in our old building broke, students cancelled appointments or didn't show up at all. I was already running late when my cell phone rang. A friend called to tell me that she had been diagnosed with cancer. My heart sank. At that moment, nothing else mattered.

Sometimes an unexpected and urgent demand reminds me of what's most important. Suddenly it was clear to me. The headaches of the worn-out building and the daily mishaps had been wearying, but hearing my friend's voice in a vulnerable moment put everything else into perspective. Her life as she knew it was not going to be the same.

Living through seasons of life, times of winter and times of spring, I find peace in discovering that even before I was created God knew every part of me, of my friend, and of all that breathes life. Knowing we are of God gives us zeal and energy to do what might seem impossible.

O God, when we reach for the distractions: the comfort food; the caffeine to take the hurt, fear, or anger away, remind us that only you can give us peace. Remind us that you knew us before we knew you and that you called everything you created good. Amen.

Do what you do so well. Get me out this mess and up on my feet.
(THE MESSAGE)

When I first came to the Wesley Foundation at San Diego State University, there was an older student who lived out of his RV. As we became acquainted, I found out that nobody in his family had graduated from college. He was working hard in school but had no family support.

One day this student came bursting through the doors of the Wesley Foundation. When I saw him, I could tell that he was in a lot of trouble. I listened while he talked. He had fallen behind in his homework and was getting over a cold. The incident started when he had worked the night before class and then overslept. He needed to produce a paper quickly, so he had pulled his paper together from information on the computer. When the professor called him in to ask him about his sources, he panicked and compounded his mistake by not admitting what he had done.

The student was facing academic charges for plagiarism. My first question to him was, "How do you feel about what you did?" He made excuses. I listened and then told him that I couldn't help him. He remarked, "I thought this is what you do. You help people."

I replied, "I do help people. But I can only help you when you can admit to yourself that the path you chose was not honest." He started to cry, and I held his hand. I said that I could not know the outcome, but I assured him that he would have to face this alone. In the end, he was put on probation. Admitting his wrongdoing, being humble and cooperative with the process— these approaches strengthened his case and his character.

Help me, O God, when I am my own worst enemy. In all things that I do, let me always be able to celebrate what you do in my life. Amen.

You are my mighty rock and my fortress.

What is your sanctuary? a favorite garden spot? a place you go to feel safe? Is it a museum or a library, a famous spot or an off-the-road mark? Where is your place of safety? Often, we seek sanctuary or a fortress in times of distress or difficulty. The psalmist understands what it means to seek shelter.

I have traveled to many places in the world. I have seen famous pillars, toured fortresses, and viewed impressive architectural design. These monuments exude great awe and strength. Yet a fortress does not have to be a mansion or a castle from medieval times. Nor does our strength come from having money.

One place that is truly a sanctuary for me is my home. I am thankful that I have a home to go to after an exhausting day at work. I even have a favorite room where I hang out with my dogs. I have books that surround me, a recliner that I love to curl up in, and a blanket I cover up with while I read or watch a good movie.

When I need to be restored, I take inside myself the God who is my pillar and sanctuary. In moments of exhaustion, I go to trusted people or pets and a space that can help me focus again. My dogs remind me of the gift of unconditional love, the recliner is the gift of comfort, and my blanket envelops me with warmth. All these gifts come from the one who loved us before we were even created. God is the strong pillar and the secure fortress where we find strength and comfort in all times of life.

God, who hears our silent tears and cries with us, give us comfort and relief from times that give us pain and grief. Surround us with your arms and remind us that we are not alone. Even in tough situations, be the source of strength that we can lean on to find everlasting peace. Amen.

I'm a resident of southern California, but I came from another part of the country, so experiencing wildfires is truly a frightful event. When one fire swept through the area, I was only a few blocks away from being evacuated. I was on edge, listening to the news reports, trying to decide whether to pack or not, and staying indoors and afraid. Time passed, and I put the fires behind me.

Then one night, flying back from a meeting in Tennessee, I was seated next to a woman who was reading what looked to be an interesting book. It was an interactive workbook in which she could check lists and write as well as read. She was so absorbed in the book that I became curious. I asked her about the book and she showed it to me. To my surprise, the book was from her insurance company. They had given it to her because she had lost everything in one of the San Diego fires. The workbook helped her try to remember everything that she had lost and to describe and list it.

We started a conversation about the fires, her story, and where she was in her life. When she began to talk about the lessons she had learned from the fire, she pointed out that life as she knew it was forever gone. There was no use going back and trying to piece all that together. Her treasures of family heirlooms, family pictures, and antiques could never be replaced.

In the midst of grief, the woman realized that what she needed most was exactly what she already had. Her family was safe. She still had a job.

Today's reading is about a time when the people are afraid. In everyone's life there comes a time when you have to put your trust in what is solid. Accidents happen, disasters come. In the midst of that, Jesus is the foundation pointing to God who cannot be destroyed.

O Designer of our souls, help us clear out our lives and focus on what you have created. May we hold dearly only what is of your design scheme. Amen.

This story tells of a woman who for many years had an ailment that kept her bent over. In today's world, many people live bent over because of illness, disease, or accident. This bent over woman had been ridiculed and excluded. Some people didn't want to risk being around her. Some thought that she was strange, not beautiful. Some speculated that her condition must be God's punishment for something.

Because the woman couldn't raise up to see people's faces, she probably knew them by their voices. Perhaps she had learned where to step to avoid tripping over rocks. She knew the footprints of her neighbors. Her intuition made up for her lack of motion. She could probably tell which people were up to no good. Her story is our opportunity to reflect on how persons who are "bent over" view the world and how different our views are from theirs.

One student at the Wesley Foundation had cerebral palsy. The other students learned a lot about her circumstances by being around her. She had difficulty holding a cup, so she requested that when they served her a drink they also provide a straw. It took her time to complete sentences, but she made excellent contributions to conversation and had a sense of humor. When she was a part of the group, everyone enjoyed talking with her.

This student saw her condition as a part of who she was. How she was created gave her different perspectives on life situations that others might not see. I learned from her. I was thankful for her witness and the lesson that she taught me about those with different abilities.

God, you create each one of us. Remind us that, in all of our human forms, we have something to bring to your creation. Let what we do glorify your name. Amen.

He placed his hands on her, and right away she stood up straight and praised God.

Sometimes our emotional state or mental state keeps us "bent over." We allow others to manipulate, intimidate, and even victimize us. When we allow others to have that kind of influence over our lives, we can be bent or broken. We are robbed of life-giving power when we focus our energy on surviving the next hit or sidestepping the next mind game or running away from the neighborhood or company bully.

The bent over woman in the scripture had lived with her hurt for a long time. You might expect that people would be grateful that Jesus could help her. But that is not what happened. The crowd of people who watched Jesus heal the woman in front of the synagogue complained loudly. Jesus had broken sabbath laws to heal her on this day. When the bent over woman could finally straighten up her back, what she saw must have been clear: the religious institution was bent over and suffering under the weight of its own laws.

As a people of faith, let us be free from those things that bend us to the point of breaking. Let us not judge or limit the power of God's work in a given situation. Let us not perpetuate customs and rules that keep others in our faith community, or in our larger world, bent over and broken.

O Divine One, show us the way to help others find freedom from living bent over. Free us from the bent-over places in our own lives. We ask for the healing and the courage Jesus can give. Amen.

Reflections of Love

AUGUST 23–29, 2010 • NANCY U. NEAL

MONDAY, AUGUST 23 ~ *Read Jeremiah 2:4-13*

This scripture was written during a period of political and military unrest for the people of Judah. They had been overcome by the world's superpowers. They had forgotten God and were influenced by other religions. They had broken the covenant by their idolatry. God compares God's self as the spring of living water, which the people have forsaken. They had dug their own cisterns that cannot hold water, and they are left with no hope. We live in a very different time today, but we still have a tendency to dig our own cisterns and provide for ourselves without trusting God.

I remember a cistern at my grandmother's house that held water that the gutters from the roof fed to the cistern. She had no refrigeration, so the butter and milk and perishable foods were lowered into the cistern to keep cool. This worked until the rains did not come and the water was not replenished. This cistern was never like the spring of living water that could be relied upon forever. We humans try to be independent and trust in our own abilities using our own resources to provide for our needs. But that is not what God wants.

Life becomes so much more rewarding when we let go and let God, who loves us infinitely, give direction to our lives and participate with us in our daily walk. How much more desirable it is to look to the spring of living water than trust in our own cisterns!

God, we come into your presence with humility and love. Thank you for your unconditional love, which enriches our spirit and helps us drink from your spring of living water. Amen.

Charter member of Harvester United Methodist Church, Land O' Lakes, FL and one who has journeyed eighty-one years getting better acquainted with God

Morning is breaking. This is the day the Lord has made; let us rejoice and be glad therein. What a wonderful way to start the day. Think of all the opportunity it holds. You can embrace the stillness of a new day unfolding. You can take a little time to wake up and count your blessings, to anticipate what the day holds. You may consider the contacts you will make and the mark that you can leave to bless someone else.

Sometimes the influence you may have on another life might only be the eye contact you make, the smile you offer or your greeting of "Good morning." Sit on your porch and enjoy a cup of coffee. Watch the light and shadow of the rising sun play against the trunk of a tree or the branches of leaves as they begin to take on autumn colors announcing a new season.

The years come and go. We live and love and give and share. We see death make its claims and new babies follow with new hope and enjoyment. We count our blessings and we are thankful for life, for God's love for us, for the ability to read a good book that enriches our life, for being able to create something beautiful. We thank God for the blessing of touching a child's face and singing to them, watching their face absorb the song. It is a breathtaking experience.

You can turn on the music, hear the beauty in actual sound—or your love and thoughts can create their own music. All the gifts of love and challenge; of hard work, sacrifice, and endurance teach us the wonderful lessons of life. They help us grow and increase in wisdom and insight. This we gain one day at a time, morning upon morning as we live and move and have our being.

Dear God, thank you for your love. Amen.

In many scriptures God reminds the people, "I am the Lord your God, who brought you out of Egypt, out of the land of slavery." God fed them manna and provided for their needs. God did not forsake them. Over the years they were influenced by the strangers they encountered as they were captured and taken into Babylonian exile. God did not leave them—but they left God.

Thousands of years have passed and still we do the same thing. God gives us free choice and lets us exercise that choice. God releases us to our own will. We make choices and try to live our lives according to our own thinking. We forget God and God's love for us. It is only when we start to sink in our own mire that we cry out for help. This is the story of our search for God and God trying to reveal God's self to us and to establish a loving relationship with us.

To ignore God, to forget God, to put distance between us and God—this is the pathway of disappointment. When we forget to love God with all our hearts and our neighbors as ourselves, we lose our way.

God desires—cries out, even—for us to listen. God desires—cries out, even—for us to follow God. God even promises the "finest of wheat" and "honey from the rock." Surely, in the midst of all the voices around us with their competing claims—surely we can heed the voice of God. God loves us without restraint, the way good parents love their children. God longs for us to love God in return. To love and be loved is a natural response. May we hear God's voice, follow God's lead, and be blessed with God's finest wheat and honey from the rock.

God, we feel your loving presence in our lives. Be with us this day, that we may be your presence in the world. Amen.

People in the times of the early church walked or rode animals to get from place to place. A long journey meant that they might have to search for a resting place at night. They sometimes slept with other traveling groups and caravans or with armies.

Because they were so vulnerable as travelers, they were encouraged to show hospitality to others, and to entertain strangers in their midst. In entertaining strangers, God says, they could well be entertaining angels unaware. They were encouraged to have sympathy for prisoners and for people who were suffering. They were taught to honor their marriage and to keep their lives clean from the love of money, to be content with what they had and to understand that God would not leave or forsake them.

We say with confidence that God is our helper and that we will not be afraid. It takes a lot of trust to live this attitude. We may suffer at the hands of our enemies, but we are assured that if we give God first place that God will never forsake us. Our spirits will be fed and lifted up and we will be enriched for eternity.

Hebrews tells us that if we Christians love each other the way God loves us, then our love will overflow and encompass others. And when that happens, we are living in constant praise of God. Jesus Christ, the one who is "the same yesterday and today and forever," will lead us into deeper discipleship and deeper praise. Through Christ, we can continually offer praise to God.

Loving God, we lift our hearts to worship you and to say thank you for your love and help in sustaining us. May we respond by loving you in return and loving each other as we journey through life. In Jesus' name. Amen.

The scripture in Hebrews is clear: Let love dictate your actions. When you see strangers, look upon them as God's children. Put them at ease if you can. Communicate to them a spirit of caring and concern. Reach out, if only with a smile. You never know the concerns or hurts they may be carrying. If you can somehow touch their spirit with awareness, gentleness, and kindness, you have made contact beyond the physical level. Perhaps you can reach their spirit no matter how briefly, so they will be enriched and lifted up.

Caring for my husband as he struggled with Alzheimer's, I was astounded by the people God put in my way to help care for *me*. Some were there with a kind word when I needed it most. Others brought food that nourished me and my husband. Still others seemed to know just when to call or stop by. And all of them witnessed to me of the love God has lavished on the world.

This is what God can do through us: God can spread God's love to our brothers and sisters. If we are made in the image of God, we share a kinship in the spirit that allows us to worship God in spirit and in truth. This is what God wants from us, to love God with all the love God has given us. We become one together when we share God's love with each other. A smile, a gentle touch, a kind word, and loving deed can make all the difference.

God has so many ways to bless us. Let us rejoice and praise God.

Take my heart, my hands, my love, dear God, and bless them to honor you and to serve others. Amen.

On one occasion when Jesus was going to the house of a leader of the Pharisees to eat a meal on the sabbath, they were watching him closely.

This is one of the experiences Jesus had wherever he went. It's a simple statement—they were watching him closely—but their watching was loaded with scrutiny, doubt, criticism, and distrust. He was tested by Satan. He was interrogated by the governing authorities. He was betrayed by Judas. He was denied by Peter. Always, always, he was carefully watched.

Yet still Jesus went about his teaching, no matter whether it was well received or thoroughly rejected. He warned people about placing themselves too high on the guest list, lest they be asked to go to a "lower" place. He said—to people who didn't really want to hear it (people very much like us)—that the exalted would be humbled and the humble exalted. He rewrote the guest list by urging people to invite not only their friends who could repay their hospitality, but also the "poor, the crippled, the lame, and the blind."

Jesus knew that he was being watched. He used every opportunity to teach about the meaning of life, to encourage people to live life for others. He challenged people to love God and serve neighbor. Do this, Jesus says, and the way will be opened for that day when the kingdom will come.

After all these years, we sometimes still don't get it. We judge, criticize, mistrust, and doubt. Yet Jesus keeps inviting us to love God and serve others. When we hear and accept that invitation, we are drawn closer to God and to one another.

Gracious God, we want to respond to your love by being loving to your children. Help us to see each other in the light of your love for us and love each other accordingly. Amen.

Humility is valued not only by Christianity but by all the world's major religions. Presidents and poets, athletes and generals, popes and rabbis all write of the importance of humility. In the life of faith, humility is seen as a critical key to a closer relationship with God.

Humility, some religious authors write, is essential to the spiritual life because it helps you to know where you come from, to see where you are going, and to remember before whom you will ultimately stand. This humility, however, comes not from putting yourself down or from downplaying who you are. Humility is not a matter of choosing a seat at the table that is lower, in hopes of being asked to come up to a higher place.

True humility is that which *frees us from preoccupation* with ourselves and thus frees us to be present to God and present with others. This is the kind of humility Jesus refers to in Luke. When we put self aside and think of others instead of wanting the place of honor for ourselves, we are responding to Jesus' teachings.

In our life's walk, we recognize the arrogance of someone who is always grabbing first place or who wants to feed his own ego. In this kind of arrogance, one person must win and the other must lose. Happiness for an arrogant person is fleeting. It is only in knowing what it means to walk humbly with God (Micah 6:8) that true happiness is found.

Jesus says, "For all who exalt themselves will be humbled, and all who humble themselves will be exalted." Seek humility. Lead a life free of preoccupation with yourself. Walk humbly with God.

We want to be a reflection of your love, O God. Make us humble. Show us the way to walk with you. Amen.

Allowing God to Shape our Lives

AUGUST 30–SEPTEMBER 5, 2010 • DAVID M. WILSON

MONDAY, AUGUST 30 ～ *Read Jeremiah 18:1-11*

As a child, I recall visiting my aunt, a full-blooded Cherokee and a master Cherokee potter. She helped revive the ancient art of Cherokee pottery in Oklahoma, studying designs and the traditional way that Cherokees created their pottery.

Each of my aunt's pieces of pottery is unique. She prides herself in knowing that her work—of all sizes, shapes, and colors—is unique. As her nephew, I am proud of her and her work.

Jeremiah went to the potter's house and there he saw the potter working at his wheel. This reading gives me a glimpse of how God has created God's people. Like the potter, God has fashioned each of us into different beings. God has been intentional; no two of us human beings are alike. God says to Jeremiah, "Can I not do with you, O house of Israel, just as this potter has done?" We have been fashioned and created out of the image of God, who created us so that we may be the vessels for the transformation of God's world.

God, show me your image in each person I see today. Amen.

Conference superintendent of the Oklahoma Indian Missionary Conference, and member of the Choctaw Nation of Oklahoma

As a preacher, it seems that I am always on alert for sermon illustrations, especially those that relate to Native American culture. My aunt and my cousin, both potters, came to a conference retreat to teach a course on making pottery. While observing the ease with which my aunt and cousin making pottery, I asked my aunt a question. "What happens if the pottery doesn't come out like you wanted?

My aunt replied, "When I begin to make a piece of pottery and take the clay in my hands, it sometimes has a mind of its own and does what it wants. At that point I work and rework the clay with my hands until I get the shape I want."

As Jeremiah watched the potter at work, he saw that the piece the potter was making spoiled in the hands of the potter. Rather than becoming aggravated or starting over (as I have done before), the potter simply took the piece of clay and reworked it into another vessel, as it seemed good to him.

The prophet reminds us of this metaphor of God as the potter and God's people as the clay. While we often have our own ideas of how we will serve God and God's people, God reworks us and uses us as God sees fit. For some, God may refashion one time. For others, God may refashion over and over again.

Who of us has not had regrets over something that we did or did not do in our faith journey? What would we give to "do over"? God allows us to care for those regrets through the forgiveness that is offered through Christ. God also allows us "do overs" as we listen to God's prompting and allow God to reform, remold, and refashion our lives for the good of God's world.

What keeps you from allowing God to refashion and remold your life?

Today's technology enables us to be in touch with one another every moment of the day. The Internet, cell phones, iPods—all conspire to eliminate a person's attempts to be left alone. When I get online to check e-mails or to work, persons on my buddy list and those not on my list, know that I am online. In the midst of some activities, there are times when we desire not to be found, to enjoy the solitude of a moment. Sometimes I need to be left alone while working online!

The psalmist did not have to deal with technology in his time. However, he recognized early on that no matter where he goes, what he does, and what he says, God knows his business. It is as if the psalmist says, "God can even finish my sentences for me!" The psalmist recognizes that God knows when he sits down, knows his thoughts, and knows everything about him.

The psalmist describes a most intimate relationship with his Creator. He is overwhelmed by the Creator's desire to have such an intimate relationship with him. The psalmist responds, "Such knowledge is too wonderful for me!"

Despite the need and desire to be left alone at times, this reading from Psalm 139 serves as a powerful reminder of God's desire to be in relationship with God's people.

Relationships are important to most Native Americans. *All my relations* is the phrase that we utter as we enter the sacred lodges. The phrase means that all relations are remembered in our ceremonies.

We may wonder why God would desire a relationship with us. We may ask, "Who am I to deserve the love of God?" Our answer comes in the form of God's greatest gift—Jesus Christ.

What distractions keep you from experiencing God's love?

From Wakan Tanka, the Great Spirit, there came a great unifying life force that flowed in and through all things—the flowers of the plains, blowing winds, rocks, trees, birds, animals—and it was the same force that had been breathed into the first man. Thus all things were kindred and brought together by the Great Mystery." These were the words spoken long ago by a great Ponca Chief, Luther Standing Bear.

Chief Standing Bear's words remind me of the words of the psalmist. All around is the beauty of what God has created. He is unable to separate any of God's creation. Like the psalmist, Standing Bear seeks to acknowledge and praise God despite the fact that the work of God cannot be described or explained. Yet so great is God's creation, the psalmist has to try to describe it, has to acknowledge its greatness to God.

The work of God, the Great Mystery, is so wondrous that the psalmist can only begin to summarize the work of God. "How weighty to me are your thoughts, O God! How vast is the sum of them!" Even if the psalmist tries to count the thoughts of God, he cannot.

The Great Mystery is that unifier of our souls, our minds, and our hearts. It matters not that we cannot understand or fathom the nature of God. All we are called to do is to recognize the awesome and magnificent nature of our God and let God continue to do what God knows is best for us.

Both Standing Bear and the psalmist acknowledge that although the ways of God cannot be explained, what matters is that we acknowledge God's presence in our lives and in the lives of those around us. God remains ever present, ever loving, ever true.

Creator God, may we trust in your ever-present mysterious ways each day of our lives. Amen.

This most personal letter written by Paul presents a rare opportunity to read something he wrote that we have almost intact. Paul writes to Philemon, one of his Christian converts, after Paul encountered Onesimus, one of Philemon's slaves.

Slavery in the Paul's time was pervasive. While slavery in Roman times was not race-based (as it was later in the United States), it was nevertheless cruel, abusive, and degrading. But Paul does not come right out and tell Christians to release their slaves. This is quite troubling. We might expect Paul, who believed that following Christ meant becoming a new person, to demand that Philemon free Onesimus. Some commentators say the reason Paul did not call for Onesimus to be freed was his earnest belief that Jesus' return was so close at hand that his coming would take care of slavery.

Instead, Paul asks Philemon to take Onesimus back as "no longer a slave, but more than a slave, a beloved brother." He urges Philemon to reconcile with Onesimus and welcome Onesimus as he would welcome Paul.

Paul encourages Philemon to be reconciled with Onesimus, to start over, to be willing to do something radically different. This short book of Philemon reminds us that we are all brothers and sisters in Christ. As brothers and sisters, we are called to look at our relationships in new ways and to be reconciled with one another.

With whom in your family, your church, or your work do you need to be reconciled? What stands in the way of this reconciliation? What help do you need from God or other Christians to begin this reconciliation?

This passage from the Gospel of Luke is a difficult one. Jesus comes across as harsh, demanding that those around him give up everything to follow him. He asks them to be willing to live under the threat of death and to suffer. They must give up their possessions. How can any person deny his or her family to follow?

Samuel Checote was one of those who gave up everything to follow Christ. The Muscogee Creek citizen traveled with his people during the forced removal to Indian Territory. The government and church had been hard on his people before and after the removal. So, when his people set up their government in Indian Territory, one of the first laws they enacted was to make it a penal offense to become a Christian. The penalty for converting was forty lashes.

Despite the law, the young Checote would still preach and teach the gospel. He was caught preaching one day and the Creek Light horsemen began to administer the penalty. As they whipped him, they demanded, "Will you give up your Christ? Checote replied, "You may whip me, but nothing can separate me from my Lord and Savior Jesus Christ!"

Samuel was echoing Jesus' words on the way to crucifixion. Those who followed weren't really sure where he was going. Jesus reminds the people that there are costs involved in following him. It is not an easy task or an easy life. However, Christian people should not be afraid of the cost and sacrifice of following Christ. Even when we falter and fail, Jesus the Christ walks before us and behind us to lead us and to pick us up along the journey!

Who do you know who has made sacrifices for their faith?
What sacrifices have you been called to make for God?

Samuel Checote went on to become a great leader in the Methodist church and in the Muscogee Creek tribe. He was licensed as a pastor at the first session of the Oklahoma Indian Missionary Conference. He presented a resolution that year to translate the scriptures into the Muscogee Creek language.

As a Methodist Church elder, Samuel was responsible for creating many churches among his people. He also became the Principal Chief among his people. One of his first actions was to work toward absolving the law that made it a penal offense to become a Christian. The law was absolved a short time later. Today the second largest number of Indian Methodist churches in Oklahoma is among the Muscogee Creek people.

Samuel Checote suffered for the sake of his people. Despite the harsh treatment by the early missionaries, Checote himself understood the true nature of Christ to be that of love, compassion, and mercy. That is what he wished to share with his people about Christ.

That is what God calls each of us to do. God calls us to look beyond our comfort zones, our safety zones, and ourselves. God calls us to be the vessels of love, compassion, and mercy for those who have not experienced Jesus the Christ.

Chief Dan George, a former chief of the Tsleil-Waututh Nation in the Burrard Inlet, British Columbia, tribe once said, "My friends, how desperately do we need to be loved and to love. . . . With it we are creative. With it we march tirelessly. With it, and with it alone, we are able to sacrifice for others." With the love of Christ, we march on.

Creator God, we march on with you today, vessels of your love. Amen.

Standing in the Gap

SEPTEMBER 6–12, 2010 • MARGARET FLEMING

MONDAY, SEPTEMBER 6 ~ *Read Luke 15:1-2*

This fellow welcomes sinners.

Jesus is right in the middle of a struggle between the haves and the have-nots. The haves are the scribes and Pharisees, who believe they have already received all the grace they need. They have become self-reliant and proud, taunting Jesus for his choice of dinner companions. They are lost, and yet do not know it.

It is the have-nots—"the sinners"—who recognize their need for God's grace. Society constantly reminds them that they are not good enough, not worthy, and so their hearts are open and receptive to God's love. They are lost, and know it full well.

I sense that same tension within the church. The pews in our churches and the love in our hearts are too often reserved for friends and family. We rebuff the shy greetings of strangers. We ignore the poor and snub the socially outcast. A dear friend of mine, who is a convicted felon and whose wild appearance belies his gentle heart, refuses to attend church anymore having been so often rejected there. I long to invite him to go with me, and yet I worry that there are those who might wound him with their stares. I am caught, like Jesus, in the middle of the struggle between the haves and the have-nots.

Gracious Jesus, you have felt the push and pull of the crowd. You have endured the judgment of the mob. You know the anger factions that seek to rip apart your very body, the church. Open our eyes, that we might see you in all of creation. Give us words of peace for those rejected by the world. Amen.

A life-long Episcopalian and member of All Saints Episcopal Church in Montgomery, AL, serving as an Assistant Attorney General and Chief of the Constitutional Defense Division of the Alabama Attorney General's Office

Which one of you, having a hundred sheep and losing one of them, does not leave the ninety-nine in the wilderness and go after the one that is lost until he finds it?

As a little girl on shopping excursions with my mother, I would sometimes wander away from her watchful eye. She taught me that if I ever became separated from her—in a crowded department store, for example—I should simply stand still and wait for her to find me. It was an act of radical trust. I knew that my mother loved me and that she would not stop seeking until she found me. And so I was always content to stand still and wait for her. I remember a store clerk seeing me standing alone and asking if I was lost. "No," I responded, "I'm just waiting for my mother." I was never hesitant to obey that rule. Time after time, she sought me out and found me.

This passage from Luke comes in response to the grumbling Pharisees and their failure to attend to the weak and poor. The stories Jesus offers are wondrous stories of God's divine mercy and unbounded joy, God's deep commitment to searching for us until we are found.

When our cares and concerns distract us and separate us from God, God calls us to be still and wait. God never stops searching for us, and God's loving presence will find us, if we relax and let the anxious voices inside us calm down.

Waiting for God in this manner requires radical trust. We must believe that our gentle Savior desires our company. We must know in our hearts that we are the beloved of God. We must believe that God desires to find us, even more than we desire to be found. We must trust that if we wait, God will come to us and carry us home.

Loving Shepherd, help me to be aware today, when my cares crowd around me, that you are seeking me. Quiet my anxious heart, I pray, to rest in you. Amen.

Or what woman having ten silver coins, if she loses one of them, does not light a lamp, sweep the house, and search carefully until she finds it?

We are not told why "all the tax collectors and sinners" were drawn to Jesus. We only know his gentle and encouraging response to them: Jesus affirms their worth. They are as precious as silver, and God puts everything aside to seek them out. What gracious words for the ears of those who feel worthless and lost—even as they are seeking God, God is seeking them!

The Creator of heaven and earth never stops seeking any of us. God longs to establish any equally close relationship with those we find it most difficult to love—those who abuse the innocent, and even those who rape, kill, torture, or neglect. How is it possible that the God of the universe, in a display of infinite compassion, actively seeks them? What is it God sees in them? Is it possible that God loves them with all the passion and longing that is extended to us? Is there a place at God's holy table for those who have wandered so far from grace?

Often in my prayers, I remember the victims of injustice and oppression. I neglect, however, to pray for the powerful oppressors—those who long for God's peace, yet whose passion for God has been misdirected and whose souls are clouded. We must be vigilant in our prayer for such persons, for their transformation is necessary if God's will is to be done on earth, as in heaven.

Gracious God, you proved your love for us, in that while we were yet sinners, Christ died for us. Help us to extend our hearts to others, so that your infinite goodness and mercy may be manifested to all. Amen.

Fools say in their hearts, "There is no God."

How disillusioned and corrupt God's people have become! The strong devour people "as they eat bread." They are without focus. Their hearts are restless for a God who has ceased to exist for them, and their lack of faith manifests itself in acts of cruelty and self-centeredness.

It is easy to lose our focus when the problems of our everyday lives crowd around us. We put off contemplation and reflection as things we'll do when the chaos around us ceases, when we feel more like praying, when we are less stressed, less anxious. We surround ourselves with the noises of telephones and televisions and computers—even the voices of friends—simply to drown out the still small voice that calls to us from the God-shaped chasm that is within us. When we do take time out for a moment of prayer, we hurry through it. Our lips move but our distracted minds wander back to our earthly cares.

We should not be surprised at the weeds that spring up in our soul's garden, take root there, and produce the fruits of darkness—pride, envy, lust, greed, sloth, gluttony, anger. We should not be surprised when we rebuke ourselves time after time at the end of the day for losing our tempers, or for overeating, or for our rising credit card debt. Our lips may acknowledge God, but our very lives have begun to deny God's existence.

Merciful Savior, my passion for you is the thing that will bring me back to life and complete me. How often have I left your daily invitations to join you in life's journey unopened—like junk mail? Don't stop seeking me. Pursue me, for I long to be found by you. Amen.

I looked, and lo, the fruitful land was a desert, and all its cities were laid in ruins before the Lord, before his fierce anger.

These passages describe a God filled with fury and destructive force. It is hard to comprehend that this God of wrath is the same gentle Shepherd who guards us from harm. However, anger and love can be two sides of the same passion.

I had just moved into a new house. I sat down before the gas fireplace, ignited the logs, and dimmed the lights to enjoy the firelight. My eleven-year-old cat, who had never to my knowledge seen fire before that moment, joined me on the floor.

I watched as the flames danced in her curious eyes. Without warning, she jumped headlong into the fire. As she landed on the hot brick ledge above the blaze, I leapt to turn off the gas logs in the pitch-black room.

I then did what any good mother would do—I climbed into the fireplace, stuck my head up the chimney, and grabbed wildly in the darkness. Just as the cat jumped down into the tiny space between the fireplace bricks and the brick wall, my hand closed around one hind leg. I stood up and lifted the sooty cat with my sooty hand.

As the reality of the danger set in, my anger began to shake me from head to toe. I was furious! I had almost lost her to a black abyss between two brick walls that could easily have taken her life. I was amazed at the breadth of my anger, which I later realized was directly proportional to my love for her.

I came that night to understand Jeremiah's intensity in a surprising and different way.

Loving Shepherd, your passion for us is beyond our imagining. We cannot fathom the pain you experience when we are apart. Forgive us when we stray, and bring us safely home. Amen.

For my people are foolish. . . . They are skilled in doing evil, but do not know how to do good.

Recently I spent the afternoon with friends at Callaway Gardens, near Pine Mountain, Georgia. Relaxing on the beach, we were delighted to see a mother goose with her young. As the geese wandered toward us, a toddler approached and tried to pet the young ones. The protective mother goose responded as one might expect, and the toddler ran away in tears.

Also watching were some older boys, around nine or ten years old. Amused by the fury of Mother Goose, the boys began to prod the young geese. Mother Goose ran wildly at them. They laughed and tormented the young geese with new enthusiasm. Within me, I sensed anger rising. The abuse of the weak by those in power stirs my wrath. Before I could speak, one friend's voice rose, more contained than my own voice would have been: "Boys. That's enough. Stop."

Her gentle reproof was born of a deep compassion for the suffering mother goose, and her tone communicated the anguish in her heart. The boys' enthusiasm soon waned, and they ceased their campaign of terror. They were good boys, and had needed only a gentle reminder.

Afterwards, I thought how great God's wrath must be against us when we abuse our power and when we exploit the poor to maintain our extravagant and comfortable lives. And yet, I could also hear God's ever-present, tender, and welcoming words: "Come unto me, all you that are weary and are carrying heavy burdens, and I will give you rest." (Matt. 11:28).

Gentle Savior, you call us to be your firm voice in the darkness. Forgive us for our failure to stand with you beside the victims of hunger, injustice, and oppression. Give us courage to speak your compassionate words of justice and mercy. Amen.

Christ Jesus came into the world to save sinners—of whom I am the foremost.

Paul's transformation was radical. He was renewed, conformed to the image of Christ. His old behaviors—"a blasphemer, a persecutor, and a man of violence"—were stripped away. He was made new and given a vital ministry. Despite the indwelling of God's Spirit and the fruit of his transformation, however, Paul never lost sight of his need for God's grace. Paul knew that it was not through works that he was made new each day, but by God's grace.

It is part of the great mystery of God, that as we become more aware of our belovedness in God's eyes, we are also more keenly aware of our own undeserving nature. The more we are conformed to the image of Christ, the more convinced we are of our need for God's forgiveness. To live with both—to humbly acknowledge our undeserving nature even as we are embraced by our loving God—is to experience the fullness of God's grace and love.

God's grace bridges the gap between grace-filled sinners and self-righteous persecutors, and between those who are in power and those who are oppressed. It takes courage to stand with God in the gap, acknowledging our failings while proclaiming God's love for all. But that is the gift we bring to the world. The story of our brokenness and God's constant mercy is our part in the ministry of reconciliation.

Loving God, it is your healing grace that the world craves. Grant us courage today to stand with you in the gap, admitting our faults and proclaiming our belovedness, that we might demonstrate for others the hope of reconciliation and the promise of your mercy. Amen.

It's Sunday . . .
But Jesus Is Coming!

SEPTEMBER 13–19, 2010 • JAMES N. WATKINS

MONDAY, SEPTEMBER 13 ~ *Read Jeremiah 8:18–9:1*

Author Tony Campolo's most famous message declares, "It's Friday, but Sunday's comin'."

Jesus has been unjustly charged and condemned to die. It's Friday, but Sunday's comin'! He has been brutally beaten, stripped and nailed to a cross and sealed in a tomb. It's Friday, but Sunday's comin'!

The message builds to a powerful conclusion when Pastor Campolo simply shouts, "It's Friday!" and the congregation responds, "But Sunday's comin'!"

But it's Sunday and throughout the world today an estimated 923 million people will go hungry. Over 40,000 children will die from preventable hunger and disease. Two thousand people will contract HIV/AIDS. Our world still faces death and cruelty following the resurrection of Jesus Christ.

The people of Israel were living in the gap as well—between God dramatically freeing them from Egyptian captivity and awaiting the promised Messiah. So, in the meantime, they cry out "Is the LORD not in Zion? Is her King no longer there?"

In this week's scripture readings, we walk the long journey between God's promise and its fulfillment. But there is hope! To paraphrase Dr. Campolo, "It's Sunday . . . but Jesus is comin'!"

God of hope and promise, lift our eyes to see you at work in this world. Amen.

Communications pastor at College Wesleyan Church in Indiana, author and speaker

Yesterday we meditated on the gap between God's promises and the fulfillment of those promises. In today's reading, the psalmist struggles with two issues that still torment believers: unanswered prayer and unpunished evil.

Enemies have invaded Israel, defiled the Temple, and reduced Jerusalem to rubble—despite fervent prayer. And God seems in no hurry to punish those kingdoms that refused to acknowledge him.

Today we pray and anoint the sick—and they still die. We pray for God to stem violence and terrorism—and the killings continue. We pray for justice for the poor and weak, for the corrupt to be brought down—and the wicked prosper.

In Psalm 79, the writer is tempted to give up. "This is what the wicked are like—always carefree, they increase in wealth. Surely in vain have I kept my heart pure; in vain have I washed my hands in innocence" (vv. 12-13). Have you ever felt that way? I have.

But the psalmist held on to hope that someday prayers would be answered; evil would be punished. The psalmist believes this: God, whose fierce love for us does not tolerate our faithfulness also has such great compassion for us that God won't let us go, no matter what.

Finally, our reading today concludes: "Help us, O God of our salvation, for the glory of your name; deliver us and forgive our sins for your name's sake." It may seem an odd twist—the psalmist here indicates that what's really at stake while we wait for God's deliverance is God's own reputation and character! How can God, who loves us so much in spite of our infidelity, not rise to the opportunity to save God's own name? Deliverance, then, is sure.

God, help us to look through our current situation to the love and mercy you pour out on us. Amen.

Waiting is hard work! Sitting in a "waiting" room mindlessly thumbing through old magazines as you wait for the nurse to call out the name of your sick child. The numbness of waiting for test results that will change your life. Waiting for a teenager to come home. Waiting for God to bring a prodigal child home.

We're not alone in our struggles with waiting. Psalm 4 is categorized as an "individual lament."

Others of the Psalms cry out, "Do not hide your face from your servant; answer me quickly, for I am in trouble" (69:17); "They cried for help, but there was no one to save them—to the LORD, but he did not answer" (18:41); "My God, my God, why have you forsaken me?" (22:1).

Commentators suggest Psalms 3 and 4 are written against the background of Absalom's rebellion against his father David as well as betrayal of some of David's former supporters who have turned his "glory into shame."

But the psalmist provides hope and some practical things to do while we wait:

1. Know that the Lord has set us apart as his own.
2. Search your heart for any anger or sin related to this waiting period.
3. In your anger—or frustration—do not sin.
4. Be silent; listen for God's encouragement and instruction.
5. Trust in the Lord.

While David is in the midst of conflict, while he is waiting for God to act, he is confident that one day his heart will be filled with "greater joy." He will "lie down and sleep in peace; for you alone, O LORD, make me lie down in safety."

Father, remind us that we are yours, and help us to trust in you as we wait for you to act. Help us, by faith, to look forward to a future with "greater joy." Amen.

Yesterday's meditation was based on a psalm that called for God to answer the prayers of the people. Today the scripture petitions God for broader concerns: that all will be saved, that faith requires knowledge of the gospel, that, while we pray for those in power, we must remember that their power is temporal and temporary.

New Testament Christians were living under the occupation of pagan Rome, whose political leaders oppressed the new Christians. And yet, this letter to Timothy asks the faithful to "pray for all who are in high positions" so that Christians "may lead a quiet and peaceable life in all godliness and dignity."

As Martin Luther King Jr. was organizing the civil rights movement against official prejudice in the United States, he urged his followers to make sure they did more praying than protesting. In his letter from the Birmingham jail, he insisted that "self-purification" precede any "direct action."

God's power face-to-face with the world's authority was never more evident than when Laszlo Tokes, a bishop in the Romanian Reformed Church, began speaking out against the Communist regime in his country. When government officials tried to force him out of his church flat and then tried to attack him and his pregnant wife with knives, his supporters peacefully created a ring of protection that grew to thousands. These peaceful, prayerful demonstrations would eventually result in the 1989 collapse of the Communist government.

God, give wisdom and guidance to leaders worldwide. And give us wisdom and guidance to grow in the knowledge of faith. Amen.

Many of Jesus' parables are as current today as they were two thousand years ago, none more so than this one from Luke 16: "There was a rich man whose manager was accused of wasting his possessions" (NIV).

Millions of people have lost money in the recent worldwide economic crisis. Some of those losses were the result of poor or dishonest management. Other losses were the consequence of, as one legislator accused, "arrogance, incompetence, and greed." And some of the worst losses were the doing of criminals like Bernard Madoff, who swindled individuals and institutions out of billions of dollars.

Luke 16 continues our theme of injustice. But strangely, in this unique parable, Jesus seems to commend the incompetent manager of being "shrewd." In first-century Palestine, it was common for managers or agents of the rich to loan out their masters' money, charging extremely high interest in order to pocket a portion of it for themselves. Some commentators believe the manager in this parable reduced the debt to the principle only and forfeited his own cut. In so doing, he retrieved the rich man's money and ingratiated himself to those to whom he had loaned the money.

In that case, Jesus does not commend the steward for being "unjust," but rather affirms him for acting wisely in the midst of the financial crisis. Jesus' parable, then, seems to be telling us to be prudent in the way we use our money. And yet, there is something more here. God exhorts us to mind the way we handle things both large and small, for following the easy way in the management of both our financial wealth and of our faith will leave us out in the cold.

Lord, guide us in all things. Amen.

Clients of Bernard Madoff, former head of the NASDAQ stock exchange, trusted him to invest their money for a promised ten percent return. Mr. Madoff, however, did not invest those clients' money for over ten years, but paid older clients with newer clients' investments. Inevitably, this so-called Ponzi scheme collapsed, and Madoff pleaded guilty to bilking his clients out of more than 50 billion dollars. Such a sum boggles the mind. But it is worth keeping in mind that Madoff started misusing his clients' funds on a much smaller scale.

First, he set up a *hedge fund*, a particular kind of investment fund open to a limited number of investors and operating outside of the rules and authority of the Securities and Exchange Commission (SEC). Next, Madoff skirted the New York Stock Exchange rules and regulations by using the Cincinnati Stock Exchange to handle electronic buying and selling. He also offered "payments for order flow" at a penny a share for brokerage firms running stock trades through his company. Critics called them simply kickbacks. Essentially, Madoff apparently made a career—and a very large fortune—by cutting corners and criminally mismanaging other people's money.

Most large scandals start small. Innocent flirtation turns to more intimate contact, and eventually to an adultery. The occasional use of drugs or alcohol turns into the regular use of these drugs, and finally ends in a life of addiction. And simply cutting corners financially can one day land a person in prison.

In contrast, Jesus promises, "Whoever can be trusted with very little can also be trusted with much." The little choices determine a lifetime of consequences—good and bad.

Lord, help us to be honest and ethical is all our dealings with our families, businesses, and communities. Amen.

Jesus made a career of drawing distinct lines in the sand: "If you are not for me, you're against me." "You have heard that it was said, 'Do not commit adultery.' But I tell you that anyone who looks at a woman lustfully has already committed adultery with her in his heart." And one of his most famous distinctions: "You cannot serve both God and wealth."

The King James Version uses the word *mammon*, the Greek transliteration of a Hebrew or Aramaic word meaning, "that in which one trusts." United States coins are engraved with the motto, "In God We Trust"; but for many today, a more honest motto might be, "In Money I Trust" or perhaps "In Me I Trust."

In whom do you trust? Jesus makes clear that nothing other than himself and his message are worthy of our trust. "Therefore everyone who hears these words of mine and puts them into practice is like a wise man who built his house on the rock. The rain came down, the streams rose, and the winds blew and beat against that house; yet it did not fall, because it had its foundation on the rock. But everyone who hears these words of mine and does not put them into practice is like a foolish man who built his house on sand. The rain came down, the streams rose, and the winds blew and beat against that house, and it fell with a great crash" (Matt. 7:24-27, NIV).

We can so easily lose our wealth, our strength, and health, or our loved ones. As Christians, we simply cannot ground our faith in anything of this world. So when we are tempted to put our trust in money—or in anything but God—let us remember Jesus' call, over and over again, to trust only in our strong, loving, and gracious God.

God, help me to remember: there is nothing as sure and secure as my relationship with you. Let nothing come between us. Amen.

Hearing God's Voice

SEPTEMBER 20–26, 2010 • WESSEL BENTLEY

MONDAY, SEPTEMBER 20 ~ *Read Jeremiah 32:1-5*

All of us would like to hear God's voice speak audibly and clearly. I suppose most of us would prefer to hear God say things that we would like to hear. I would be thrilled to hear a voice from heaven telling me: "You are loved," "You are blessed," or "You are right." It would great if God told me that my views on contentious issues were without fault. Of course God loves us and blesses us; this is essentially the gospel we proclaim. Now for the challenge: God does not always agree with our perspectives.

In fact, speaking on God's behalf may land us in a great deal of trouble.

The prophet Jeremiah found himself in this predicament. How do you tell a king that God was going to allow his enemies to overthrow him and occupy his land? Can you imagine Jeremiah asking himself whether he heard God wrong or misinterpreted what God had said? Listening to God is a difficult discipline. It involves prayer and discernment—and this is especially true when you are acting as God's mouthpiece for those around you.

Do you know if there is something God wants to tell the world through you? Right now, take some time to focus—really focus—on what God is saying to you. Be prepared, though. Standing up for God's revealed truth may land you alongside Jeremiah, confined to the courtyard of the guard.

Almighty God, I pray that I will hear you speak clearly. Amen.

Minister of the Glen Methodist Church in Pretoria, South Africa, author, and lecturer on ethics at the University of South Africa

Wasn't it enough for God to tell Jeremiah to share bad news with the king? Now God was telling Jeremiah to purchase land that was soon going to fall into Babylonian hands! We have to admire Jeremiah's faith. Not only did he make political enemies, but now he was about to make the worst investment decision of his life—all because God told him to do it.

In today's reading, we further explore what it means to listen to God's voice in the midst of controversy. During my studies, I came across two Latin terms that significantly shaped my theological understanding. The first term is *sub specie temporis* meaning "from the perspective of temporality." The second is *sub specie aeternitatis*, meaning "from the perspective of eternity." I suppose many of the things God says do not make sense to us simply because we do not share God's perspective. From Jeremiah's temporal perspective, purchasing a piece of doomed real estate is a problem. From God's perspective the people of Judah will once again inhabit this land—and that's a promise.

It is not always possible to see our lives from God's perspective, but we must try. As you pray and explore the will of God for your life, trust that God can see further than you can. Hold on to the conviction that God's voice does not come without promise. Yesterday you may have found yourself with Jeremiah in the courtyard of the guard. Today as you obey God's impossible or irrational commands, you may very well find yourself playing your part in that which God sees, but others fail to see.

Almighty God, you call us to do many irrational things—to love our neighbor, to bless our enemies, to deny ourselves, and follow you. We trust that you see what we cannot see. We place ourselves in your hands. Amen.

The psalmist does not hide his assurance of God's presence. He is so certain of God's involvement in his life that he dares to sing aloud, for everyone to hear, placing his confidence in his God. Considering what we shared about Jeremiah in the last few days, we may feel tempted to warn the psalmist not to take these words too lightly. Would the psalmist still be able to sing this song if he were standing in the courtyard of the guard with Jeremiah? Yet, this "celebration of assurance" is every Christian's goal—to live with this measure of conviction that God is truly with us.

A friend of mine once told me that the word *faith* is spelled R-I-S-K. Faith in God is a risky business, but what joy we get when we know that God is near no matter what life throws at us! Not only is God near, but God is our shelter, a place of protection. This kind of faith is easier said than done. In times of crisis people often prefer taking charge of their own lives instead of trusting God with their problems. Both Jeremiah and the psalmist encourage us to practice a faith of surrender, trusting that God is not vindictive or malicious but loving, caring, and concerned for our well-being.

As you have listened to God this week, you may have found yourself in the courtyard of the guard or in a place where you await God's promise of salvation. Today accept the invitation to surrender yourself so that you might find yourself enveloped in God's arms of love and protection.

Almighty God, as I face today's challenges and responsibilities, I give thanks for the assurance of your presence. Give me courage to surrender all into your hands, and with the psalmist, praise you as my refuge and my fortress. Amen.

How do you picture God when you pray? What do you imagine God thinking when you bow your head in prayer? The view of a God who is far away, far removed from this world, implies that God couldn't really be bothered with our prayers. In fact, we would need to earn God's attention by praying correctly, offering the expected sacrifices and performing the right rituals. The psalmist's God does not treat his own prayers like that. This God not only pays attention to our prayers but eagerly awaits them. Furthermore, God promises to respond to the psalmist's prayers even should he find himself in times of trouble.

During this week we have considered different experiences of *hearing God*. Today's reading reminds us that when we pray, God *hears us*. What would our spirituality be if we heard God clearly but had no assurance that God shows interest in our thoughts and feelings? Knowing that God hears his prayers enables the psalmist to proclaim with boldness that he is able to place his trust in God (91:2). The psalmist knows that God listens to his prayers not only on special occasions—at bedtime or at worship— but that God actually anticipates conversation with him.

These words of the psalm are comforting and reassuring: "Those who love me, I will deliver; I will protect those who know my name. When they call to me, I will answer them." The psalmist knows that God is true; God has promised to be true to us as well.

As you take time during this day to hear God speak, picture God eagerly waiting to hear you speak. Pray honestly and with the assurance that God accepts whatever you have to say with a generous measure of love.

Almighty God, I stand in awe at the knowledge that you eagerly await to hear what I have to say. Take my words and thoughts and transform them to be an act of worship. Amen.

Knowing that God speaks to us and having the assurance that God hears our prayers can be like a breath of fresh air in our spiritual walk. It certainly paves the way to have an open and honest conversation with God. Paul speaks to Timothy about another great challenge in our faith—being content. I am constantly aware that my prayers and the prayers of others often imply a general feeling of discontent. Our constant requests for better health, financial success, fruitful relationships or a bigger car suggest that we are not happy with what we have or who we are. What does God say when we offer prayers that center exclusively on our own material "wants"?

This text reminds Timothy that to try to live the godly life is to strive to walk closer to God, to be faithful in our commitment to the Almighty, and to express love without reservation. No material object can achieve this for us. After reading this portion of Paul's letter, I can imagine Timothy's conversation with God changing. The focus of his requests may begin shifting, moving away from asking only for material things. He may be beginning to emphasize his yearning to participate in God's acts of grace, love, and generosity.

How does this passage affect the content of your conversation with God? It might be a good idea to keep your Bible open to this passage as you pray. Glance at it repeatedly during the course of your prayer. Allow it to guide you as you express yourself and listen to God. You may find that as you strive toward the "greater" things that Paul describes, you will grow, becoming more content and thankful for what you have and who you are.

Almighty God, you know my needs and I place them in your hands. I pray that in this day I may become rich in righteousness, godliness, faith, love, endurance, and gentleness. Amen.

Jesus does not give the rich man a name. The beggar is named Lazarus, meaning, "God has helped." In our societies the dynamics seem to be the other way around. We know the rich and powerful by name, but the poor and marginalized are often little more than statistics. The irony in this difference is that we often consider prominent people to be "God-blessed" and those who experience difficult circumstances to be "God-forsaken." Like Paul's admonition in yesterday's reading, in this text Jesus warns that an over-dependence on material things leads to a superficial, and often, lonely life.

Although this is a parable, we can find both the rich man and Lazarus in our communities. We even find these persons in ourselves—the self-absorbed and selfish part of us and the part of us that survives solely on God's grace and providence.

The rich man in Jesus' parable realizes too late that his attention was at the wrong place. If only he had listened when God spoke. He goes so far as to negotiate with God to speak more audibly to his loved ones so that they would be spared this terrible place of desolation. This hell he experiences does not seem to be a place of punishment for a selfish life, but the place where his choices led him. If only he had listened to God, he may have been challenged to love his neighbor more. The rich man's hell is a place of regret. Lazarus, on the other hand, can look back on his life and truly testify to the fact that "God has helped."

As you plan and journey through your day, surrender yourself to God's guidance. It is a blessing to come to the end of the day with little or no regret. It is a blessing to come to the end of the day and celebrate the assurance of God's arms enfolding you.

Almighty God, may my life in this day celebrate your grace and providence. Amen.

What must God do so that we will hear God's voice? To what extremes must God go to get our attention? The rich man pleads with Abraham to make a special effort to warn his brothers about their coming fate. There is an ironic twist to this story. The rich man asks that Lazarus be sent to them to deliver the message, for they will surely listen to him. This is the same Lazarus the rich man failed to notice or flatly ignored. We may want to ridicule the rich man for his lack of insight, but we need to tread here with caution. Do we expect God to speak to us only through a sermon or a church worship service or the reading of the Bible? Maybe we expect something more extravagant, like handwriting on a wall or angels appearing out of nowhere, declaring the will of God.

What if we slowed the pace of our lives long enough to look around us carefully? Perhaps we would not only hear God speak but also act on what we heard.

What is God saying to you when you encounter a person in poverty? Is this not Lazarus speaking to us, bringing a message from God about our commitment to loving our neighbor? God speaks to us constantly through the people we meet, through the situations we face, and in the various activities that define our world. Today is Sunday. In addition to listening for a word from God from the preacher, listen carefully for a word from God through the people with whom you worship.

Almighty God, on this the sabbath day, may your voice speak to me from surprising places and through unexpected people. Amen.

Faithful Remembering

MONDAY, SEPTEMBER 27 ~ *Read Lamentations 1:1-6*

Disaster has befallen the kingdom of Judah. Babylon and its allies have conquered Judah and taken many of its residents into exile in Babylon. A poetic hymn, Lamentations remembers this event and provides a collective liturgy. Some suggest that Lamentations is authored by a woman or group of women. This makes some sense in that women are the "professional" mourners in Middle Eastern society. Indeed, the portrayal of Jerusalem as a princess or bride who has lost her place, her husband, and her protector is an experience with which women of the time would be viscerally familiar.

In a patriarchal society, there is no devastation worse. The woman's life goes on, but she has lost all standing in society. There were commandments that widows and orphans (as well as the stranger in their midst) were to be cared for, but a major charge of the prophets was that Israel had been more than negligent in fulfilling this duty.

The author says the disaster is God's punishment for this negligence of duty. And it is true: Israel's sin and intransigence has made it complicit in the suffering of Israel's people. There is no way around it—Israel has contributed to its own demise. This does not, however, erase all the pain and destruction, the murder and the ruthlessness of Israel's enemies. Even now, God is with God's people.

God, help me to be aware of your presence and your desires for my life, whether I am joyful or grieving, riding high or sinking low. Hold on to me always, I pray. Amen.

Computer programmer and co-owner of Soul Desires Bookstore in Omaha, NE, with wife Susan Davis

Psalm 137 is written from the perspective of those at the other end of the forced march into Babylonian exile. The opening verses are some of the most heartrending and beautiful poetry ever written. One can feel the powerlessness of the people whose only response to the taunting requests of their captors to sing is to refuse to sing, to hang their harps in the trees. Yet, I do not believe they gave up the singing. I would guess that like captives and exiles the world over from slave shacks to concentration camps to "resettlement" villages, people such as the exiled Israelites have gathered in the dark, as far from prying ears of smug captors as possible, and continued to sing.

Why do I think that? Because song is the most potent form of remembering. And verses 5 and 6 are all about remembering. "If I forget you, O Jerusalem, let my right hand wither! Let my tongue cling to the roof of my mouth. . . . " With these declarations of human remembering comes a poke at God. Mount Zion, site of the Temple, center of Jerusalem, "seat of God on earth," God—they all get bundled together by poets and other people. People can substitute one for the other. The poet is declaring the community's faithfulness in remembering not just Jerusalem but God. The implied questions linger: Is God faithful? Does God remember us? After days and weeks and months and years of singing remembrance, the community is asking: "God, can you hear us this far from your temple?"

God of all that is and was and ever shall be, help us to remember that you are not confined to a place or a time or a situation. Open our eyes to your presence in every circumstance in which we find ourselves. Amen.

To what end do we remember? We remember to honor the dead, to learn the lessons of the past, to help define who we are, to fuel a struggle for justice. I would suggest that in the religious context, we also remember to heal and to celebrate in the presence of God.

Without God, remembering can easily be twisted into the stoking of our anger and our lust for power and revenge. We have seen this play out in recent times in the regeneration of memories six hundred years old in the Balkans and the horrific events that followed in Serbia and Kosovo and Croatia. We have seen it in Rwanda. Shiite against Sunni in Iraq. Sometimes I can hear overtones of this in our commemorations of the events of 9/11.

Cognitive studies in recent years have demonstrated that the simple act of thinking about revenge triggers ancient pleasure and reward centers of the brain. The last half of Psalm 137 swiftly descends into the dark pleasures of revenge for the poet, whose unbridled anger leads to a gruesome testament to the dangers of memories maintained with no desire to heal. So fervently is the psalmist remembering (lest we forget) that the poet never hears God speak a word that turns the poem around. This is unusual in the Psalms. Since God seems absent and inattentive to Israel's needs, the poet demands that the least God should do is to remember the vile deeds of the Babylonians and the Edomites who participated in the destruction of Jerusalem. It is a call for God to continue the cycle of revenge and retribution between peoples rather than heal them through God's presence.

Jesus, who in death opened the possibility of life for the whole world—not just for "good" people—unstop our ears when they are full of our angry voices that we may hear your word of peace and reconciliation. Amen.

THURSDAY, SEPTEMBER 30 ~ *Read Luke 17:5-6*

"Increase our faith," the disciples desperately demand of Jesus. Were you to ask me when this imperative was given, I would have said it either happened in the boat during the storm or when Peter was trying to walk on water to Jesus. Luke, however, places the exchange between the disciples and Jesus at a time when things are actually going quite well. Attendance is up. Giving is up.

Jesus is in a teaching mode, however, and has just made his expectations clear. He starts in Luke 16: be obedient to God and not financial success; do not intentionally create the social equivalent of widows by divorcing; care for the needy without the aid of a miracle; if people break the mutual trust of a relationship with you, forgive them regardless of how often they aggrieve you. All these expectations are tough! Where is God in all that? Isn't God supposed to bless the faithful? Increase our faith, indeed!

According to Luke, Jesus' response to this outburst from the disciples is a remarkably obscure lesson about mustard seeds, mulberry trees, and teleportation. Given the lesson of Lazarus and the rich man a short while before, I don't think Jesus is suggesting any supernatural event will occur as a result of the disciples' faithfulness. No teleportation. Rather, faith has a cumulative effect like weeds (mustard) that through the persistence of their small seeds over time can overrun a garden or an orchard, and even push more substantial plants off of the land. Faith is about nitty-gritty, sometimes unpleasant, always persistent, mostly unheralded, oftentimes unrewarded actions at the heart of life.

God of the atom, God of the universe, make your desires known in our living; in the moment-to-moment actions, responses, decisions that are the substance not the surface of our being. Amen.

These verses are ones you will rarely hear preached from a pulpit. Some cultural unpacking is necessary. For most people of the industrialized world, slavery is repugnant at its very core. And for me, growing up in the populist and egalitarian world of the plains, I expect to thank everybody for doing their job. That's just good manners.

But in Jesus' day, slavery was as ingrained in the social fabric as electricity is in ours. Practically everyone either was a slave or owned one. You didn't have to be wealthy to own a slave. A master would not thank a slave nor prepare food for the slave because he or she had already done enough.

In this parable, God is the master and the disciples are the slaves. So what position do we have from which to expect anything of God? Being a faithful slave is not about getting special treatment. On the other hand, being a faithful slave is not about being worthless—just ask the master who needs the work done. It is especially worth noting that, unlike the 1% of the population who were actually wealthy enough to have leisure, most masters toiled right alongside their slaves. In this analogy, God is toiling right along with us.

When we come to the end of the day, do we expect God to prepare our meal? Do we expect milk and honey from God for doing what was our job? Do we act out of our faith in God or out of our faith in a system of rewards?

God, you have blessed us with our lives and the bounty of this world in which there is plenty for all when we have done your work. Help us celebrate your presence and your work. Amen.

We see only glimpses of Timothy's situation in this letter, but I am left with the image of a reluctant evangelist. Perhaps Timothy is facing dissension in the churches assigned to his care. Perhaps he has felt on his shoulder the hand of the law or the hands of sanctioned thugs. Perhaps he has been in jail or knows brothers or sisters in the faith who have died for their beliefs. Whatever the cause, Timothy has been infected with timidity. We can hardly blame him. Our desires for a comfortable life and a successful career reflect his dilemma long ago. I can hear his thoughts: *Where is God in this? Why are we suffering? I'm not sure this is what I signed on for. Where is the milk and honey?*

The author seeks to reassure this reluctant evangelist. In a graceful and careful way, Timothy is given the tool of remembering. First the author remembers the relationship with Timothy and the grief Timothy had at their parting. Then he remembers the sincere faith of Timothy, his grandmother Lois, and his mother Eunice. These heaped-up memories are not to pour guilt on Timothy but to point him to a way of remembering his relationships and his faith. Timothy is reminded to rekindle the gift of God's healing that is within him. Here our readings come full circle to the inverse of Psalm 137. The benefit of remembering with God is the restoration of the divine spark within us. We can think that spark is all but extinguished when times are hard and we are worn down and despairing . . . but be assured, it is not.

God of grace-filled memories and memories that heal, help us to remember the powerful faith of our forebears and, at times, of ourselves. Bring us again, we pray, from timidity to courage. Amen.

This book was probably authored by someone writing in the early second century in the spirit of Paul, as was the acceptable practice of the time. At this time, different camps of believers held to widely different belief systems. And, also during this time, official persecution of Christians was escalating. And so the questions arose: Why do Christians suffer? Is it for our sins, or do we suffer for the gospel? What is it in our lives—or in our faith—that brings so much suffering?

When you read the whole letter you see the author's great concern with right teachings, with Timothy's heritage of faith, and with his nurture by the divine gifts of love and self-discipline. But the book states that Timothy had to put his Christian heritage at risk for the sake of the gospel.

The author makes an astonishing claim: "For this gospel I was appointed . . . and for this reason I suffer as I do." The call of the gospel can, in fact, lead to suffering in one's life. Though sin brings suffering, so too can the gospel. This is not to say that the gospel call will invariably mean suffering. It does mean that the gospel will not deflect suffering. Responding to the divine does not change the realities of the world we live in—hardships come and go, successes rise up and pass away. What changes is our ability to move through it all. Moving forward in love and self-discipline, we always remember the one who "abolished death and brought life and immortality to light."

God, fill us with your spirit living in us. Help us remember to kindle, nurture, and guard in our time, in our days, the power and love and self-discipline you have given us. Amen.

Peace in the Neighborhood

OCTOBER 4–10, 2010 • DAVID JAMES MORENO C.

MONDAY, OCTOBER 4 ~ *Read Jeremiah 29:1, 4-7*

The prophet Jeremiah tells the people of Israel who are in exile in Babylon to build houses, plant gardens, and start families. When I first read this scripture I thought that Jeremiah was telling those in exile to accept their oppression. Exile and the oppression that accompanies it are harsh and ungodly. How can anyone suggest that we accept it?

Throughout history, and today, too many people have lived and continue to live in exile. It is a tragic and harsh reality of our world. Many innocent people have suffered exile: the segregation of African-Americans, the Jewish internment and Holocaust, the Japanese internment of World War II, displacement of indigenous people across the Americas, the atrocities of Darfur.

So I did not understand what the prophet was telling his people. But, a line from the movie *Shawshank Redemption* helped me see what Jeremiah means. In the movie about unjust imprisonment, two friends are talking and one says to the other, "Get busy living, or get busy dying." This is good advice; we all are sometimes in danger of dying from the burden of frustration, anger, and hostility.

When we find ourselves in exile, Jeremiah tells us we must remember that we are not abandoned by God. Listen to the wisdom of the prophet. Work for the welfare of your community; in this you will find peace and you will bring peace to your community.

Lord, be with those living in exile, and help us all embrace your presence in our lives. Amen.

An ordained elder in the Rio Grande Conference of the United Methodist Church serving as a campus minister at the University of Texas Pan American and South Texas College

My mother experienced exile both as a member of her community and as an individual. She was born in Belfast, Ireland in 1920, during a civil war. Random violence from shootings and bombings often killed or injured people. She and her family were persecuted. During World War II, the family home was destroyed in a bombing raid by Nazi war planes. My mother and her family were both exiled and homeless by the cruel reality of war. The pain of exile was prevalent in her stories and in her life.

During the war, my mother met, fell in love with, and married my father. He was a United States soldier stationed in Belfast. After the war, they moved to San Antonio, Texas. Once again she found herself in exile, although this was one of her own choosing. She was away from her home and family, living in a foreign land. My father, a Mexican American, had brought my mother to his predominately Spanish-speaking community. My mother embraced her new home, but it was not Belfast and she had difficulty adapting. She was away from her family and often lonely.

Exile is experienced in different ways. People can be banished from their homes and families, or their countries may be occupied by foreign governments. Moving to a new land, working with people who are different from you, being struck by a debilitating illness—all these can leave us feeling exiled. Despite all our hardships, we can come to understand God is with us. The prophet Jeremiah enlightens us by his words: "Build houses and live in them; plant gardens and eat what they produce. Take wives and have sons and daughters . . ."

My mother lived with the powerful knowledge of God's presence in her life. In it she found guidance, comfort, and purpose. Civil war, world war, separation from her homeland and family—none of this separated her from God.

Lord, let us always know your presence in our lives. Amen.

Two years ago, on May 3, at 6:30 p.m., I received a phone call from my brother. When I answered the phone my brother said simply, "It's over." I knew exactly what he was talking about. I had been expecting the phone call, but still it took me by surprise. My brother was calling to tell me that our mother had just passed away. She had been ill for years; the last few months were strenuous. It was a painful passing.

She died surrounded by those who loved her. My brother, sisters, and several grandchildren were comforting her and praying as the time came. When my brother called and said, "It's over," he wasn't only telling me that our mother had passed away; he was saying that my mother's suffering was over.

She had lived a difficult life. I know she understood Psalm 66 well and she could claim these verses as her own: "For you, O God, have tested us; you have tried us as silver is tried. . . . You laid burdens on our backs. . . . We went through fire and through water."

Yet my mother understood far more of Psalm 66 than just these verses. It's true—she felt heavy burdens on her back. But she also had a deep joy in her heart. She was a wonderful model of what a Christian should be. She taught me that being a Christian was more than a Sunday duty; I learned that Christianity is a way of life. She was a generous woman, helping strangers and those less fortunate.

Despite all her hardships, my mother loved life. She enjoyed family nights of fun and games, loved to tease others and be teased, and confidently knew that God's love and presence were her strength and comfort. She embodied the psalmist's call to make a joyful noise, show glory, and give praise.

Make a joyful noise to God. Sing the glory of God's name. Say to God, "How awesome are your deeds!"

Faith is a frequent topic of sermons, Bible studies, and discussions among Christians. Usually the reference is to our faith in God. But here Paul talks about God's faith in us.

For the past several years, I have had the pleasure of visiting my dear friend Manuel Guerra on a regular basis. Manuel, retired and in his late eighties, is one of the board members who signs checks for our campus ministry. For me, going to Manuel's home for signatures is really just an excuse for me to visit with him. During our visits, we have talked about many things—church, ministry, politics, family. Our talks have been humorous, touching, heartfelt. However, I do not recall our ever talking about faith. Still, I know he has faith in God, and I know God has faith in Manuel.

Manuel has experienced his share of difficulties. There are two that changed his life greatly. He suffered a serious accident while in the army, and he deals with the physical pain to this day. That is difficult. But perhaps his greatest sorrow is the loss of his wife, Dalinda. Manuel and Dalinda loved each other deeply. He misses her in ways he can't talk about.

These kinds of loss—of physical health, of a life-long love—often lead people to doubt God's presence in their lives. It is at these times when our faith may falter.

But the apostle Paul tells us that God has faith in us—no matter what. Because I know Manuel, I know Paul's words to be true. I am struck by the joy that radiates from Manuel. His joy is a visible sign of his faith in God and God's faith in him. It is a blessing to know Manuel. It is this blessing—God's faith in us—that gives us the strength, wisdom, and courage to endure life's hardships and serve God despite those circumstances.

God, help me understand your faith in me and help me respond faithfully to your love. Amen.

The ten people Jesus healed in this scripture must have suffered greatly. Because of their affliction, they were outcasts of their community. They approach Jesus before he enters the village because they were not allowed in the village. They must have looked appalling to the people around them. They had no place to bathe; their clothes were old, torn, and dirty. Their open wounds looked horrible and smelled bad.

Yet Jesus has great compassion for these people and does not reject them as the rest of society had. They speak briefly and Jesus sends them away healed. As the ten are leaving, one realizes that he has been healed, and he returns to Jesus. He falls at Jesus' feet and thanks God for healing him.

Of the ten, the Samaritan is the only one to come back to Jesus. The other nine do not return to offer their gratitude. I have always wondered why Jesus would be concerned with the actions of the nine. I believe that Jesus was trying to make a point when he asked about the other nine. Jesus not only wanted to heal the lepers; he wanted to be in relationship with them.

Jesus knew what was at stake for these people, and he was offering them much more than a cure for their affliction. He was offering them a better relationship with God. This relationship offered forgiveness of sins, healing of inner wounds that were cast on them by society, and comfort in dealing with the other burdens of life. Only in relationship with God can we receive these gifts. That is perhaps why Jesus asked, "Where are the other nine?" It is an invitation to accept God's relief from burdens and to receive healing of illness and inner wounds.

Accept God's forgiveness. Praise God, celebrate God, offer God's peace and be grateful.

Thank you, Creator God, for the healing and the peace you have given to me and to the world. Amen.

SATURDAY, OCTOBER 9 ~ *Read Luke 17:11-19*

I have never had a serious illness so I cannot relate to the suffering and pain of the lepers. Their suffering was particularly harsh during the time of Jesus. If you suffered from a physical aliment or an illness with visible wounds like leprosy, you were chastised and alienated from the community. In the story we read today from the Gospel of Luke, ten lepers approach Jesus so that Jesus would heal them. Jesus does not turn them away as society does. With no sign of any rejection, Jesus heals all ten.

Though I have experienced no serious illness, I have needed Jesus. I have sinned against God and God's people. I have had injuries that needed healing. I have been in situations where I do not know what to do. I have needed God's wisdom. There have been times when I had to do difficult things. I have needed God's strength. There are times I have felt turmoil and needed God's peace. There are times when I have been hurt by the struggles of life or by the actions of others. I have needed God's tender love. I have come to God like those ten lepers, and I have been healed.

I am ashamed to say that sometimes I have been like one of the nine who did not show gratitude. I just went on my way taking God's wonderful mercy, God's healing power, God's strength, God's peace, and God's love—with no thought of expressing gratitude to God. I regret my actions; God has given me so much, and I know I cannot live without God's presence in my life. I am resolved to be like the Samaritan who came back and thanked God. Thank you, God. I celebrate your presence in my life!

God, you are gracious to me. Help me to be grateful to you. Amen.

Being a neighbor means we have a responsibility to one another. It means showing respect to each other and helping one another. And, generally, when we talk of being a neighbor, we are referring to those people who live near us.

However, the biblical notion of neighbor is much broader. It requires that we recognize our global obligation to be neighbors. Yet too often we ignore our responsibilities to others. Our concern should include those who live near us as well as those who live across the ocean. If we consider all those who live near us as our neighbors and those who live in other countries as our neighbors, then we are responsible for taking care of all of the world's people.

According to the psalm, suffering is universal. We suffer when we lose jobs, when loved ones die, and when we are debilitated by disease and poor health. Life is full of suffering, and we often feel alone and in exile. But God dwells amongst us. By recognizing God's presence and God's promises, our perspective changes from despair to hope, and then to gratitude—because through God we gain insight, wisdom, and peace.

If the nine lepers we read about earlier this week had understood that Jesus was offering more than healing, that Jesus was offering a better way of life, then it would have been ten lives that would have been changed, ten families blessed, and many neighbors served.

When we celebrate God in our lives and we are grateful, we bring love, pardon, faith, hope, and joy. And then we will surely have peace in the neighborhood. "Make a joyful noise to God all the earth."

God, make me aware of your presence and grateful for your love. Help me live my life so that I may bring peace to my neighborhood and to the wider world. Amen.

Covenants, Communications, and Charges

OCTOBER 11–17, 2010 • BEATRIZ FERRARI

MONDAY, OCTOBER 11 ~ *Read Jeremiah 31:27-34*

The days are surely coming, says the LORD, when I will make a new covenant with the house of Israel . . . I will be their God, and they shall be my people.

A new day and a new covenant. No less than this is the vision and the promise of the prophet Jeremiah to the people of Judah and Israel—conquered, captive, dismayed and dispersed. The message runs through chapters 30 and 31 in what has been called the book of consolation.

The message, however, is not just about land ownership and real estate. Jeremiah's message signals a departure from the old covenant to the establishment of a new covenant, which will be written on their hearts and which works from within.

The promise becomes experience: God, by the Holy Spirit, continues writing God's law on our hearts. As we feast in fellowship with God and one another, we become the covenant renewed.

What Jeremiah means is that the words of scripture are not static, old and dry. Scripture is, instead, a witness to a living God, a forgiving God, and a God who reaches out to us with a new and startling covenant—a covenant written on our hearts.

God of powerful words and actions, write your covenant on my heart today. Help me carry your words in my heart and make them plain by my actions. Amen.

Director of the Mutualista Hospital Evangelico in Uruguay, former president of the Evangelical Methodist Church in Uruguay

I work in a home for the aging, and during the last two years we have been living in a place that we do not hesitate to call "a corner of paradise on Earth." The power of life and creation is around us: in the centuries-old trees, in the flowering of the garden plants, and in the colorful variety of birds and other living beings.

And, when the sun has rolled over the horizon, and the moon and the evening star begin to shine, "there is no speech, nor are there words . . . (but) the heavens are telling the glory of God." And we feel that we are in communion with the Creator, giving thanks for another day.

In every place where any of us live, we can find "a corner of paradise on Earth." Joyously seek it in the sky, the sun, the moon, the running water, a tree, a garden, or a flower. A sacred "corner" awaits you.

And yet, even there, we, like the psalmist, also look for the word of the Lord addressed to us in our situation, confronting us and consoling us, guiding us. It is the *trustworthy* and *radiant* word in the law of God. Otherwise, "who can detect their errors?" Then, admiration and contemplation turn into confession: "Keep back your servant also from the insolent; do not let them have dominion over me."

This psalm displays three forms of God's communication with us humans. The first is creation, with all its power and beauty. The second is the law in the written word. The third is personal confession and therefore all prayer.

Let the words of my mouth and the meditation of my heart be acceptable to you, O Lord, my rock and my redeemer. Amen.

The reading for today is one stanza in an acrostic design on the word of God. God's commands, decrees, statutes, ways, and precepts are epitomized in verses 97 through 104.

The sung word of God is the center of this meditation from the daily experience of the pious believers in the Hebrew scriptures. If we approach these powerful, poetic lines with open hearts, they can be a means of worship wherever—culturally or geographically—we find ourselves.

Even though the word of God confronts us and calls us to change our ways, the final influence God's word has on us is one of delight: "How much I love your word! How sweet are your words to my taste, sweeter than honey to my mouth!"

As I was preparing this meditation, I received a letter addressed to me as the national distributor of the *The Upper Room* in Uruguay, from a Honduran convict in a prison in the United States. It illustrates beautifully the ways the word reaches human minds and hearts.

> Beloved sister in Christ, the peace of the Lord be with you . . . and with all those who labor to promote the gospel. . . . I am in prison because I disobeyed the call of my Lord. And here, in prison, it happened that I reconciled myself with the Lord. And I want to say thanks to you and to others who write pamphlets. . . . I try to cultivate myself, to follow their advice from the Word . . . . Most blessing for many here is *The Upper Room.* . . . this is why I write to you.

How do I receive and respond to the written word of God through its many forms and channels? What can I do to share the word of God through scripture, publications, and devotional works?

But as for you, continue in what you have learned and firmly believed . . .

These are the words of the apostolic tradition, the charge to "presbyters" (or "elders") and teachers like Timothy.

Timothy, the son of a Greek father and a Jewish mother, was taught the scriptures by his mother, Eunice, and his grandmother Lois. He became the favorite disciple and the apostolic companion of Paul during his trips and incarcerations in prisons (Acts 16:1-3; 2 Tim. 1:5).

The subject here is the word of God, as mediated through the scriptures and through the witnessing community. The word comes to us not only through the writings but also through human preaching, witnessing, and teaching.

Today's reading reminds us that it is not enough to be acquainted with the scriptures through our family and the church. It is the word of God that *equips* us to be witnesses for righteousness in a world that is not different from Timothy's times.

There is an instructional quality to the word of God: "All scripture is inspired by God and it is useful for teaching, for reproof, for correction, and for training in righteousness." The word of God gets us ready to live a life of faith.

The charge is for all of us teachers, pastors, parents, and others in the faith community. It is our job to pass on the teachings of God, to encourage the study of the word, and to allow the word of God to equip us all for witness in this world.

God, help us to hear your word and to learn from you what it means to be a person of faith in this world. Amen.

These past days of covenants and communications have led to a final charge that sounds like a clarion: Preach the word! Where does the admonition occur? "In the presence of God and of Christ Jesus who is going to judge the living and the dead."

The word is clear: the good news is to be communicated and the word is to be proclaimed. No matter what. "Whether the time is favorable or unfavorable. " This is not an optional program or an elective course; it is a core requirement. This one is mandatory, students!

People need to know the good news; the gospel is for them all. And good news is to be shared. This is true for every Christian believer. But this charge is particularly addressed to the presbyters, who had been called and ordained for this ministry, as is the purpose of these "pastoral letters."

Yet the preaching of the word is not limited to Sunday proclamation from the pulpit in a temple or in a church. It includes listening and sharing and counseling: we are to "convince, rebuke, and encourage." And all of this has to be done with unfailing patience.

The author anticipates times when people "will not put up with sound doctrine . . . and will turn away from listening to the truth and wander away to myths." Illustrations of this are as near as the next glossy magazine or high-definition television that seduces your field of vision. The time described has also arrived across our globalized world, far beyond the distribution of this book. *All* of us need to open ourselves to this the apostolic demand: Preach the word.

Help me, O God, to do my part in the apostolic mission of passing the good news in my own time and place and to give personal support to those who are called to the ministry of your word. Amen.

Yes, stop reading after three verses. Now pretend that is all you are given of the story. You know only that the judge is questionable; the widow is persistent; and she would sure like a little justice in relationship to some third character in the story. Picture that this scene takes place where you are in 2010. Provide a middle and an ending to the story that could teach your neighbors and friends something about the necessity to pray and not become discouraged.

Be imaginative. Either tell your story aloud (as though to a gathering) or jot it down. Go ahead—set your book down and allow yourself a little creative time.

There is something Christlike about making up a good tale that teaches faithfulness. Jesus is a fabulous fable maker and a stellar storyteller. He could give us another ten commandments or an additional one hundred purity laws but instead gathers us into a big circle and launches into a profound parable.

Jesus doesn't legislate one-size-fits-all statutes. He tells stories. Some of these tales convict; some inspire; and still others communicate different things to different people. With a little openness and trust, each of us can see ourselves somewhere in these truth-illuminating vignettes.

Through the dynamic changes in my life, I could be the disrespectful judge one week, the persistent widow a second, and the third character soon thereafter. Awakened by the wisdom of it all, I can be made new. Tell me the stories of Jesus that I long to hear.

Gracious God, I sit centered in a sacred place before you. Help me to find or remember a parable of yours that will speak to me today. I pray that you will encourage and guide me just now, that I may hear your voice. Amen.

Then Jesus told them a parable about their need to pray always and not to lose heart.

In trying to make the point of persistence in prayer, Jesus touches a very real and sensitive situation: the condition of widows, totally dependent on the protection provided by the law. Jesus himself denounced the Pharisees who "devour widows' houses" (Matt. 23:14). The widow in this story had to face both the "opponent" in the suit and an unjust judge to whom she makes her demand: "Grant me justice against my opponent."

The widow had only her plea for justice. This was the only action available for her. Her stubbornness won over corruption, carelessness, and the temptation to give up.

Jesus asks his disciples, "Listen to what the unjust judge says. ('I will grant her justice, so that she may not wear me out...') And will God not grant justice to his chosen ones who cry to him day and night?" Jesus is not equating but *contrasting* the one with the other. The God of Jesus, as with the God of the prophets, is in solidarity with the poor and oppressed. Where might you see the workings of God's justice for the poor and unrepresented today? In Central America? In Africa? Los Angeles? Detroit? Mumbai?

Christians are challenged to pray with persistence, once and again. This is what prayer is about. The parable is essentially an encouragement to continue in prayer, so that we might get through difficult times of waiting in our lives and our history. Don't give up. Don't lose heart.

God, help me to be unfailing in prayer, no matter what. Give me both persistence and patience, and help me to grow in boldness. Amen.

Infinite Mercy, Boundless Blessing

OCTOBER 18–24, 2010 • ANN E. RIVERS

MONDAY, OCTOBER 18 ~ *Read Joel 2:23-27*

Joel is a moving litany of praise, promise and prophecy that celebrates, above all, the enduring and everlasting nature of God's grace toward us. In the book of Joel, water—in all its sustaining nature—is also seen as symbolic of God's grace. The crops that have been utterly destroyed by locusts are now, at last, growing again because the autumn rains have come.

Then, as today, water has been essential to sustain life and growth. Throughout the world's history, people have suffered and died of thirst and subsequent starvation. In developing countries where drought is prevalent most of the year, crops fail and basic foods cannot grow.

Suffering falls upon us all. Many of those in Zion who suffered greatly must have cried out, "Why, God? Why me?"

Even today, we cry and still the book of Joel speaks to us: Yes, the time of judgment is near. But those who return to God with their whole hearts, who repent with fasting and weeping will find mercy and grace from a God who is slow to anger and "abounding in steadfast love" (Joel 2:13).

Perhaps God is saying to us now, as then, "Remember me? I am still in your midst." Perhaps it is time for us to recall the roots of our faith and make a new commitment.

Heavenly God, you pour out undeserved blessing upon us. Help us to remember that every good and perfect gift comes from you. Amen.

Founding member and church historian of First United Methodist Church in Land O' Lakes, FL; early childhood and special education teacher

God's people have barely survived drought and starvation. God has promised abundant restoration. They will no longer be hungry but will praise the name of their one Lord God. There will be no other God, and they will never again suffer shame.

God has restored their physical welfare and has now turned attention to uplifting their spiritual lives as well. God promises to pour out the spirit upon them and to draw them closer to God. People of all ages and social classes will receive gifts of prophecy, dreams, and visions. Then faith will increase.

God promises to show portents in the heavens and on earth, so that they may not forget their one true God. Joel 2:31 says: "The sun will be turned to darkness and the moon to blood before the coming of the great and dreadful day of the LORD " (NIV). Throughout history people have been threatened and often devastated by natural phenomena. Many of their fears were realized as they suffered earthquakes, fire, flood, and famine, often considering them punishment. We humans have no explanation for such catastrophes.

The day of the Lord has often been identified as the Judgment Day, when the Lord will come to gather believers, and the unsaved will be cast out. But Joel 2:32 assures us that everyone who calls upon the name of the Lord will be saved. How, when, and where this day will take place is a mystery to us. We love God because God first loved us. We choose to follow God's leading.

Thank you, Lord, for revealing yourself to us through signs and portents. Thank you too for the gift of your Holy Spirit. We choose you. Amen.

The Lord reigns! This is the strong message of Psalm 65, an awesome song of praise and allegiance to God. The writer gives thanks to God for forgiveness, quality of life, deliverance, and hope. God's power is displayed by the mountains, the seas, and the people God has created. God brings salvation and happiness to the entire universe. God is in absolute control.

Psalm 65:8 says, "Those who live at the earth's farthest ends are awed by your signs; you make the gateways of the morning and evening shout for joy." We believe that many signs in nature represent God's warnings, assurances, or promises.

Many have celebrated the beauty of these spectacular gateways in paintings, poetry, and song. They have compared them to the beginning and ending of earthly life. I, much less talented, take countless photographs, and I can never quite capture the true depth of their beauty.

In my mind's eye, I see the gateway of dawn, the sun rising swiftly through dynamic changes of scope and color, energizing us. At the same moment in time, a glowing gateway at the opposite end of the earth is lowering its benediction of peace and rest as its pastels slowly deepen, and darkness falls.

I have been privileged to travel to faraway places and to view these splendid gateways of heaven from mountains, oceans, and deserts. Every one of these "moveable feasts" lifts our souls. We want to shout out in joyful praise for the earthly glories God reveals to us, reaffirming God's grace and faithfulness toward us.

It's impossible to imagine how much more resplendent heaven will be. There will be no night there, and all of God's people will sing endless praises around the throne.

God, you have showed us great things. You are worthy to be praised. Help us this day to live life awash in your joy. Amen.

Do you remember the 3-D movie glasses that thrilled us so when we were younger? How about those children's stories in which a character becomes excited by looking through rose-colored glasses? Or the fantasy stories our parents read to us about pirates or pixies or some daring adventure?

For some reason, as we grow older, we sometimes lose a sense of the wonder all around us; we can even blunt the beauty of God's creation. We lose that sharp edge of sensitivity to the kaleidoscope of seasonal changes God provides for our enjoyment. Psalm 65 reminds us of how wonderfully God provides for the creation. The psalm coaxes us back to color, excitement, and wonder.

Transplanted many years ago from the hills of Pennsylvania to the plains of Florida, I had lost my memory of how dramatic autumn can be. This year my family and I went back to Pennsylvania and saw the fall foliage at its peak. We drove along roads under an archway of trees in glorious array. Mountains of full color rose on every side, contrasting with sculptured acres of spruce trees in precise rows. Cattle, standing in tiers on high hillsides, reminded us of familiar scriptures.

From our friends' two-story, mountaintop house, we watched in wonder as the sun set across the ridges of mountains spread as far as our eyes could see.

Yes, I've been to the mountain and viewed God's creation with new awareness and deeper appreciation. What wonders God has wrought for us! I can also almost hear God's delight when we look up and see the wondrous works of God's hands in this world.

Divine Creator, help us to keep our eyes wide open. We don't want to miss anything. Amen.

During his final imprisonment in Rome, the apostle Paul, in a letter to his spiritual son Timothy, compared his life as a Christian to a libation poured out to Christ in devotion and sacrifice. (Whether this letter was written by Paul or by some of Paul's devoted students after his death is unclear.)

Known as Saul before he was struck him down on the road to Damascus, Paul had been unrelenting in his persecution of early Christians. After his conversion, he dedicated himself to spreading the gospel of salvation. During his journeys he suffered loneliness, pain, beatings, imprisonment, and martyrdom.

Paul's use of the phrase "I am already being poured out as a libation" echoes other places in his writings when he has used this image to portray the intensity of his life's witness and the end of his life. In the last half of that same verse, Paul says it even more directly, "the time of my departure has come."

The Hebrew scriptures mention numerous references to libations. The patriarch Jacob dreamed of a ladder with ascending and descending angels. God appeared, promising Jacob the surrounding land. Awakening, Jacob raised the stone that had been his pillow, poured oil upon it, and named the place Bethel, House of God.

Today, as members of the body of Christ, we continue to participate in sacraments of libation. We are baptized with water; anointed or consecrated with oil; and observe Holy Communion, partaking of bread and wine.

When Paul faced the end of his life, all had abandoned him. All, that is, except God. Paul says that God stood by him and gave him strength. He was, Paul said, "rescued from the lion's mouth" (see Ps. 22:21).

Lord Jesus, give me courage to relinquish that portion of myself that I am holding back, so that my life may be a libation to you. Amen.

It's a lonely place for a Christian who is desperate for positive answers in a hopeless situation; to be unwilling to submit your will to God's probable no and to say "Thy will be done!" I'm recalling a fifty-year-old memory that stirs up a conviction of guilt for my rebellion against God. It is a regret I've borne all through the years.

I didn't doubt God's power but wouldn't accept that God might refuse me the only answer I wanted. Our seven-month-old son was in critical respiratory distress. Three pediatricians had given up and told us that our baby boy would probably not survive the night. It was my night of deepest despair. The only answer acceptable to me was that my son would live! I refused to pray, "Thy will be done!" Some say that true hell is total separation from God. I was there, in that terrible black void, alienated, unwilling to submit to God's will.

As I sat in agony in that hospital room, I was unaware that night that a group of prayer warriors in our neighborhood were on their knees praying for our family during my hours of deep despair.

The next morning we learned that our baby had barely survived a two-hour convulsion during the night. Through God's grace and with tender nursing care, he survived. Today my son is a healthy family man, retired from military service, leading a productive life.

My amazement continues to this day. God does not forsake us, no matter how weak our trust, no matter how rebellious our hearts.

Almighty God, we believe. Help our unbelief. We give you thanks that we are never totally alone. Amen.

Jesus told a parable about two men living at the opposite extremes of Jewish society. We know the story as "The Pharisee and the Publican." An alternate title might well have been "In a Lonely Place."

Two men went up to the Temple to pray at the same time. One, a Pharisee, was a member of society's highest class, learned in religion and the law, pious, wealthy, and powerful. He boasted of fasting and tithing and observing the law.

By contrast, the lowly publican lived in fear as a social outcast. Because he extracted dues from his Jewish brethren on behalf of their Roman oppressors, he was a pariah in his own class. If you are already on the lowest rung of the social ladder, you can only look up for mercy and forgiveness. His humble prayer of remorse was sincere, heartfelt, desperate—and more acceptable in the eyes of God, who justified and exalted him.

The sanctimonious Pharisee had no clue that God treasured humility above position and possessions. He did not realize it, but he too was in a lonely place and not justified in God's eyes. Often God's most diligent servants, taking on roles of leadership and responsibility, are seduced by power and self-importance.

We must ask ourselves, "Who is really in charge here?" "Whose work are we really supposed to be doing?" God exalts those who humble themselves and seek God's face. Oftentimes it's hard to be humble. The lure of power, position, and the trappings of material society seduce many away from the close relationship God seeks with us.

Today's reading guides us to the place of prayer where God can meet us. That way begins, "God, have mercy on me, a sinner."

O God, forgive our foolish pride. Help us come to you today humble and asking for mercy. Amen.

Trusting God
When Things Are Tough

OCTOBER 25–31, 2010 • JAN JOHNSON

MONDAY, OCTOBER 25 ~ *Read Habakkuk 1:1-4*

Remember the old saying, "If you can't say something nice, don't say anything at all"? Christians often interpret this to mean, "If you can't pray something nice, don't pray anything at all."

With prayer, this is exactly the wrong advice. We are free to speak to God about the things that *really* bother us, rather than just "religious" issues or the things we think God wants us to think about. Habakkuk's example encourages us to do this. Not to pray about the things that anger us, hurt us, or confuse us locks God out of the deepest corners of our lives.

God wants to engage us even in the midst of our troublesome times. It is not only acceptable, but it is desirable that we go to God with questions such as "How long?" and "Why?"

But does it help to ask such questions? Yes, it does. It helps because it honors God as the companion of our soul—the one to whom we run for help. Also, such prayer helps us learn to dialog with God. We may even revise our prayers, asking God, *"Is there anything else you want me to know?"* God knows things we don't. God can help us understand things we don't understand on our own. As we pray these questions and wait on God, something important may come to us. Or, we may experience the comfort and companionship of God even more intensely. And even when nothing seems solved, through prayer our commitment to God is strengthened.

O God, show me how to trust you, even with my complaints.
Teach me to trust you as the companion of my soul. Amen.

Author of *Invitation to the Jesus Life* and *Enjoying the Presence of God* and speaker, living in Simi, CA

What is it that gives you that "everything's going to the dogs" feeling? Current events? Cultural analyses? Relationship disappointments? Talking to a young person . . . or to an older person? Habakkuk is in that sort of mood where things just aren't right as he complains about the desperate conditions around him.

But Habakkuk isn't just being crabby. He's attentive, even vigilant, about how God might speak to him. In fact, he understands that God is giving him something to do: to write down what he hears. He waits with alertness and stations himself where he can see the horizon. In this attentiveness, he hears God respond that an answer is coming at "the appointed time."

God doesn't tell Habakkuk exactly what will happen. Instead, God explains what sort of person will endure this present time. It won't be the proud person who endures, for pride is about trusting in one's self. Instead, we trust in God and live by faith. In this statement, God invites us to trust, just as God has moved through all of human history with the same invitation and challenge.

The trust to which God calls us is not a timid trust. It is a bold, courageous trust that is written large so that even a passing runner can read it. It is a deep and hearty trust, one that leads us ever closer to God.

In the midst of life's confusing calamities and perplexing current events, can we stand alert and attentive? Can we ponder, with faith, what it would look like to trust God in the next ten minutes? When we trust God in this experimental way, we often find that life looks different—even though circumstances do not change. That's because trusting God focuses us on God's faithfulness. It helps us *endure.*

What would it look like to trust God for the next ten minutes?
How might my life be different if I were attentive to God?

What is the greatest compliment you could receive? What are things about yourself you'd be glad for people to notice? My guess is it's probably not about being *righteous*. Why? Because the idea of being *righteous* is not popular these days. We might even think of a righteous person as someone who's boring, not in touch with real life, and probably not merciful for those who aren't quite so righteous.

But the biblical idea of righteousness is very different. It speaks of an attractive, inner goodness that you can count on because it involves justice and fairness (*tsad-deek'* in Hebrew, *dikaiosune* in the Greek Old Testament). Think of someone you've known (or a character in a book or movie) who's deeply good in a beautiful, alluring way—somebody you admire and respect. People like this—truly righteous people—are those we can trust deeply because they are faithful and true. They keep the promises they make, even when it's difficult to do so. They work hard to live in right relationship with all who are around them. We are blessed to have people like this in our lives.

It's important that we understand and treasure the idea of *righteousness* because righteousness is a central attribute of God. God has that deep goodness through and through. God's righteousness is not about pride, but mercy. It's not about rigidity, but stability. It's not temporary and fleeting; it's sure and everlasting.

Learning to trust in God's righteousness and care for us can sometimes be hard—especially when things in life are tough or challenging. Learning to trust in God's righteousness and care for us is a lifelong walk. Today, this week, give God a chance to shower you with the joy and strength that come from God's eternal love and righteousness.

As you go through your day, call to mind often God's promise to care for you in all things.

How do you feel when you see people taking the low road, cheating, taking advantage of people, or using shortcuts to get ahead? These people value winning over character and ethics.

Today's psalm moves back and forth between how good and wise God's ways are and how the psalmist's foes have forgotten this. The psalmist's plight seems small and despised: "Trouble and anguish have come upon me." It's enough to fill anyone with self-pity, but the psalmist reacts much differently.

Instead of being overcome with self-pity, the psalmist is consumed by zeal for God, and God's commandments fill the writer with delight. The psalmist understands that life really does work best when we live by God's ideas. The writer believes that integrity and kindness really do produce a good life, that love and peace really do bring contentment, that humility and self-control create an unbeatable sturdiness and reliability.

How different this is from the cynicism of our age: Do unto others before they do it to you! Others' pessimism has not penetrated this psalmist's soul. The passage seems to say, "So what if I'm small and despised? I still remember your precepts. So what if trouble has come upon me? I still delight in your commands."

This psalm paints a picture of invincible trust that refuses to be conquered by the suspicion and scorn of the age. It's tempting to dismiss the psalmist as a Pollyanna, but in truth what we see is a strong example of what it means to persevere in trusting God.

Inspire us to trust you, O God. Amen.

When we hear deep truths or experience great blessings, there is in all of us the need to respond in some way to the truth or the blessings we have received. This was certainly true for Paul. When he speaks of the grace God shows us—the ideas that have come to us or been taught to us, the people who have shown us little mercies, the beauty of our surroundings that have spoken to us—he acknowledges our need to respond to God in gratitude (vv. 2-3). Gratitude follows grace. We become grateful for the grace we receive.

In this passage, it is the grace of God that has empowered the Thessalonians to trust God and to love each other well. So Paul points this out, which is good because people don't always notice the grace of God working in their lives. Because the Thessalonians had been suffering persecutions (see 1 Thess. 2:14-3:5), hearing this passage read aloud in their community (as letters were read) may have caused them to weep. Seeing that kind of gratitude, hearing someone's deep thankfulness—this can be a humbling and empowering experience.

What do you need to celebrate today? What are you grateful for today? What might you notice in the congregation of which you are a part that is evidence of God's grace: Who has moved ahead when they had reason to fall behind? Who has gifted you with love and generosity? How has God been at work softening hardened hearts? How have people shown love to each other? Who is suffering but bearing it and even seeking God in the midst of it? As you notice these things, give thanks to God for them.

Lead me to see your grace working in others, O God. Guide me in expressing my gratitude for it. Amen.

Imagine sitting down at a table with an unsavory criminal or having a conversation with someone who has just swindled your widowed grandmother. Can you see yourself eating a meal with someone who's been convicted of embezzlement?

It strikes us as scandalous. Jesus too must have scandalized both religious leaders and casual onlookers when he welcomed Zacchaeus, a cheat and one of the most unpopular men in Jericho. He was not just a tax collector. He was the *chief* tax collector. He was the one who set the tone of Rome's taxation. Such persons were commonly cheats, over-charging and making money on the side.

What drove this notorious person to be so inquisitive about Jesus? What was it that made Zacchaeus feel he *had* to see Jesus? Was it Jesus' deep, inner, attractive goodness? Was it Jesus' reputation? Was it his way with people?

And what did Zacchaeus think Jesus would think of him, would say to him? But Jesus—ever the one to gaze at hearts and penetrate them, ever the one to speak to those whom others avoided, who welcomed the forgotten and should-be-forgotten—engaged this disreputable character and broke all rules of hospitality by inviting himself to dinner.

It would really be like Jesus to do that sort of crazy thing, wouldn't it? And what might we learn from watching Jesus and Zacchaeus? It is clear that Zacchaeus began his relationship with Jesus as a seeker, and he persists in pursuing Jesus—but Jesus, too, seeks out Zacchaeus. And it is Jesus who saves Zacchaeus. Jesus, Zacchaeus's savior, shows us the way to trust. But trusting Jesus is a very exciting life. This trust and faith may, by the grace of God, help us to reach out to people with whom we might not ever think of sharing a meal.

O God, lead me seek you the way Zacchaeus sought Jesus. Amen.

Normally when people grumbled about Jesus hanging out with less-than-ideal folks, he told a parable. But before Jesus can respond to the crowd's criticism, Zacchaeus does. His response shows that he recognizes Jesus as Lord. This realization results in Zacchaeus's deep repentance—a repentance that is more than simply sadness and regret. His repentance led him to give half of everything he owned to the poor. He promises to return what he had stolen from the people he harmed, and then he does something truly amazing: he makes restitution of *four* times what he stole.

Zacchaeus's lifestyle will take quite a dip because of this—no more opulent housing or rich food. To Zacchaeus's friends, this must have looked scandalous. But a reduction in lifestyle isn't a problem for Zacchaeus, for today *salvation* comes to his house. And it is salvation in its fullest sense. It means that God's power has delivered Zacchaeus—and us—from old ways of life, from valuing the wrong things, from sure death by thousands of daily wrong choices. Salvation comes with the sum of God's blessings, and this is what Zacchaeus gains. He *receives* more than he has given up. Now he will be able to look people in the face rather than see only the eyes of their contempt. Now he can become a member of the community again. Now he can find peace and joy.

Zacchaeus trusted Jesus in a radical way. So much of his identity had involved his shrewd way of collecting money and his lavish lifestyle. Now he has a clear picture of who he will become: rich in good deeds and secure in God's empowering love.

What have you struggled to give up that you know is holding you back in trusting God? Certain habits or possessions? Trying to control certain people or situations? Certain beliefs about yourself? Call on the image of Zacchaeus sitting in the tree, seeking salvation from Jesus.

Stand Firm, Hold Fast

NOVEMBER 1–7, 2010 • GREGORY PALMER

ALL SAINTS DAY

MONDAY, NOVEMBER 1 ~ *Read Haggai 1:15b-2:9*

Like many of you, I have not paid attention to Haggai, one of the post-exile prophets. But this second shortest book in the Bible is worth paying attention to. The Jewish people had spent several generations in Babylonian exile and now were free to return to their homeland.

But can you ever really go home again? Jerusalem had changed, and the people had changed. While in captivity they were sustained by a recollection of their homeland.

When the people returned and saw the temple in Jerusalem, they were discouraged and sad. They were home—but home had changed. We ourselves have seen people return to their homes after natural disasters. It is a heart-wrenching sight to watch them pick through the debris of the symbols of their life and work following hurricane, flood, fire, and tsunami. The prophet's words ring "Who is left among you that saw this house in its former glory? How does it look to you now? Is it not in your sight as nothing?"

But if we stop here, if we continue to gaze upon the disaster, we will come out from the cycle of despondency. Thank God we are never left alone to sift through our debris. God remains faithful and is in our midst saying, "Yet now take courage," one and all, "for I am with you." Ultimately, we abide where God abides.

God, in our despair make your presence known all the more. Give us courage. Renew our lives. Amen.

Resident bishop of the Illinois Great Rivers Conference of the United Methodist Church

God reminded the returned exiles that despite the ruin they saw, the divine presence was sure. When we are sure of God's sustaining presence we are able to take on any task, to claim any future. As God's people looked upon the rubble of the former Temple and their own depleted numbers it was likely hard for them to grasp the notion of rebuilding. Discouragement was natural and understandable. Yet God says, "Work, for I am with you." From any other source it might sound like a pious platitude. But God has a track record, not only with Israel, but also with us today. We can speak of God's faithfulness and power from experience, not hearsay.

Many tasks we face may seem at first and even second glance impossible. We look at what is before us and catalogue the resources at our disposal and find the task outweighs the resources.

But if we begin a good work, we often discover that we have far more resources than was at first apparent. Indeed, our hardest task is often simply making a start. The challenge of making a start is about where we place our faith and trust. Rebuilding either a physical temple or a human life and community is an act of faith that often starts small. But what we need will be supplied to overflowing if we but commit ourselves to make a start and then to trust the God who "once again will shake the heavens and the earth."

But God isn't willing to stop there—with a good beginning rooted in faith. No, instead, God is bold to say, "The latter splendor of this house shall be greater than the former." God is bold enough to say it. Are we bold enough to believe it?

Thank you for never abandoning us, God. When we must start over, help us to do so in the assurance of your love, presence, and power. Amen.

This psalm is about praise. The psalms invite and teach us how to praise God and how to stay connected to God through praise in good times and in bad times. God is worthy of our praise even when our hearts are broken and our heads are bowed in sorrow. A popular gospel praise song that has blessed many has as its title "Praise Is What I Do." Embedded in the lyrics of the song is a phrase that sticks with me: Praise is who I am.

I want to tell you just a bit about why I can't help but praise God. God is a mighty Creator, and I see extraordinary testimony to the greatness of God in the created order. I marvel at the splendor, creativity, genius, and mystery of God's good creation of which I am a part. What I have seen in creation causes me to throw my head back and say with full throat, "How great thou art." My praise empowers me to act as a steward for creation in responsible ways.

I also praise God for the gift of salvation in Jesus Christ. God is always seeking the best for God's creation. In the life, death, and resurrection of Jesus Christ, the creation has been freed. None of us is forever bound to a cycle of sin and death. We have been set free in Jesus Christ to live new lives that glorify God in word or deed.

Finally I praise God when by any worldly standard it might seem spurious to do so. Praise of God is not conditional on my outer circumstances; my praise is driven by God's constancy. The "stuff" in my life notwithstanding, God remains faithful. This is who God is—faithful and steady. And so "my mouth will speak the praise of the LORD, and all flesh will bless [God's] holy name forever and ever."

Let me praise you, God, with my lips and my life. Amen.

Have you ever felt "set up" by a question put to you? Especially when it's a question from a detractor? It is not a good feeling. In our sensationalized media age I often get the gut feeling that questions that could be geared to help the public engage in civil discourse and make wiser decisions are instead intended to embarrass or entrap. Jesus of Nazareth was not immune to this tactic. His detractors often seemed to pose questions intended to trick, trap, and tie him up.

Honest inquiry that seeks to pull back the layers of knowledge and complexity is always in order. The church should be a community confident and humble enough to encourage the search for deeper knowledge and truth. Only then can we live faithfully toward the one who is "the way, the truth, and the life."

The text before us today is apparently not intended to shed light, deepen knowledge, or inspire faith. Jesus has entered Jerusalem and is in the midst of delicate encounters. The Sadducees pose a question that assumes a tenet of faith they in fact do not affirm—resurrection. Sometimes great opposition and discourtesy come not from the irreligious but from the religious who are insincere.

What the religious leaders who fought to entrap Jesus missed was this: they missed the very core of who Jesus was. The Sadducees asked a question that Jesus dismisses as of "this age." His answer shows quite clearly that the questioners are so preoccupied with the old religious system that they can't see anything new. In fact, they can't see the "new thing" that is standing right in front of them: their question (and their insincerity) blocked their view of the God who is "not of the dead, but of the living."

Dear Jesus, you are the way, the truth, and the life. Help us to know you and to see the new thing you are doing. Amen.

Hold on. This passage is not the basic Golden Rule that you learned in first grade. This passage is stronger than that. It is a teaching about a complete reversal of values, about the risks of being a Christian in the time of God's reign and rule. It is a challenging word that Jesus speaks to his disciples—then and also now, indeed in every age. "When the world is righted, here is how things are going to be. Here is what you can expect." He addresses things both spiritual and temporal. He blesses and he also says "woe." Depending upon how you see yourself today, these words of Jesus may be comforting and hope-filled—or they may be disquieting and cause much distress.

No one is left untouched. Even if you see yourself as one "who is hungry now" but who "will be filled," there is no promise that your association with Jesus is less likely to cause others to hate, exclude, curse, abuse, and strike you or otherwise seek your undoing. This Golden Rule is actually specific counseling for dealing with your enemies.

And as such, the gospel makes sweeping demands on us. We can't just get over our anger at someone—we must actually *forgive* them. If someone takes our coat, we must *give* them our shirt too.

This kind of sweeping demand of God puts me in mind of a story in the Middle East from 1968. An American rabbi was shot by a Palestinian terrorist while visiting Jerusalem. The rabbi's family struggled with forgiveness. At the trial for the Palestinian, a remarkable thing happened. The rabbi's wife said, "I forgive Omer for what he did." She then asked the State of Israel to forgive him also. When the court adjourned, the two families embraced. Perhaps this is what the hard work of God's coming reign looks like.

O God, help us surrender to the authority of your reign that we have seen in the life, death, and resurrection of Jesus. Amen.

The writer of this epistle is addressing matters of pressing concern for its audience. The community is clearly alarmed and anxious. So the writer moves quickly to steady things by urging that the flock "not to be quickly shaken in mind or alarmed." This anxiety has been stirred by those who believe that the day of the Lord is at hand.

In every age there are those who see current reality and read into it that the end is near. Some of these may be well-meaning proclamations about the future. Thinking ahead is not necessarily a bad thing—but thoughtlessly announcing doom and gloom most certainly can be. Such announcements ought to come not from anxiety and fear but from the calm of God-centeredness. We do not do our best work when fueled by fear and anxiety.

And so the writer gives some reassurances: What awaits those who have been led astray by a bad teacher is not the same thing that awaits the one who remains faithful. We must, quite truthfully, remember who we are and whose we are. The writer is clear: "For this purpose he called you through our proclamation of the good news, so that you may obtain the glory of our Lord Jesus Christ."

When change, fear, or anxiety come, we must keep this in mind: God's great love, God's salvation, and God's faithfulness will lead us to confidence, growth, and the peace that abides in God's arms.

Our purpose does not change. Our methods and strategies may change. The tools we employ may vary. But our purpose— to be a sign of God's love and reign in this world—is unchanging. In the words of an old African American spiritual, "Comfort your hearts and strengthen them in every good work and word."

By your grace, dear God, keep us steady in your work and word. Amen.

I have sometimes had a bit of push back when I have referred to my audience as saints. Some have been quite explicit, saying, "I'm no saint." I've wondered why ordinary Christians resist the term *saint* when applied to themselves, though they may feel comfortable referring to someone else in this way.

My hunch is the resistance is less about being genuinely pious and more about how we have come to hear the term. We think of some of the noble figures in the New Testament or the writers of the Gospels. We measure ourselves against their contribution to the Christian movement, and it makes no sense to think that we have made so substantial a contribution.

But just because you think you are not a saint does not mean that you aren't one. In today's reading the writer addresses those in his audience as saints. I can't help but imagine that his hearers or readers were nothing if not a ragtag crew. So I think we might look at that term in some new ways.

Saints start out ordinary—each and every one of them. They start out ordinary; we are saints *not* because we earned our sainthood but because the risen Christ in the power of the Holy Spirit is at work in our lives in extraordinary ways.

There are no solo saints. In the New Testament the noun is always plural. We are saints in community. The community of faith is a vast one made up of those with whom we live our lives and practice our faith here and now, as well as those who have passed this way ahead of us and expectantly await us in glory.

The next time you hear the word *saint*, kindly include yourself.

For all your saints, O God, even ourselves, we give you thanks and praise through Jesus Christ. Amen.

Imagine That!

NOVEMBER 8–14, 2010 • JENNIFER E. COPELAND

MONDAY, NOVEMBER 8 ~ *Read Psalm 118:1-9*

The first commandment handed down to Moses at Sinai made things quite clear: "You shall have no other gods before me" (Exod. 20:3). God goes on to disclose a personality trait that is crucial to our grasp of this injunction: "for I the LORD your God am a jealous God" (Exod. 20:5).

At first glance we might assume this is because God dwells in delusions of grandeur or because God is insecure and covets our fickle allegiance. It turns out, however, as we continue reading the story of salvation history that God already knows what we still struggle to comprehend: we can't really depend on ourselves for survival. Even when we surround ourselves with the delusional protectors of money and might, we find our lives surprisingly vacuous. The psalmist recognizes this and gives voice to the reality that only God offers refuge.

Thus, God's jealousy has little to do with God and much to do with us. God warns us away from idols, not because God wants all of our attention, but because God knows that only God can sustain us. What would the world look like if we believed God's promise to provide for our material needs? If we no longer hoarded goods and resources, would there be enough for the basic sustenance of our neighbors? What would the world look like if we believed God's promise to save us from the hand of our enemy? If we didn't hoard and exploit, would we even have any enemies? The psalmist summons us to trust God's "steadfast love endures forever!"

God, give me the faith of this psalmist today. Amen.

United Methodist chaplain at Duke University in Durham, NC; ordained elder in the South Carolina Conference of the United Methodist Church

Homes destroyed, crops spoiled, livestock slaughtered. Family members missing or known to be dead. Filth, hunger, and grief stretch ahead with no end in sight. The world of the refugee exists in the moment, whether that refugee is in Babylon or Burundi, first-century Palestine or twenty-first century Palestine. There's not much to see in either century from the inside of a refugee camp. A different world, a new word, has to come from another place, interrupting the monochrome monotony with vibrant visions.

Isaiah offers us a new word. When viewed through the lens of faith, we can see the possibility of a different world. Dirt doesn't disappear, only the inevitability of dirt. Food scarcity does not vanish, only the expectation of incessant hunger. Death does not end, only the pointlessness of it. We must use our imagination.

We must tell a different story than the story that has been told to us; we must imagine a different reality than the reality that is shown to us. We must live a different truth than the lies laid before us. The world doesn't have to be imagined as a refugee camp. Our God comes into our midst where we are dirty, hungry, and dying to infuse our imagination with the vision of new life.

Can you see it through the eyes of Isaiah? Can you hear it in the words of the Lord? Will you live it today as if your dreams have already come true?

It is you, O God, who gives streams of living waters, like grace from age to age. We are grateful for your abundant love. Amen.

S ave us! Or, in Hebrew, *Hoshianna*. Can you hear it? Save us, *Hoshianna*, Hosanna. "Hosanna in the highest. Blessed is the one who comes in the name of the Lord. Hosanna in the highest."

We say it and we sing it. These words are our "unending hymn" united with "people on earth and the all the company of heaven." Save us. In the hymn is the implicit understanding that we cannot save ourselves. Such knowledge does not evoke resignation or despondence on our part but rather the recognition that God can save us and the expectation that God will. These truths propel us to lift our voices in praise and thanksgiving for the gift of salvation.

The gift of salvation inspires us to participate in God's truth, for God's "steadfast love endures forever." So it is that we become what we do, but only after we understand who we are. Without an understanding grounded in salvation we might think it's important to be citizens of the most powerful military nation in the world and rule all other nations. Without an understanding grounded in salvation we might think it's important to live in the wealthiest nation in the world and regulate trade so that other nations will remain poor. Without an understanding grounded in salvation we might actually think we deserve to be powerful and rich. We may think we need to be saved from "the enemy" who would destroy our power and steal our wealth, but we find instead that we must be saved from ourselves or else our power and our wealth will consume us. Save us, we beseech you, O Lord!

God, we know so little that is true about ourselves. Give us hearts to receive your truth about us, truth that can heal our pride and sin. Amen.

This lengthy speech from Jesus describes a world that we're eager to recognize in the events around us. We're not the first. Down through the centuries people have always found signs of the end times in the current events around them.

Jesus is not describing anything in these verses that was unfamiliar to his audience or that is unfamiliar to us. "Wars and insurrections," "great earthquakes" and "dreadful portents" have been around since the beginning of time. Events abound on the nightly news that easily fit into these categories. Jesus is merely describing the reality of the first century and it's a sad, but true, commentary that his descriptions aptly apply to our own circumstances.

In addition to the cataclysmic events of war or natural disaster are the more personal aspects of betrayal and hatred. Yes, betrayal does come at the hands of "parents and brothers, . . . relatives and friends," though more often it assumes the guise of broken trust: Friends renege on promises, spouses are unfaithful, parents abuse their children. All of this is a present reality, not a future calamity.

The details of the current events are incidental to our behavior. We behave the same way—or can behave the same way—in every situation because our behavior is not dictated by specific events; our behavior is dictated by our name, Christian. Because Christians can see the end of the world and already know how the story ends, we can confess a different version of the current events. And what we say, through both word and deed, is dictated not by our circumstances, but by our name—Christian.

God of present, past, and future, focus me this week on the name you have given me—Christian. Help me to live out my name, no matter what comes this week. Amen.

Busybody. What might a busybody look like in Thessalonica? It looks like people standing around doing nothing. First Church Thessalonica is awash in the expectation of God's promises coming to fulfillment in the return of Christ, the imminent return of Christ. What's left to do, except nothing? Such a languid attitude is unimaginable in our society. We are just the opposite, fixated on appointments, assignments, and tasks. Our bodies are very busy, indeed, with PDAs grafted onto our hands to keep it all straight and in order.

But is our busybodyness any more laudable than that of the Thessalonians? They are sitting around doing nothing to participate in the coming reign of God, while we are scurrying around doing everything *except* participating in the coming reign of God. There, perhaps, is the true definition of the busybody—one immersed in one's self whether that self is waiting around on God to do something or scurrying around deflecting God's presence in his or her life.

What if we lived as though the reign of God is already present, not something we have to wait for and not something we can ignore? Would we sit around doing nothing? Hardly—we would live into God's promises. Would we scurry around keeping busy all the time? Hardly—we would participate in kingdom building. Is there any reason not to live into God's promises right now? Is there any reason not to participate in kingdom building right now? Such work reflects righteousness, not idleness. Such work espouses purposefulness, not busyness. Such work flows from the tradition we receive from the life of the one whose work embodies our salvation.

Gracious God, give us faith that plunges us into life. Help us recognize the work of your kingdom right now and to join in that work. Amen.

A testimony is "telling somebody what you have seen and heard and confessing what you believe about it." It happens in courtrooms all the time: we put someone on the witness stand and instruct the person, "Please tell the court what you saw." Jesus' instruction to us during our times of trial is no different. Please tell the kings and governors, the keepers of the institutions, what you saw. Tell them what you heard. Tell them what you believe about it. Such a definition assumes we'll tell the truth. It's not a testimony if you lie; it's a violation of the ninth commandment.

But telling the truth begins with what we look at and to whom we listen. We can't testify if we aren't paying attention. By the time we get this deep in the Gospel of Luke, we ought to know how to pay attention, if we've been paying attention. A prostitute sneaks into a banquet hall and shows greater hospitality to the guests than the wealthy church officials hosting the party. Did you see that? A tax collector, also known as someone who sold out to the system, turns out to be a person of great generosity who tithes an astonishing 50%—better than a Pharisee at only 10%! Did you hear about that?

We could pay attention to Luke, and then we could pay attention to the world around us, looking for those places where God is at work in the world transferring grace and transforming lives. What do we see? What do we hear? What will we say about it?

God, let my testimony today be alive, energetic, and focused on the work you are doing in the world. Help me speak the truth in all my actions. Amen.

What, exactly, does peace look like? Is peace merely the absence of violence? If so, then we could instigate peace by taking the tentative step of stricter gun control or the bold step of nuclear disarmament. We know, however, that peace is far more than the absence of violence, so while gun control and nuclear disarmament might be worthy accomplishments, they don't represent peace. Jesus promised us peace (John 14:27), but then said we wouldn't recognize it among worldly definitions, especially if we identified his peace only as an absence of violence.

But neither is peace idleness. Isaiah is very specific about all the things we will *do* in the midst of our peaceful lives: build homes, plant vineyards, raise children, live long. Peace, it seems, is very specific for the one inhabiting it, but perhaps it is best captured in the words "my chosen shall long enjoy the work of their hands."

My father is a gardener, farmer, and sometimes carpenter; my mother is a quilter, embroiderer, and sometimes cook. The work of their hands produces tangible results for them and those they love, but interestingly their longtime enjoyment of these accomplishments has nothing to do with the drudgery of work. In their peacefulness, manifest through the tangible experience of retirement, they have time to "enjoy the work of their hands." The peace envisioned by Isaiah involves creating time and space in which to do the things that bring us great joy. It is a time when God's character will be reflected in all nature's being completely at peace with itself. Isaiah's beautiful vision of peace, of the New Jerusalem, puts all things in perspective.

Grant me, O God, the eyes to see your New Jerusalem. Amen.

Reign of Christ

MONDAY, NOVEMBER 15 ~ *Read Jeremiah 23:1-6*

Woe to the shepherds who destroy and scatter the sheep of my pasture! says the LORD . . . you have not attended to them. So I will attend to you for your evil doings, says the LORD.

These were hard words. But those were hard times. These words were addressed to the leaders of the nation, both political and religious, who were the "shepherds" of God's people. During the forty years of his prophetic ministry, Jeremiah had to deal with incapable kings and false prophets in the midst of the most trying times for the nation.

The prophet points to the coming of a descendant of David, "a righteous Branch . . . (who) shall execute justice and righteousness in the land." Jesus would not fulfill the political expectation of a king in the image of David, but he would proclaim the righteousness of the kingdom of God (Matt. 6:33), and he identified himself as the "good shepherd" who "lays down his life for the sheep" (John 10:11).

No wonder the church introduced the terminology of shepherding for its own mission in the world and for its ministry within the body of Christ. A main point of the Protestant reformation was, precisely, the recovery of the "priesthood of all believers." All of us are both objects and subjects of shepherd-like caregiving—both pastors and flock. May we hear these words and follow their call.

Shepherd, help me today to look for your presence and to accept my part in the shepherding. As you nurture and care for those around me, may I do my part to love them also. Amen.

Bishop Emeritus of the Methodist Church in Uruguay

"Blessed be the Lord God of Israel, for he has looked favorably on his people and redeemed them. He has raised up a mighty savior for us in the house of his servant David."

This passage came to be known by the Latin title of "Benedictus" ("Blessed be"), and also as the song of Zechariah (the father of John the Baptist). It is part of the collection of hymns celebrating the coming of Jesus in the first two chapters of Luke. First comes the song of Mary, then the song of Zechariah, next the song of the shepherds of Bethlehem, and finally the song of Simeon at the Temple.

What better way for the coming of Jesus to be anticipated and celebrated than by singing! It is like the sun's rays announcing the break of day. The birds begin to sing, one after the other. The trees and the garden become the concert place for a new day.

The coming of the long-awaited Christ—with the hope of a new time of the reign of God among humanity—is celebrated by songs of anticipation, in the hope and expectation of justice and peace. The reign of Christ as celebrated in these songs brings something more lasting than just another political kingdom and more incarnate than an otherworldly salvation. Justice and peace in human relationships are essential in the messianic expectations of prophets and the people who celebrate in these gospel songs.

Our voices sing out, song after song from our Christian hymnody. Great is our God! Blessed be the Christ! Praise and honor, at all times and in every day!

Our God of grace, come to my life and make me a singing bird in this new day. May I sing with my own feelings and voice, as well as with borrowed songs and tunes—like a mockingbird! Amen.

And you, child, will be called the prophet of the Most High; for you will go before the Lord to prepare his ways.

Zechariah was an old man—a priest in the service of the Temple, and his wife was an old woman. They were both beyond any reasonable age for child-bearing. The fact that they finally had a son was a powerful motive to celebrate the end of sterility and the beginning of a new life for the family. But the birth of that baby was more than a family event; it was part of God's plan for the people, in the line of the messianic expectations.

This son of a senior couple was going to prepare the way of the Messiah. Zechariah took the occasion of his son's birth to affirm his expectations of a special mission for this child. John would, one day, "give knowledge of salvation to his people by the forgiveness of their sins."

Before this song of Zechariah began, its singer had been temporarily mute, terrified by the visitation of an angel. But now he had found his voice, and a prophetic voice at that. Zechariah was now ready to tell the world how John would "go before the Lord to prepare his ways." These words were powerful and held much hope to Zechariah's listeners. These words still speak powerfully to us today. They fill us, too, with hope.

Our God of grace, thank you for my life. Help me to discover my part in the life of my family and in the working of your kingdom in this world. Use me however you will to prepare the world for your coming once again. Amen.

May you be made strong with all the strength that comes from his glorious power, and may you be prepared to endure everything with patience, while joyfully giving thanks to the Father, who has enabled you to share in the inheritance of the saints in the light. He has rescued us from the power of darkness and transferred us into the kingdom of his beloved Son, in whom we have redemption, the forgiveness of sins.

The apostolic writer—Paul or one of his collaborators—is addressing the holy and faithful at Colossae. He piles up the language of power and strength to underline the working of the power of God in the experience of the believer.

This experience is not our doing; it is God's action in us. As the passage continues, it is clear that it is God who "rescued" us from the dominion of darkness and "transferred" us into the dominion of Jesus Christ. Have we lifted ourselves up by our bootstraps and made a place for ourselves? No. God has "enabled" us to share in the inheritance of the saints in light. By the prevenient, justifying, and sanctifying grace of God, we are a redeemed and forgiven people.

God is *for us* and God is *in us*. What glorious things God does *to us*. It becomes a happening! In our text this manifestation of the divine power is not displayed in spectacular events but in endurance and patience, particularly in face of opposition from outside. Redemption meets human need and transforms human experience.

My God, I am conscious of my needs. The way you have provided for my need of endurance, forgiveness, and transformation is beyond my understanding. Somehow, through your grace and love, you have reached me through your son Jesus Christ. Thank you, loving God, for your works of love. Amen.

[Christ] is the image of the invisible God. . . . In him all things in heaven and on earth were created, things visible and invisible . . . in him all the fullness of God was pleased to dwell, and through him God was pleased to reconcile to himself all things, whether on earth or in heaven, by making peace through the blood of his cross.

Today's passage is a Christological poem—a solid piece of New Testament theology—addressed to a young Christian community. They are living in a time with a hostile cosmological view. This worldview was filled with evil powers in heaven and on earth, surrounding and dominating human lives.

Today millions still live in the midst of that cosmology of evil powers, even though the predominant cosmological vision is based on growing astronomical knowledge and the continued development of scientific and technical tools. The recent Nobel Prize in physics suggests a further distancing from first-century cosmologies. It was awarded to researchers using intra-atomic indicators to estimate that the age of the cosmos is in fact thousands of millions of years.

The message of the Colossian Christology is right on target. It proclaims a God who is not alien to our human situation. Our God suffers, through God's historically incarnate son, and with each and every human being who suffers. The cross is at the center of the world and at the center of our spiritual life. As the French physicist Blaise Pascal said, "Jesus is in agony until the end of the centuries."

God, how great is your love. The gift of your son to be our savior is most wondrous. Help us to know, deep inside ourselves, the depth of your care. May it evoke from us, from the depths of our souls, deep gratitude and wonder. Amen.

They crucified Jesus there with the criminals. . . . They cast lots to divide his clothing. And the people stood by, watching. . . . The leaders scoffed at him. . . . The soldiers also mocked him.

Here we have a crucifixion compact. *They* crucified him: the religious and political rulers, the soldiers, and the bystanders, including disciples who betrayed and denied him.

"They" means "us." We are people like them. The same forces that took Jesus to the cross are still at work with our own participation: religious and political authorities ruling over millions of believers; economic and financial powers dividing among themselves the riches of the earth, robbing from the people; military and terrorist wars destroying human lives (both those who attack as well as the innocent); and people who have become simply "watchers" of what is going on in the world. Just as it was in the story of the crucifixion long ago.

We crucified him then and we still crucify him now. What we do to others we do to God and what we do to God's creation we do to God the Creator. If Christ is to truly reign in our lives, we have to take a good, long look at this whole dynamic.

And "we" means "me." "Were you there when they crucified my Lord?" we sing. Yes, I'm afraid—the answer is yes. We were there. I was there. We are still there.

Again we sing: "The Messiah dies cut off for sins, but not his own." For me, for you, for all of us, Jesus died.

My gracious God, help me today to be a faithful disciple of Jesus Christ. Help me to use all my potential for good. Help me to suffer with grace any portion of pain or injustice. Expand your reign in my life. In Jesus' name. Amen.

REIGN OF CHRIST

Then Jesus said, "Father, forgive them; for they do not know what they are doing."

Right there, at the crucifixion, the redeeming power of the cross is in action. The cross is the intersection of God's love and our sin.

One of the criminals who hung at Jesus' side responds to Jesus' manifestation of love with a sprout of faith: "Remember me when you come into your kingdom." And, before dying, the convict heard the word of triumphal welcome into God's home: "Today you will be with me in Paradise." Here is an opportunity for us to enter the scripture, asking that God remember each of us. Sensing that we are recognized and remembered, we can begin to acknowledge God's love.

We may be part of those for whom Jesus prayed, "Forgive them for they do not know what they are doing." He intercedes for us. God's love is always nearby. It becomes a fact—an experience—if we are ready to accept that we are guilty and need forgiveness. Right where we are. We can then "accept that we are accepted," as theologian Paul Tillich said in a famous sermon.

This is the power of the cross. It is the living symbol of God's transforming love and reign in our lives and in our community of faith. It has the power to become real and personal for us. It has the power to change our lives. It has the power to change the world. This is the greatness of God's love.

O God, remember me. Help me to receive your love and accept your forgiveness. May I come to accept that I am loved. Amen.

The Coming of the Kingdom

NOVEMBER 22–28, 2010 • BRENDA VACA

MONDAY, NOVEMBER 22 ～ *Read Isaiah 2:1-5*

I remember my father pulling out the *Thomas Guide* whenever we were going on a trip. This dusty book seemed to be the key to many far-off places and, indeed, it was. But things change over time. I now have a GPS navigator on my cell phone. I even used it once when I was at a conference in Arizona with clergy friends to get us to the Grand Canyon. We did not have a map, but this GPS navigator somehow pinpointed our current location. I just had to type in "Grand Canyon," and voile! Instant directions to one of the Seven Wonders of the World!

I wish I could tell you that we have a fabulous device with GPS for the Christian path. No church or denomination has a GPS navigator for keying in your current location to get clear instructions on how to safely arrive at your desired location. Instead, we have a magnificent set of stories in our sacred scripture that point in the direction we need to be headed. And, thankfully, we have prayer and the Holy Spirit, to help guide us on the journey. But there is no manual or *Thomas Guide* to give us the exact steps as we trudge along the road. Instead, God is asking us to pay close attention to God's teachings so that we may follow in God's paths.

We will know that we have finally arrived at the mountain of the Lord when we see swords turned into plowshares and spears into pruning hooks! War no more! This is what it means to walk in the light. This is what it means to live in God's house.

Loving God, as I try to live and walk in this Christian journey, help me to follow in your paths so that I might know your ways all the days of my life. Amen.

Pastor of Nueva Vida Ministries in San Francisco, CA

My brother John is a heavy sleeper and always has been. We grew up in Los Angeles in a time when it seemed like there was a major earthquake twice a year. Inevitably earthquakes occur at ungodly hours, three or four in the morning. Each time, as our family scrambled to squeeze between thresholds or under tables, someone would ask, "Where's John?" Eventually my brother would emerge (usually after the quake subsided) rubbing his eyes, asking, "What time is it?"

In his letter to the Romans, Paul is eager to remind his friends: "Salvation is nearer now than when we first believed." Perhaps Paul was writing of a chronological time that he believed would actually arrive at any moment. But let us consider our salvation as John Wesley did: as a journey.

There was a time in our faith journeys where we were not aware of the love of God. During this time, God watched over us with prevenient grace—the grace of God that arrives before we are even conscious of it. Then comes justifying grace—it comes when we realize we believe—the moment we first open our eyes to God's reality because of Jesus' teachings. The rest of the journey is sanctification—or as Paul would identify it, our salvation coming "nearer."

Once we are awake to God's loving grace, we cannot go back to sleep. We cannot pretend that it does not exist or push the pause button while we have our good time. We cannot afford to doze off on this grace because to do so would mean living in spiritual darkness. And if we are living in this spiritually dark place, how can we possibly recognize the light when it greets us in the morning?

God of life and light, help me to be like Jesus, who clothed himself in light and lived his life out loud in praise to your holy ways. Amen.

WEDNESDAY, NOVEMBER 24 ~ *Read Psalm 122:1*

In countless churches across the United States, and probably around the world, this verse greets churchgoers every Sunday as they enter the sanctuary, "I rejoiced with those who said to me, 'Let us go to the house of the LORD'" (NIV). Every time I visit a new church or attend a committee meeting, I stop at the entrance of the sanctuary to get a first impression and more often than not I find these words.

We have to admit, these words are powerful and joyful. They signify a group of people being glad to go to a familiar place, the house of the Lord. But what of those who are not invited? What of those children of God who do not know where the house of the Lord is?

During this season of Advent—this season of eager anticipation and of radical hospitality—I have to stop and ask with whom are we rejoicing? Who is being left out? I know a day laborer in San Francisco who lives under the freeway near my home and church. I am constantly inviting him to church or social gatherings. Often he admits to me that he does not dare enter the church or the parsonage for fear of being judged— judged for what he is wearing or because he has not been able to take a shower for the week. Unfortunately this has been his experience of "church" many times over.

We must realize that we are living in a different time. Some people can no long assume that church is a safe and welcoming place. We must be willing to be the ones who say, "Let's go," as Jesus so often said to friends and strangers. We must be willing, especially during this season, to be a loving people who go and seek those on the outside.

Gracious God, you welcome me and love me. Help me to be the arms and heart of Christ in my corner of the word. Amen.

THANKSGIVING DAY, USA

Today is Thanksgiving, a day when many gather around tables to celebrate family and to give thanks to God for the blessings of the past year. Yet it can be a difficult time for many, filled with unpleasant memories of past wrongs or painful reminders of isolation and loneliness. Holidays have a way of dredging up old feelings, no matter how much we anticipate the goodness of the day. Sometimes holidays are more than we can bear.

I know some people who close their eyes to special occasions of all kinds—birthdays, weddings, Thanksgiving, Christmas, New Year's. Hurt at some time in the past, they have convinced themselves that they are better off without the big hoopla of celebrations. They are essentially asleep to the possibilities of positive experiences with loved ones or even strangers. But cutting ourselves off from experiences and relationships is no way to live our lives. After all, this is real life.

Paul urged his friends in Rome, "Wake up!" Wake up to what? And why wake up now? These words call us to live in the light of Jesus' teachings. And *now* is the time because we do not know exactly when salvation will come . . . because salvation is not something that we possess. Salvation is something that possesses us.

And, yes, being awake to this love and sharing this love with others means that we are putting our hearts on the line. Yet, there is salvation and power in this kind of vulnerability— the power of love to overcome all obstacles. It is the same power that quickens the coming of our Savior.

Jesus, as I break bread with loved ones or strangers today, awaken in me your divine love. Let me know that I am yours. Amen.

When I ordered Internet service at my new home, the sales person gave me a four-hour window of time during which the technician would come to install my cable service. I hated it. The same is true when you order other kinds of utility services or UPS or FedEx. The dreaded four-hour window: 8:00 a.m. until noon, or 1:00 p.m. until 5:00 p.m. No matter how you slice it, it is a chunk of your day when you'd rather be doing something else.

As twenty-first century people, especially Americans, we want things fast and we want them to arrive precisely at the expected time. Christians are not exempt. We don't like surprises, and we definitely don't like being caught off guard. Even the four-hour window is better than no window at all. We at least can emotionally prepare ourselves to expect when something is about to arrive. That way the house can be clean; the dog can be on her best behavior; and you can look your most presentable as you open the door.

Yet our scripture today urges us to stay on guard. To keep watch. To be alert. Because we do not know the appointed time. We will not get a four-hour window that will let us know "the coming of the Son of Man." What does this mean? It means that we must be ever conscious of the coming kingdom. It means staying connected to God and trusting in God for all things and at all times.

God of all time and place, let me live today ever conscious of your presence in my life and in the world. Amen.

There is a woman named Betty who prays for peace every Sunday. She has been doing this for as long as I have known her, and certainly since the wars in Iraq and Afghanistan began. She stands up every Sunday and raises up her prayer concerns for the week. She adds without fail, "And, as always, for peace."

I do not know Betty's political persuasion. I do not know if she believes in just war or if she believes that no war is ever just. I do know that Betty is faithful and that she believes week after week that she is responsible for praying peace into the world. She is absolutely convinced that she is responsible for praying for the "peace of Jerusalem" and for all those she knows and loves.

Betty reminds me that I cannot be apathetic to the violence and hatred happening around me. I am responsible for it. You are responsible for it. We are accountable to pray peace into this world for the sake of God's coming kingdom. No matter our political persuasions, our nationalities, our theology, our call at all times is to pray for peace. Praying for peace will indeed signify that we are living in the spiritual Jerusalem. It will be a sign that we stand at the gates of God's holy city and that we seek God's kingdom first. When we claim peace in Jesus' name, it will come.

Prince of Peace, guide and guard my heart as I pray and work for your kingdom. Amen.

FIRST SUNDAY OF ADVENT

There is a popular bumper sticker I see often in the San Francisco Bay Area, "Jesus is coming. Look Busy." I imagine many people put this sticker on their car to poke fun at the Christian concept of the "last days." The underlying message of this bumper sticker seems to be *I'll just take my chances that if God does come, I can always manage to look Christian at the last minute.*

Our scripture passage likens the coming of Jesus to the story of Noah. Noah is a man who certainly keeps busy while the rest of the world's inhabitants go along their merry way, "eating, drinking, and marrying." Now, none of us would profess that these things are evil or sinful. Quite the opposite! We love to do these things.

But what if our lives become completely focused on these things alone? What happens if my whole life's purpose is looking for something good to eat, looking for the best bar in town, or searching for Mr. Right. Sooner or later, I will wake up and realize that I have lived my life only for myself.

Noah is a great example of Advent living. He had the communication lines open with God. He focused on godly things. And he lived for others. Remember, he didn't build that ark for himself or even for him and his loved ones. He brought every kind of creation onto that boat with him. What a feat! To live a life that matters means focusing on the things beyond our own survival and desires.

God of our salvation, help us to focus our lives on you. Let us walk this day in the way of Advent. Amen.

The Shared Yearning of Hope

NOVEMBER 29–DECEMBER 5, 2010 • FAITH WALKER

MONDAY, NOVEMBER 29 ~ *Read Isaiah 11:1-10*

Solomon was a slave in Texas during the Civil War. While he picked cotton, he dreamed of a day when he could have his own land. When he crawled into bed exhausted at night, he prayed for a day when he could own the roof over his head. When he was up before sunrise to do his master's bidding, when he took whippings, and when his son was sold to another plantation, he longed for justice.

On June 19, 1865, known as Juneteenth in Texas, Union general Gordon Granger read aloud in Galveston the Emancipation Proclamation originally issued on January 1, 1863. That day, about 250,000 slaves were freed. Imagine that moment of hearing the news.

Justice is coming! Those enslaved are now free! In that instant, you don't have your own land, meat on your plate, the master's education, or a paycheck. But you do have this news, and it changes you. To this day, communities in Texas celebrate Juneteenth.

This powerful Advent text from Isaiah is about justice. It is news that God is bringing justice into the world. It can't be stopped. We haven't yet experienced the peaceful world because peace depends on justice that hasn't yet arrived. But it is coming! Justice is promised! Peace is promised!

God's news changes everything about who we are. And this news changes everything about the world. Convinced by God's vision, we can become those who work to make it a reality.

Loving God, help us to hear your promise of justice. Amen.

A religious scholar and writer who lives in California with her dogs and enjoys hiking and travel

God promised to send a descendant of King David as a leader and sign. This leader, imbued with God's Spirit, a person with wisdom and understanding, comes in fulfillment of God's promise to the Israelites. This leader fulfills God's intent and promises. The powerful sit down with the weak. Children are safe. Unscrupulous people stop hurting others, and people experience safety because God's justice prevails.

As a young priest in El Salvador, Oscar Romero performed the duties typical of a Roman Catholic priest. He was shepherd to his flock. He administered the local parish, gave homilies, and served the Mass. When his country was embroiled in war, he didn't want to get involved. War was no solution to the problems. Then government troops occupied his town, raped and murdered men, women, and children, and took whatever they wanted. Members of his town slipped away and joined the guerrilas. Romero was unable to get help from the government to stop the suffering and violence. But the scriptures gave fresh inspiration to his preaching. It is plainly written in Isaiah that God takes the side of the poor and those who suffer.

When the town was under attack, Romero offered protection to all the people. Daring to speak against violence and calling for an end to corruption and inequities made him a target. One Sunday morning while Romero administered the sacraments, a hired gunman entered the church sanctuary and gunned Romero down in the front of the people.

The words Romero preached were seared into lives of the common people of El Salvador. God has promised justice for the poor. God will send leaders to care for the poor and their rights. And justice will come.

Dear God, when we are reluctant to tackle big problems, remind us of those who suffer. Let us hear your call for justice. Amen.

It isn't easy for Christians to live in harmony with one another. Sometimes only the words of scripture and familiar hymns seem able to bind together members of the Christian family who fail to agree on many other points. According to biblical scholar N. T. Wright, Paul is saying that the gospel creates a community that is called to live a new way. The renewed community seeks to live in harmony under God's steadfast guidance and encouragement.

James and Keith removed the front door of the church. They laid it across sawhorses at the front of the church for a worship service for church delegates and friends from all over the world. The minister covered the door with a cloth and set out bread and grape juice for Holy Communion. The church was filled to overflowing, the Word was proclaimed and the sacraments were celebrated. "All who desire to follow Jesus and intend to lead a new life in love and charity with your neighbors, come and eat." The choir sang; music filled the sanctuary.

The service concluded and people left—people of every hue and color, many nationalities, gay and straight, men and women, right through the open doorway. The worship service had been powerful. We all had been called to live a new way as a renewed humanity. We had experienced the presence of God.

As I passed where the door should have been, it was clear to me: without the door, there was no way to keep people out. There was no barrier. I felt like shouting down the street, "Hey, you are welcome! Everyone is welcome!" When the Lord's Table is a door, we can't keep people out. Everyone is welcome.

Dear God, help us open our doors even wider to experience the renewal that you can bring to us in community. Amen.

This psalm was written as a prayer for the king of Israel. Just as people today want good leaders at the helm of a nation—who will be fair, put down oppressors, lift people out of poverty, and help justice-seekers flourish—the people of Israel prayed for their king to lead them in these ways. These words describe one aspect of what we seek in the Messiah. We believe that when Jesus showed us what God's love is like, it included setting injustices aright and restoration of justice, the necessary condition for peace.

Caesar Chavez, inspired by his Christian faith and impassioned by the suffering of farm workers, stepped forward to lead his people, to alleviate poverty, and to make the food system more humane. Chavez stopped picking grapes to organize and lead the United Farm Workers. Farm workers needed a spokesperson and leader; Chavez was willing to try.

Chavez grew up as a migrant laborer working the fields of western states. He lived in migrant camps with inhumane conditions, shared water faucets, no clean drinking water and cups, filthy toilets, and sometimes showers without water. Pay was poor. Fields had no toilets. Some work required handling cancer-causing pesticides without protection.

To take on these issues, Chavez needed help from consumers. Aided by Dolores Huerta, Chavez organized a grape boycott to ask people to care about the working conditions of farm workers. People marched the dusty roads of California; consumers boycotted grapes; and eventually farm workers won better conditions. Caesar Chavez Day is celebrated in eight states on his birthday, March 31.

"He will defend the afflicted among the people and save the children of the needy; he will crush the oppressor" (NIV).

God, when I can't be a leader, help me to be a follower. When I can be a leader, help me be a good leader. Let me answer the call to work for justice. Amen.

The Shared Yearning of Hope   349

The key to understanding Romans is Paul's experience of God's righteousness, a concept far broader than being right or moral. We are called to participate in God's vision and to welcome Jesus, the bearer of this vision. God's righteousness refers to the in-breaking of justice in human affairs, the essential ingredient of a peaceful world. God's righteousness is fulfillment of promises made to Abraham. God's promises do not fail, and, in the end, justice prevails. The letter to the Romans imagines a world of justice and peace, welcoming and inclusive, centered in a confession of faith in the name of Jesus Christ.

God makes "righteous" or gives legal status to and defends those who, like orphans and widows, had no one to defend them. This legal status spreads equality and implores Christians to "welcome one another . . . just as Christ has welcomed you."

Zoe was a transgendered woman looking for a place to worship and to be accepted for who she was when she discovered our church. After many conversations, group meetings, and outreach activities, she came to our church one Sunday morning. People welcomed her, but the day that the mother-daughter dinner was announced, I feared she would be left out. So I invited her. We agreed to be mother and daughter for the event, and interestingly enough, after the event, we felt like mother and daughter. What had begun as a gesture became a relationship.

My boundaries stretched when Zoe became a friend, but they expanded again when we became "mother and daughter." I confess that words of scripture opened my mind and heart to this new possibility. I confess the power of Jesus to take me out of my comfort zone and into new places to "welcome one another."

Come, Lord Jesus, into my heart. There is room in my heart. Amen.

John the Baptist, a cousin of Jesus, was an independent desert man. He didn't dress like a businessman, fisherman, farmer, or Pharisee. He had a strange outfit made of camel hair.

John was a few months older than Jesus, a preacher without credentials. John and Jesus were familiar with passages from Isaiah and the Psalms about God's promises concerning the fulfillment of a time of peace and justice for which the Israelites had longed.

John thought that God's fulfillment would come when the people confessed their sins, repented their ways, and began to bear fruit worthy of the changes in their lives. His message reached some, and their lives began to show good results. They confessed their sins, came to him to be baptized.

However, when many Jewish religious leaders started coming for baptism, John figured that something was up. They wanted the benefits of John's message without actually doing the hard work. Some only wanted to rest on their pedigree as genuine descendants of Abraham. But John saw no time for delay. Right now, God would examine their lives. If they weren't "producing good fruit," they would be treated like barren fruit trees that are cut down and burned.

Where's the fruit? That's the question for us. In John's time, in the time of the early church, in our own churches in this Advent season, are we growing fruit for the harvest?

Dear God, help us sort out the work we need to undertake in our lives to bear a full and rich harvest. When our church is confused and our ministry is unclear, bring your message to us again in the birth of Jesus. Amen.

SECOND SUNDAY OF ADVENT

Before the economic crisis and global recession of 2009, many of us had a comfortable life. When the bubble burst, it changed life situations. We all knew people who lost investment funds, pensions, jobs, or homes.

One Sunday morning a Jewish restaurant owner, himself affected by the economic downturn, was moved by seeing poor people walk past his restaurant. They could not afford his meals. He came to a Christian church and offered to open the doors of his restaurant on Easter and provide free food to the poor if members of the congregation would serve it.

The pastor said, "Rearrange your Easter Sunday plans. Bring your friends to help. We need to do this." Margaret Mead has said, "A small group of thoughtful, committed citizens can change the world. Indeed that is the only thing that ever has."

John the Baptist baptized people so that they would give up their sins, but he points to an even more powerful next step. John the Baptist calls us to repent and claims that Jesus "will baptize you with the Holy Spirit and fire," a judgment process that separates wheat from chaff in our lives. This is not just a personal message. Our lives must bear fruit in community, and the renewed community needs to live in justice and peace. Just as gold must pass through a refining fire to be made pure, we must pass through experiences that burn away impurities. Walking with Jesus, we can go through hard times, join hands with others, and change the world.

God, we long for your Messiah. Help us turn around our lives, clean up our messes, and receive your incarnate love. Help us never to underestimate what a community can do when it comes together. Amen.

Greater Wholeness,
Deeper Holiness

DECEMBER 6–12, 2010 • JORETTA L. MARSHALL

MONDAY, DECEMBER 6 ~ *Read Isaiah 35:1-7*

Walking in high desert country, I was astounded to see a tiny flower blooming in the midst of the rocky, hard earth. It had been given just enough shelter, water, and nourishment to show forth in splendor. It added to the wholeness of the desert by its surprising presence.

Spiritual writings sometimes offer images of the desert as a quiet place—a dry spot—where little grows. Often they move us to imagine a place through which we must wander in endless, drab shades of brown and light green—until we arrive someplace else. Yet there is great beauty, surprise, and joy found in the midst of the endless stone and dirt.

Using the image of a *living* desert, Isaiah invites us to envision a world where the blind see, the lame "leap like a deer," and the speechless "sing for joy." Likewise in Advent, we are invited to imagine and anticipate a world that takes us by surprise. We move into a life of greater wholeness in God's presence. Yearning for this wholeness, we sometimes have to pass through the fear of not knowing.

But Isaiah reminds us to be strong. New things will spring forth.

Where do you yearn for God's surprising presence? How is God inviting you toward greater wholeness in this season of anticipating Christ?

Professor of Pastoral Theology, Care and Counseling at Brite Divinity School in Fort Worth, TX; ordained United Methodist elder in the Rocky Mountain Conference

The search for the right road led me down the wrong path. I was trying to find a street that would take me west, but I ended up on one that took me north. Thinking I could take a couple of turns and reconnect with the street that would take me west, I found myself on a string of dead ends and winding paths. One path led me to the top of a hill with a view that was simple, yet stunning. How often I try to find the "right" road, only to end up on a journey that is less direct. When I am open to the surprises of God's spirit, my lostness moves me to a highway of grace.

No matter how many times I read this passage from Isaiah during an Advent season, new insights arise. This time I wonder about this highway that is for God's people, where "the redeemed shall walk." This feels to me like an invitation to walk in holiness. This "Holy Way" requires more than reading scripture or praying or attending church. Holiness also involves daily attitudes and postures that we carry into the world around us and that invite us to anticipate God's surprising presence and grace on the journey, whether our path be direct or over many hills, winding curves, sustained vistas, and deep canyons.

Wherever we travel, God is present. What makes the Holy Way different is our intention to live in ways that keep us in conscious relationship with God's sustaining grace in the midst of our everyday lives. Isaiah suggests that on the Holy Way we discover a joy that is deep and a renewal of our souls in holy gladness. Walking in holiness, we find a road to reunion with God. The vista is beautiful.

How is the God of the Holy Way inviting you to journey in holiness?

A pew in my home reminds me of the small country churches in which my family grew up. There I witnessed the blessings of God through people who stood by my family in the midst of everyday experiences as well as in those moments of life that seemed unbearable. My grandmother was the local postmaster in one of these villages, and the post office was located in the home that my immediate family shared with her. I grew up at the post office and in the church and knew them to be gathering places where people related the stories of their lives.

Those within the community gathered to share the pain, grief, and sadness of lives marked by illness or poverty or despair. Likewise, they shared the joy of having enough money to plant new crops and celebrated children who were healthy and relationships that were strong. Tears were shed, and stories were told. Underneath it all was a deep and abiding belief that God was present and that God was involved in transforming the world in some new way.

Those memories remind me of the God whom Mary names as the one who transforms the present and the future. This Magnificat praises what God has done for Mary and will continue to do through her. It "magnifies the Lord." This God would transform the stories of her life and the lives of the generations to come, reminding many of the blessings of God. In addition, the Holy One would bring a new order to the world, creating new patterns of relating by bringing down the powerful and raising up the lowly.

God of holy transformations, as we move through this season of anticipation, may we continue to give thanks for the holy changes that you bring. May the world be transformed through them and through your grace-filled blessings. Amen.

The days seemed endless and short as I tried to accomplish too many tasks and respond to too many commitments. The activities were important in light of the call to lift oppression and work for justice. Yet, I was often left weary because things did not seem to change fast enough. The care offered did not seem to be enough to change the world. There was no room for rest, let alone praise. What I slowly came to realize was that because I was not resting in God's grace, my holiness and wholeness were lost in my doing.

Holy living moves us to recognize and claim that God's activity in the world is important, but it is not dependent on any of us individually. God's work requires moments to slow down enough to engage in praise that rocks the depths of our souls. Working hard to bring God's justice, we sometimes overlook our souls and lose our wonder and praise. Both holiness and wholeness are in jeopardy when we put our trust in our own doing rather than in God's presence and activity.

Advent brings an invitation to live in ways that are holy in order that we might recognize and praise the coming of wholeness to the world through justice and release. Taking time during this season to praise God's activities in the world revives each servant's soul in ways that give renewed energy. Then, together, we can watch over the stranger and uphold the widow. In so doing, we find ourselves meeting the psalmist and raising our voices together, knowing that God will reign "for all generations"—not just in this moment.

God, you are the one who keeps faith forever, offering us wholeness. May our words of praise come from the depths of our holy living. Amen.

Patience is a hallmark of the holiday season. We tell children to be patient until Christmas day. We ask those who are poor to be patient while we try to gather offerings to meet their needs. In all seasons, we encourage those who are eager to change the world or the church to be patient until things will be in the right place to create change without chaos. Patience toward solutions to complex problems like suffering, poverty, and war? We all seem to want those answers right now.

And then we get a word from James, who reminds us to be "patient . . . until the coming of the Lord" and to "strengthen your hearts." James's encouragement does not mean that we need to put up with things that are harmful and destructive, nor does it mean that suffering comes our way to prove to us that God is compassionate. Strengthening our hearts requires a new kind of patience.

James reminds us that the quality of patience is part of our holiness. Patience is not simply endurance. It is a way of actively believing that God is making something new. And, as the writer goes on to say in this short letter, we are to participate in moving the world toward deeper expressions of wholeness. Holiness and wholeness are integrally connected.

James's call for patience in this passage isn't about patience as virtue. Instead, this kind of patience refers to a way of faith that sees and knows, despite current circumstances, that God will come.

"The coming of the Lord is near." How do we wait with a sense of holy patience while taking important actions to bring the realm of God on earth? What are we waiting for?

Loving God, we wait with patience even while we are eager to change the world around us. Bring your realm into our personal and corporate lives that our waiting may result in deeper gifts of wholeness for all of your world. Amen.

An invitation that I did not seek arrived at my door and caused me to wrestle with a decision. In the process of discernment I began to wonder if this opportunity was the one I ought to consider? Or, was there something else to which God was calling me? How would I know? Was this God's call or was I just seeking something that I wanted? Besides, where did I get this notion that what God wants for me is so very different from what I might want for myself? What I knew in the depth of my spirit was that discernment was called for in the midst of my eagerness to make a decision.

John—and those listening to him—wondered if Jesus was the one they had been waiting for. When asked, Jesus responded not by defending himself or by adamantly claiming his place. Instead, he pointed toward those around him, reminding them about what they had seen and experienced in his presence. Jesus brought new visions of wholeness to the world as he healed the sick and brought relief to those who suffered. Was this the one they anticipated? Is this the one we expect to experience during this season?

Christ comes to offer wholeness for the whole world. This is at the core of our Christian faith. Through healing the sick, bringing sight to the blind, and offering a new relationship with God, Jesus embodies the one. We wait in Advent, recognizing that we have experienced the God who has been present in Jesus' healings and who is also part of our own healing. Jesus is the one who will continue to offer the world a new kind of wholeness.

Christ, we know that you are the one. Let our waiting for wholeness be touched by the reminder of your healing already done and that yet to come. Amen.

THIRD SUNDAY OF ADVENT

My best friend often reminds me that I have lost my way or that I have forgotten to prepare for the presence of God in my life. Like John the Baptist who pointed others toward the healing and wholeness found in Jesus, my friend counters the stories of despair and hopelessness with those of genuine and faithful hope. Just as John reminded the people to live in ways that were holy, I am often reminded to return to spiritual disciplines that prepare me for the wholeness God offers.

John lived a life that bore witness to holiness and wholeness. Although his dress and way of living in the world drew comments from our New Testament writers, it was not this that illustrated John's yearning to live a holy life. He provoked others to look to the coming of Jesus by capturing the imagination of those around him. John invited people to be prepared for the coming of the one.

John the Baptist is not inconsequential in the Gospels. He prophesies the way toward holiness and is a messenger for the kind of healing and wholeness incarnate in Jesus' life. John's holiness prepares him to meet this Jesus who brings good news, heals the sick, and invites people into a fuller relationship with God.

Jesus says, "No one has arisen greater than John the Baptist; yet the least in the kingdom of heaven is greater than he." No one greater? The least is greater? These words give us a dissonant glimpse into how radical Jesus' coming is, into how radical the path ahead will be.

John, and now Jesus, invites us to prepare the way, that all might experience wholeness in new ways.

Gracious God, we believe you are the one who invites us to live lives that are holy. Fill us with your redeeming love that we might experience anew the gift of the wholeness you offer. Amen.

The One We've Been Waiting For

DECEMBER 13–19, 2010 • CYNTHIA A. WILSON

MONDAY, DECEMBER 13 ～ *Read Isaiah 7:10-16*

It was moving day! The van had been loaded, the car filled with gas, the bags of snacks and good music were prepared—as were the maps! The detailed maps were outlined with a marker so that my family and I would not veer from the main path. But even as I placed the key in the ignition, I was still asking God for a "sign." Have I made the right decision to relocate? Did I hear you correctly? Are you sure, God?

Then it hit me. Jacob lost a whole night's sleep wrestling with his sign. Jonah ended up giving heartburn to the magnanimous sign of a whale. As if manna, quail, and pillars of fire were not enough, Israel spent forty years in the wilderness waiting for *more* signs.

When God offers King Ahaz a sign, Ahaz says, "I will not put the LORD to the test." (Ahaz's phony piety only suggests his lack of faith.) Just the same, Isaiah announces that God will give a sign that will offer the people of faith assurance. It is the sign of Emmanuel. It is a Hebrew word signifying "God is with us." This will be the name of a child born to a young woman.

So too Mary and Joseph will receive a sign that efficaciously leads us to a child who will be called "Emmanuel," just as God promised. Signs like this don't always give answers, but they do give the faithful assurance of the right direction. This is the way to the celebration of Christmas.

God, you are always with us, but sometimes we are afraid. Help us trust you as we seek to discern your will and do it. Amen.

Ordained Deacon at St. Mark's United Methodist Church in Wichita, KS; *Women of Color* scholar for the General Board of Higher Education and Ministry of the United Methodist Church; concert artist

In an age of exponential growth in technology, medicine, science, and education, it never ceases to amaze me how things continue to fall apart. In the church, our ostentatious approach to the preaching of the gospel has caused the church to talk much and love sparingly, to do things grander but not greater, and to replace merit with magnitude. We seem to believe we can save ourselves.

In this prayer for Israel, the plea comes forth: "Restore us, O God; let your face shine, that we may be saved." Approaching this psalm with humility and openness jolts us back to the recognition of the one who saves us. This inspiring metaphor of God's shining face can be seen throughout the book of Psalms. Here the psalmist petitions a redeeming God for provision, protection, and guidance from all that is evil.

The good news for today is of the one who *is* coming! This is the one whose thoughts are much more advanced than our thoughts and whose ways are far more productive than ours. There is one coming who will not oversee us but will shine on us and through us, making us strong and giving us life. We can rest from our overfunctioning and flashiness. There is one coming who will love us in spite of ourselves and who will bring hope to our land.

So we begin to watch for that shining face again, in the faces of pregnant virgins, brighter-than-usual stars, and even from overbooked hotels and mangers. That's the One who shall bring forth birth that "we may be saved."

Shining One! You know our efforts to save ourselves have fallen short. Your coming is a gift to us! Your presence will revive us, restore us, refresh us, and renew us! Come, Lord Jesus, come.

Our commercial, popular culture often serves up a thin gruel of media and retail trivializations of Christmas. These last ten days of Advent are a great time to add the theological nutrition and depth of Paul's letter to the Romans to our spiritual diet. In these opening words of greeting, we picture the ancestry of the people of faith in the good news of discipleship. This is substantive stuff for a hungry-for-meaning, postmodern, twenty-first century Advent.

A documentary about jazz aired on television recently. It beautifully celebrated Louis Armstrong's immeasurable impact on this distinctively American art form. Born in 1901 in the poor and violent "Battlefield" section of New Orleans, Louis's fatherless family had little food. Louis recalled his stomach regularly growling from hunger. At age seven, Louis began working for a Jewish Russian immigrant family, delivering coal to the houses of prostitution in the "Storyville" part of town. That family's mother insisted that he eat a good meal before going home each night. In gratitude for this Jewish mother's loving kindness, he wore a Star of David the rest of his life.

Consider our spiritual lives in a too-rushed Advent. A materialistic decadence—a decadence prettier and shinier than the one little Louis faced—surrounds us. Sometimes we don't realize how hungry we have been until we start getting a full spiritual meal on a regular basis. Romans presents a hearty meal for the soul—even in the first six verses. Read it again. Dine on the promises of the prophets and the power of God. Become renewed as an apostle of the One who is to come.

God of preachers and prophets, Gentiles and Jews, feed us with your spirit of holiness and hope. Sustain us, we pray, that we too might bring about the obedience of faith in this season of expectation. In Christ we pray. Amen.

In some cultures, a person brings a gift when visiting to show honor, admiration, or love. Some cultures bow. Some hug. Some kiss both cheeks. (Or at least the air next to the cheeks.) Some break into a big, sincere smile and ask "how y'all *doin'*?"

When we are serious about treating others—all others—as we would have them treat us, we approach each person as if he or she was the most important person we will meet that day. When beginning an interaction, we set a mood and a spirit for how we will relate. Approaching someone in person, body language says a lot. However, when the greeting is by a phone call, an e-mail, or a handwritten letter, honor is shown by the words we choose to use.

Writing to the Romans, Paul addresses them as "God's beloved . . . called to be saints." He then offers them both the "grace" of the traditional Greek greeting and the "peace" of the Hebrew salutation. Isn't *that* a fine "how do you do"? We can hear in his words that he was treating them just as he wished to be treated.

This is not just a season to prepare a place in our hearts and minds for the coming incarnation of God. It is a time for renewing and reordering our relationships, that we might await the Christ in each person. May we bow or hug or kiss in a spirit of expectation and hope, that the awaited One might arrive to a cheerful "how y'all *doin'*?"

Loving God, as you come into the world in new and surprising ways, help us to honor those we meet, in whom we might be surprised to meet you. Help us to so love and respect the "other" that we anticipate your arrival in each one that we meet. Amen.

Many times the scriptures give a detailed account of what a particular character has done and the role he or she plays in the Hebrew scriptures or in New Testament stories, but sometimes the character remains nameless. Conversely, with Joseph, we do know his name but we know very little about his background or trade. What a meager biography for such a major personage. Here is what we do know: Joseph is "a righteous man."

Righteousness for Joseph means having right relationships, as defined by honorable social conventions. By the norms of his time, he wants to do the right thing. He is "unwilling to expose (Mary) to public disgrace." But then a message from God comes to him through an angel. Joseph's integrity must now incorporate, take in this ongoing revelation. He stands as a person of faith, prepared to follow obediently the divine plan of a faithful God. Joseph does not doubt the divine message from the angel. He takes Mary as his beloved wife and accepts the child that she carries as the child of promise.

Our holiday preparations can also involve a wonderful mix of community gatherings, traditional expectations, and world-changing new revelations, whatever or whoever the angels are that appear to announce them. The angels speaking to Joseph echoed the words of Isaiah's prophecy, reminding us that the new thing can be rooted in something very, very old. Visions of a redeemed future coupled with sacred memories can also ground us in a glorious expectancy today. A measure of Joseph-like righteousness will help.

Grant us, God of revelation, an openness to your word of things to come, that we might not be too rigid for the sake of the proper and polite. Give us the freedom and integrity of faith to change and more forward like Joseph when your divine message comes to us. Amen.

What about these angels? The dictionary defines *angel* as "a messenger of God, a supernatural being to whom are attributed greater than human power (and) intelligence." However, when angels show up in scripture, one of two things will happen: either someone will be transformed or someone will be transferred. Genesis 16 details one of the first angelic encounters recorded in scripture. It states, "The angel of the LORD said to [Hagar], 'Now you shall conceive and bear a son; you shall call him Ishmael, for the LORD has given heed to your affliction.'" Sound familiar?

This Christmas angel appears to Joseph in a dream. A spiritual Joseph openly trusts both the dream and the angel in it, perhaps aided by a culture that made room for sacred mystery. It is tougher in our radically secular time to remain spiritually open. We need children to help us do that.

A close friend of mine tells the story of her young son's unusual angelic encounter. After reading the story of the birth of Christ to her three children, the young boy said, "Why were Mary and Joseph afraid, Mom? Angels sit in my room all the time. Actually, I think they're pretty neat." I could not help but remember the song taught to me by my maternal grandmother, "All day, all night, angels watching over me, my Lord; All night, all day, angels watching over me."

Holy One, we can become far removed from the truths of this holy season. We repent for being so easily sidetracked and world-weary. There so much to do. There is no time to read or listen to the stories again. Nor for angelic voices. Give us the wonderment and mystery of Mary and Joseph. Guide us again toward the Christ child. Amen.

SUNDAY, DECEMBER 19 ~ *Read Matthew 1: 21-25*

FOURTH SUNDAY OF ADVENT

It was my maiden voyage to South Africa. The apartheid system had just been dismantled. Not very long after my arrival in the village, I was informed that the trip would culminate with a "naming" ceremony. On the final day, I found myself singing and dancing in the village chapel, along with the pilgrims representing various tribes, and the Afrikaans.

After leading us, Nana, the matriarch of the community, moved me to the center of the circle and with great eloquence and passion, announced, "She shall be called *Toboko*—'sent from God!'" It was a moment that changed me forever. The authority and passion with which Nana "named" me moved me in some very deep place.

I admit that, since then, there have been many days when I do not feel that God should take ownership for my behavior. I stop and remind myself that I am a daughter of the One who spoke and gave life to the world and everything in it.

One's name and father's ancestry was of great significance in Jesus' day. Born in a patriarchal society where the law stated emphatically that a fatherless son was of no use, Matthew prominently situates Joseph in his story.

The law gave Joseph the right to dispose of this child; adoration constrained him to bring him up as his own. The law allowed him to turn the child over into the hands of government; devotion demanded that he cover his wife and child, even if they had to live as fugitives. Joseph had clearly heard the angel of the Lord say, "You are to name him Jesus, for he will save his people from their sins."

God, who does not leave us fatherless or motherless, we are grateful for the privilege of calling your name. Draw us together in unity, in strength, and in hope. We give you thanks, with great expectation. In the name of our Messiah. Amen.

Christ Born among Us

DECEMBER 20–26, 2010 • JAN LOVE

MONDAY, DECEMBER 20 ∼ *Read John 1:1-14 and Hebrews 1:1-12*

Students at Candler School of Theology recently asked a panel of students and faculty to speak on "Why I am a Christian." Increasingly, a variety of religious traditions and spiritual paths compete for our attention. Whether we live in cities or rural areas, most of us have opportunity to live, work, and create community with Hindus, Muslims, Jews, or people of other faiths. We can often grow in our faith in Christ and learn much about our own tradition by encountering those whose faith commitments differ from ours.

For example, among the religions of the world, Christianity is the only one that believes that God became human in order to show us the way to salvation. The first chapter of John does not provide any details of the birth of Jesus but instead jumps right into a bold assertion on which the whole Gospel is centered: Jesus is God incarnate. Jesus is God's Word. Jesus shares God's identity and character, the "exact imprint of God's very being" (Heb. 1:3). Jesus' revelation of God springs from Jesus' intimate familial relationship to God.

Jesus reveals God to us and shows the way to salvation through intimate personal relationships like those he had with the disciples and Mary and Martha, relaxed conversations like those with Nicodemus or the Samaritan woman, passionate prayer like those he prayed in anticipation of his death, and the ultimate sacrifice of giving his life.

God, help us find full and fresh access to you by receiving Christ anew into our lives. Amen.

Dean of Candler School of Theology at Emory University in Atlanta, GA

John tells us that all who receive Jesus and believe in him become "children of God." What does it mean to be children of God?

One panelist's response at the Candler forum on "Why I am a Christian" was simple: "I am a Christian because Jesus washed Judas's feet." What a remarkable and radical act, lovingly washing the feet of the one who betrays you. What an example for us! Isaiah reminds us that, as children of God, we receive God's gracious deeds, great favor and abundant, steadfast love, even though we regularly betray God. Do we in turn show God's love to everyone, even those who would do us harm?

Jesus "had to become like his brothers and sisters in every respect," including being born to a woman, the wonderful event we celebrate this week. He was fully human, just as he was fully God. As a human, his words and works as well as his life and death show us concretely the way to live our lives as children of God. His prescriptions continue to astonish us. The beauty and our familiarity with Jesus' teachings sometimes mask how hard they really are: resist evil, love your enemies, bless those who curse us, feed the hungry, visit the sick and imprisoned, be as carefree as birds and flowers.

Paul's letter to Titus in Crete attempts to pass leadership on to others and show this young associate how to guide congregations of believers, children of God. In Eugene Peterson's paraphrased verses from *The Message*, Paul encourages Titus to tell believers "to take on a God-filled, God-honoring life," to become people Christ "can be proud of, energetic in goodness."

As children of God, Christ calls us to witness energetically to the abundant love, grace, and mercy shown to us, even when it's hard.

God, help us, as your children, be more faithful followers, in word and deed, of Christ our savior. Amen.

At the very time we celebrate the gift of the incarnation, the coming of the Christ child, many families will be living with the painful reality of having lost loved ones. Recent deaths, no matter what the cause, make holidays difficult for families and friends.

Many will be mourning the loss of those killed in war. Children without mommies or daddies; parents with daughters or sons; wives, husbands, and sweethearts without their partners —these are some of the costs of war.

These costs increase significantly when we add the tens of thousands who have been wounded physically and psychologically. Most communities in the United States have families directly affected by losses in combat. In some towns and cities, particularly those near military bases, virtually everyone knows firsthand the price of war.

When we survey all the places across the world where wars are being fought, sometimes with whole societies destroyed, we stagger under the burden of trying to comprehend the full effects of this form of violence. Surely the wars we wage are an illustration of what Isaiah describes as "The people who walked in darkness . . . those who lived in a land of deep darkness . . ."

Isaiah goes on to declare, "For a child has been born for us . . . and he is named wonderful Counselor, Mighty God, Everlasting Father, Prince of Peace." Jesus' birth—the joy of new life and coming of the Prince of Peace—brings renewed opportunity for each of us to be signs of God's ever-present and unfailing love. The Christmas season is a special chance to offer comfort to all who suffer unbearable loss, all who mourn, and all whose lives must be rebuilt. Christmas invites us to witness to the light that shines in this darkness, indeed, to live as those who "have seen a great light."

Come, Lord Jesus. Bring us out of our darkness into your marvelous light. Amen.

For two decades, I was a member of congregation that periodically used the call and response litany that says: God is good, all the time. All the time, God is good.

There have been difficult periods, often around holidays, when I resented hearing this litany, much less reciting it. On occasion, I have almost choked while saying it through bitter tears and heartbreak that accompany the great challenges in life that we all endure.

Yet across the years, I have come to believe that repeating these sentences provides a profound reminder that nothing can separate my loved ones or me from God's love and the life-transforming power of redemption we know in Christ. In good times and bad, this short, rhythmic affirmation helps center my meditations on the remarkable, abundant blessings that enrich and sustain me and my faith community.

Reading Psalm 96 at Christmas time has a similar effect. "Sing to the LORD, bless his name; tell of his salvation from day to day. Declare his glory among the nations, his marvelous works among all the peoples." Living a life of thanksgiving and gratitude—not just in good times and not simply as a naïve way of escaping the hard work of wading through tough challenges—can be a powerful witness to the world.

Certainly contagious joy characterized early Christian communities. They faced more adversity than the average person, yet they had laid hold of an inner peace and joy that seemed exuberant, even radiant, spilling over for all to see. They lived the psalmist's proclamation, "Let the heavens be glad, and let the earth rejoice; . . . for he is coming, for he is coming to judge the earth."

Indeed, Jesus is coming. God is good. Sing to the Lord a new song!

God, help me be grateful for the many blessings of life and the love made known in Jesus Christ. Amen.

CHRISTMAS EVE

One good friend once said that one of the most important dimensions of being a father was that he got to play like a child with children all over again. Although he was raised in a loving home with lots of opportunity for play, from his perspective he somehow just never got enough. By playing with his own children, he could extend his childhood and make up for lost time.

Reading Psalms 98 and 148 is like being in a room of happy, giddy children—even grown children—discovering new delightful pastimes and having fun at play, grateful just to be there. Everyone and everything in these psalms is having a good time. Everybody is making a joyful noise. The hills sing. The waters clap their hands as the fish applaud. Fire and hail, snow and ice, and even the wild rushing winds praise God, as do the apple trees and cedar woods. The important people as well as the ordinary ones break forth into songs of joy.

Why all this glee, this delight, this exuberant and uncontainable joy, as with children at play? God has done marvelous things. God has shown steadfast love and faithfulness to us. Indeed, God has redeemed the whole of creation! And now, as we are reminded on Christmas Eve, God will enter the world anew through the birth of a vulnerable baby, the Christ child.

Little baby Jesus is God with us, Emmanuel. The Christ child provides access to God in ways never before possible. The Word becomes flesh and lives among us (John 1: 14). In the birth of Jesus, we meet, in Charles Wesley's words, "love divine, all loves excelling"; a savior that is "all compassion, pure unbounded love." Even the creatures and the earth itself can feel the difference. Joy to the world!

God, prepare me to welcome the Christ child and, in gratitude for this gift, live a life of love and joy. Amen.

CHRISTMAS DAY

According to the elite of the first century, shepherding was the worst job you could have. Shepherds were disparaged as lazy, dishonest people who lived on land belonging to others. Finding rest in a stable was better than sleeping out among the sheep.

But Jesus' birth in a feeding trough is a very humble circumstance too, as is almost everything in this story. God enters into human history completely helpless, as a newborn. Jesus' parents have few possessions and little experience. Mary is probably in her early teens.

Then the first to know about the birth are the lowly and outcast shepherds. "I am bringing you good news of great joy for all the people: to you is born this day in the city of David a Savior, who is the Messiah, the Lord." The shepherds are not accustomed to being the first to get such good news. When the angel of God showed up, surrounded in glory, the shepherds were naturally afraid.

Once they comprehended the message, the shepherds knew what to do next: they went to check this news out for themselves. They shared with Mary and Joseph what the angels had told them. All were amazed, but Mary kept the words and pondered them in her heart. In the midst of all the rejoicing, she quietly considered the meaning of all these wonderful events.

Once again, God enters human history through the poor and the homeless, those without social standing or power. God chooses to favor the disfavored and lifts up the humble, the lowly. Among such as these, God is with us, Emmanuel.

God, help me find the presence of Christ in surprising places and humble people. Amen.

SUNDAY, DECEMBER 26 ~ *Read Mathew 2:13-23*

First Sunday after Christmas

Christ comes to a world of terrible danger. Soon after he was born in Bethlehem, Herod ordered the deaths of all the children under two years of age. To escape, Joseph and Mary took baby Jesus and fled. They left in the middle of the night to go to Egypt where they hoped to find refuge.

Years ago in dangerous coal mines, gases like methane and carbon monoxide would build up in the shafts. Detection of these gases is difficult, but canaries are very sensitive to carbon monoxide. As long as the birds sang, the miners knew they could continue their work. If the canaries stopped singing, the miners knew they must evacuate immediately.

Like canaries that stop singing, children's deaths provide warning of a world gone terribly awry. The United Nations reports that millions of children die of poverty, malnutrition, and disease every year. In recent decades, tens of millions of children have become refugees from wars and other disasters. The multibillion-dollar commercial sex industry exploits two million children each year. More than fifteen million children have been orphaned by HIV/AIDS.

In church we learned to sing "Jesus loves the little children, all the children of the world." If we believe these lyrics, we know that each of the statistics above is a precious being entrusted to our care. They are, like the Christ child, refugees. If we embrace Christ's command to love them all, we must work to help them escape a world gone terribly awry.

God, help us love all the children of the world. Help us build communities of refuge and peace where they can flourish and sing for joy. Amen.

Epiphany's Light

DECEMBER 27–31, 2010 • ANNA LEE

MONDAY, DECEMBER 27 ～ *Read Psalm 8:1-4*

As winter's freeze hardens the ground under our feet and frost dances in icy patterns along the windowpane, God's work surrounds us with beauty each day. Regardless of the season of year, God's glory is seen in creation. Psalm 8 praises the mighty works of God in creation. In verse 3, the psalmist highlights the moon and stars that God has established with God's own fingers. The very moon that the psalmist looks at in wonder illuminates our own nights as well. The psalmist's words call us to a renewed sense of awe and wonder at God's creation.

The psalmist goes on to ask, "What are humans that you are mindful of them, mortals that you care for them?" In light of the majestic scale of creation, the author can hardly imagine how humans are significant in such a world. God shows throughout the scriptures and in our own lives that God loves and cares about humanity. God's interest in us is endless. God's care for us is immeasurable. This God, who created the entire universe, is mindful of and cares for us, mere mortals.

As we busy ourselves with life's tasks, we often miss the wonder of creation extravagantly displayed around us. When we forget to look up and around, we risk becoming isolated, forgetting our relationship to creation and forgetting that God cares for us deeply. But God is attentive to the minute details of the world, and knowing this gives us strength, joy, and wonder that carry us, day by day, throughout our lives.

God of the universe, I praise you for your astounding creation.
Open my eyes today to its grandeur. Amen.

Student at Vanderbilt Divinity School and member of Trinity United Methodist Church in Murfreesboro, TN

After the psalmist praises God's creation and marvels at the care God shows for humans, he goes on to express an understanding of a human's place in the created order. The psalmist declares in verse 6 that God has given humans *dominion* over the works of God's hands. Sadly, the word *dominion* in this psalm and elsewhere in scripture has been misused and abused throughout history. Humans have often interpreted dominion to mean that humans have the power and "right" to do whatever they wish with the world and its resources. Such a view has led to the stripping of forests for lumber, the annihilation of animal habitats to make roads, and the blasting of mountaintops for coal. In the name of consumption and human "need," our adopted behaviors have helped create the current climate crisis and other devastating environmental effects.

But viewing dominion as an invitation to use the world however we choose is a distorted understanding of what God intended. God granted humans dominion over the earth not to exploit it but to care for and protect it. Understanding dominion as sacred stewardship changes our worldview immediately. We can begin to examine our own actions in light of the well-being of all of creation. Instead of using the cheapest and fastest forms of energy, we can research and use renewable energy sources that respect the earth and meet human need. Understanding our role on the earth as steward and protector allows us to respect God's creation and participate in the full glory of God's work on earth. Surely this is a great gift to us from God.

Creator God, we are humbled to be given responsibility for your earth. Keep us vigilant that we may protect this world. Give us sharp, creative minds and willing spirits to serve you and the home you have created for us. Amen.

The opening words of Ecclesiastes 3 have been used time and again in both secular and religious contexts. Ecclesiastes belongs to the wisdom literature tradition, characterized by its universal messages and themes. Ecclesiastes 3:1-3 speaks to the universal experience of life's cycles and changes. As we approach the end of another year, we too feel the tugs of birth and death, endings and beginnings.

The writer of Ecclesiastes highlights in these verses the natural cycles of the earth. After reflecting in Psalm 8 on God's creation of the earth, it follows that God created the earth and the cycles of the earth as well. God fashioned the earth in such a way that a seed must fall from a tree and be disconnected from its source of life in order to produce a new tree and new life. God also created the steady cycles of day and night, the ebb and flow of the tides, the need to work and then to rest.

In the modern world, we sometimes try to modify or stop the cycles of creation. We create light strong enough to dismiss the dark and create fields that never have to rest in order to accomplish more. We bend rivers from their natural paths and build structures that are vulnerable in the path of hurricanes. Our resistance to natural cycles tires not only us. It tires the earth itself.

These three short verses can teach us much about living in harmony with the earth. If we are open to living in step with the earth's natural cycles, we can begin to view our relationship with the earth in a new way. Instead of directing nature to the paths that benefit us most immediately, we can follow nature's created paths and cycles designed by God to benefit all.

God, help me to understand and embrace the balance and beauty of creation. Slow me down so that I may be nurtured by the natural rhythms of the earth. Amen.

Jesus' words, as recorded by Matthew, are a serious call to examine our love of neighbor. It is easy to think we are fulfilling our call to serve others by contributing to a food bank or giving money to a homeless shelter. These things are important, but they are only the beginning. Jesus calls us to even greater action. Jesus identifies himself with "the least of these," and with that in mind our service must go much deeper. Feeding the hungry means sharing food with those who need it, but it also means addressing the systems in our country and world that cause hunger. Taking care of the sick includes paying attention to healthcare systems and access to medicines. Jesus calls us to re-imagine what it means both to meet the immediate needs of those around us as well to address the underlying causes of those needs.

As we read Jesus' words in light of the current environmental crisis, we can begin to see new visions of caring for our neighbor. People around the world suffer from lack of safe and clean drinking water. Lack of infrastructure in developing countries as well as pollution of their water sources contribute to the spread of disease. In many cities around the world air pollution creates numerous harmful physical side effects causing sickness. Our environmental decisions affect the health and well-being of our neighbors next door and around the world.

Jesus' call to love and attend to the needs of our neighbors challenges us to use our hearts, minds, and strength to care for individuals and to reform the systems that create hunger, poverty, and disease.

God, expand and enlighten my understanding of what it means to love my neighbor. Help me to serve people and change systems so that all your children have what they need. Amen.

In reflecting on a year gone by and looking forward to another, this passage reminds us that our actions on earth have far-reaching, even eternal consequences. In Matthew's Gospel, Jesus tells of the judgment of all people based on love and care of neighbor. Jesus says that those who love others will inherit the kingdom. I imagine the ones on Jesus' left hand who were told to depart from him were shocked and completely caught off guard. The Gospel says they are incredulous and ask when they saw him in need and not care for him? Jesus tells them that what they did not do for the least of their brothers and sisters, they did not do for him.

As Christians we are held accountable for our actions and way of life. The end of the year is a good time to reflect on our lives, to examine how our lives affect those around us. The decisions we make about food and transportation, possessions and lifestyle are important; we are accountable for the consequences of those choices. When we ask, "Lord when did we see you thirsty and not give you something to drink?" might Jesus reply that our negligence in polluting water deprived someone of clean drinking water or that our waste of water caused a shortage that led to someone's being thirsty? As Christians seeking to live in loving community with all, we must consider the effects of both our actions and our inaction. Our relational choices, including those with the environment, have serious consequences, ones for which we will be held accountable.

God, forgive me for the ways in which I have not lived out your call, and give me the strength and guidance to follow you more closely in the year to come. Amen.

The Revised Common Lectionary* for 2010
Year C – Advent / Christmas Year A
(Disciplines Edition)

January 1–3
NEW YEAR'S DAY
Ecclesiastes 3:1-13
Psalm 8
Revelation 21:1-6a
Matthew 25:31-46

January 3
EPIPHANY
Isaiah 60:1-6
Psalm 72:1-7, 10-14
Ephesians 3:1-12
Matthew 2:1-12

January 4–10
BAPTISM OF THE LORD
Isaiah 43:1-7
Psalm 29
Acts 8:14-17
Luke 3:15-17, 21-22

January 11–17
Isaiah 62:1-5
Psalm 36:5-10
1 Corinthians 12:1-11
John 2:1-11

January 18–24
January 18-24
Nehemiah 8:1-3, 5-6, 8-10
Psalm 19
1 Corinthians 12:12-31a
Luke 4:14-21

January 25–31
Jeremiah 1:4-10
Psalm 71:1-6
1 Corinthians 13:1-13
Luke 4:21-30

February 1–7
Isaiah 6:1-8, (9-13)
Psalm 138
1 Corinthians 15:1-11
Luke 5:1-11

February 8–14
TRANSFIGURATION
Exodus 34:29-35
Psalm 99
2 Corinthians 3:12-4:2
Luke 9:28-36, (37-43)

February 15–21
FIRST SUNDAY IN LENT
Deuteronomy 26:1-11
Psalm 91:2, 9-16
Romans 10:8b-13
Luke 4:1-13

February 17
ASH WEDNESDAY
Joel 2:1-2, 12-17 or
  Isaiah 58:1-12
Psalm 51:1-17
2 Corinthians 5:20b-6:10
Matthew 6:1-6, 16-21

February 22–28
SECOND SUNDAY IN LENT
Genesis 15:1-12, 17-18
Psalm 27
Philippians 3:17-4:1
Luke 13:31-35

March 1–7
THIRD SUNDAY IN LENT
Isaiah 55:1-9
Psalm 63:1-8
1 Corinthians 10:1-13
Luke 13:1-9

March 8–14
FOURTH SUNDAY IN LENT
Joshua 5:9-12
Psalm 32
2 Corinthians 5:16-21
Luke 15:1-3, 11b-32

March 15–21
FIFTH SUNDAY IN LENT
Isaiah 43:16-21
Psalm 126
Philippians 3:4b-14
John 12:1-8

March 22–28
PALM/PASSION SUNDAY
Isaiah 50:4-9a
Psalm 31:9-16 or
  Psalm 118:1-2, 19-29
Philippians 2:5-11
Luke 19:28-40

March 29—April 4
HOLY WEEK

Holy Thursday
Exodus 12:1-14
Psalm 116:1-4, 12-19
1 Corinthians 11:23-26
John 13:1-17, 31b-35

Good Friday
Isaiah 52:13-53:12
Psalm 22
Hebrews 4:14-16; 5:7-9
John 18:1-19:42

Easter
Acts 10:34-43
Psalm 118:14-24
1 Corinthians 15:19-26
John 20:1-18
Luke 24:1-12

April 5–11
Acts 5:27-32
Psalm 150
Revelation 1:4-8
John 20:19-31

April 12–18
Acts 9:1-6, (7-20)
Psalm 30
Revelation 5:11-14
John 21:1-19

April 19–25
Acts 9:36-43
Psalm 23
Revelation 7:9-17
John 10:22-30

April 26—May 2
Acts 11:1-18
Psalm 148
Revelation 21:1-6
John 13:31-35

May 3–9
Acts 16:9-15
Psalm 67
Revelation 21:10, 22-22:5
John 14:23-29

May 10–16
Acts 16:16-34
Psalm 97
Revelation 22:12-21
John 17:20-26

> **May 13**
> **ASCENSION DAY**
> Acts 1:1-11
> Psalm 47
> Ephesians 1:15-23
> Luke 24:44-53

May 17–23
PENTECOST
Acts 2:1-21
Psalm 104:24-35b
Romans 8:14-17
John 14:8-17, 25-27

May 24–30
TRINITY
Proverbs 8:1-4, 22-31
Psalm 8
Romans 5:1-5
John 16:12-15

May 31—June 6
I Kings 17:8-16 (17-24)
Psalm 146
Galatians 1:11-24
Luke 7:11-17

June 7–13
1 Kings 21:1-21a
Psalm 5:1-8
Galatians 2:15-21
Luke 7:36-8:3

June 14–20
I Kings 19:1-15a
Psalm 42 and 43
Galatians 3:23-29
Luke 8:26-39

June 21–27
2 Kings 2:1-2, 6-14
Psalm 77:1-2, 11-20
Galatians 5:1, 13-25
Luke 9:51-62

June 28—July 4
2 Kings 5:1-14
Psalm 30
Galatians 6:1-16
Luke 10:1-11, 16-20

July 5–11
Amos 7:7-17
Psalm 82
Colossians 1:1-14
Luke 10:25-37

July 12–18
Amos 8:1-12
Psalm 52 or Psalm 82
Colossians 1:15-28
Luke 10:38-42

July 19–25
Hosea 1:2-10
Psalm 85
Colossians 2:6-19
Luke 11:1-13

July 26—August 1
Hosea 11:1-11
Psalm 107:1-9, 43
Colossians 3:1-11
Luke 12:13-21

August 2–8
Isaiah 1:1, 10-20
Psalm 50:1-8, 22-23
Hebrews 11:1-3, 8-16
Luke 12:32-40

August 9–15
Isaiah 5:1-7
Psalm 80:1-2, 8-19
Hebrews 11:29-12:2
Luke 12:49-56

August 16–22
Jeremiah 1:4-10
Psalm 71:1-6
Hebrews 12:18-29
Luke 13:10-17

August 23–29
Jeremiah 2:4-13
Psalm 81:1, 10-16
Hebrews 13:1-8, 15-16
Luke 14:1, 7-14

August 30—September 5
Jeremiah 18:1-11
Psalm 139: 1-6, 13-18
Philemon 21-30
Luke 14:25-33

September 6–12
Jeremiah 4:11-12, 22-28
Psalm 14
1 Timothy 1:12-17
Luke 15:1-10

September 13–19
Jeremiah 8:18-9:1
Psalm 79:1-9 or Psalm 4
1 Timothy 2:1-7
Luke 16:1-13

September 20–26
Jeremiah 32:1-3a, 6-15
Psalm 91:1-6, 14-16
1 Timothy 6:6-19
Luke 16:19-31

September 27—October 3
Lamentations 1:1-6
Psalm 137
2 Timothy 1:1-14
Luke 17:5-10

October 4–10
Jeremiah 29:1, 4-7
Psalm 66:1-12
2 Timothy 2:8-15
Luke 17:11-19

October 11–17
Jeremiah 31:27-34
Psalm 119:97-104 or Psalm 19
2 Timothy 3:14-4:5
Luke 18:1-8

October 11
THANKSGIVING DAY CANADA
Deuteronomy 26:1-11
Psalm 100 (UMH 821)
Philippians 4:4-9
John 6:25-35

October 18–24
Joel 2:23-32
Psalm 65
2 Timothy 4:6-8, 16-18
Luke 18:9-14

October 25–31
Habakkuk 1:1-4; 2:1-4
Psalm 119:137-144
2 Thess 1:1-4, 11-12
Luke 19:1-10

> **November 1**
> ALL SAINTS DAY
> Daniel 7:1-3, 15-18
> Psalm 149
> Ephesians 1:11-23
> Luke 6:20-31

November 1–7
Haggai 1:15b-2:9
Psalm 145:1-5, 17-21
2 Thessalonians 2:1-5, 13-17
Luke 20:27-38

November 8–14
Isaiah 65:17-25
Isaiah 12 or Psalm 118
2 Thessalonians 3:6-13
Luke 21:5-19

November 15–21
THE REIGN OF CHRIST
Jeremiah 23:1-6
Luke 1:68-79
Colossians 1:11-20
Luke 23:33-43

November 22–28
FIRST SUNDAY OF ADVENT
Isaiah 2:1-5
Psalm 122
Romans 13:11-14
Matthew 24:36-44

> **November 26**
> THANKSGIVING DAY, USA
> Deuteronomy 26:1-11
> Psalm 100
> Philippians 4:4-9
> John 6:25-35

November 29—December 5
SECOND SUNDAY OF ADVENT
Isaiah 11:1-10
Psalm 72:1-7, 18-19
Romans 15:4-13
Matthew 3:1-12

December 6–12
THIRD SUNDAY OF ADVENT
Isaiah 35:1-10
Luke 1:47-55
Psalm 146:5-10
James 5:7-10
Matthew 11:2-11

December 13–19
FOURTH SUNDAY OF ADVENT
Isaiah 7:10-16
Psalm 80:1-7, 17-19
Romans 1:1-7
Matthew 1:18-25

December 20–26

December 24
CHRISTMAS EVE
Isaiah 9:2-7
Psalm 96
Titus 2:11-14
Luke 2:1-20

December 25
CHRISTMAS DAY
Isaiah 57:7-10
Psalm 98
Hebrews 1:1-12
John 1:1-14

December 26
FIRST SUNDAY AFTER CHRISTMAS
Isaiah 63:7-9
Psalm 148
Hebrews 2:10-18
Matthew 2:13-23

December 27–31
Jeremiah 3:7-14
Psalm 147:12-20
Ephesians 1:3-14
John 1:1-18